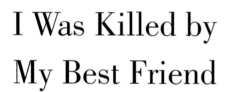

I Was Killed by
My Best Friend

I Was Killed by
My Best Friend

A Story of My Death to Sin and
My Life in Christ

Alice Leszek

To order additional copies of this book, contact:
Xlibris Corporation
1-888-795-4274
www.Xlibris.com
Orders@Xlibris.com
70098

To God who gave me strength to write this book and the strength to get through the events which took place in this book.

To my husband, Greg, who showed me confidence and encouragement throughout the process of writing this book and through all of life's highs and lows.

To Tiffany, thank you so much for your help in writing this book especially considering the troubles you went through during this process.

My Family Background

I was born in Uganda, which is part of East Africa. Uganda has many different languages, and I come from a tribe called the Baganda. We have a very large family of about five hundred. I know this because every time someone died, the family would all come for the funeral, and someone would count us. In our culture, it is usual for a man to have several wives. Many are Muslim and can have two to four wives. I know of a family member who has six wives. You can imagine how many children they have! Some of my relatives who have Christian names also have two or three wives. Many still believe in the king and queen's way. Many also still believe in family spirits and worship the king's ways despite the fact the British came and colonized everyone.

> If a man sleeps with a woman who is a slave girl promised to another man but who has not been ransomed or given her freedom, there must be due punishment. Yet they are not to be put to death because she had not been freed. (Lev. 19:20, NKJV)

I also have some relatives who are Protestants and Catholics. They only have one wife each but still have many children because there was no birth control back then. Of course, I have relatives who don't believe in anything at all; they do as they please. There are those who will have a second wife even if she is their dead brother's wife. They will marry them under the guise that they are only doing it to help the widow and raise her children. There is no divorce in Uganda, and most marriages are arranged ones. My father had eighteen children from three different wives, three of which were from my mother. I am the eldest of the three.

My Relationship with God

I can still remember the first time that I heard about God. There was a rumor going around that there was a war coming. My parents dug a hole in our backyard and put our belongings in to hide them from looters. This hole was very deep. They put plastic in it to protect our most expensive valuables that were placed there. I don't know what age I was at the time. All I remember was that I was little, had a sister, and my mother was pregnant.

Everything was fine until one day, there was so much noise and bullets flying everywhere. We fled to the woods. My father had gone to work that day, so we didn't see him; we were a group of people and children. In the woods one night, I was crying because I was so cold on the ground that my mother had laid me on. She came over to me and noticed that there was a snake next to me, ready to strike. My mother was so shocked but happy at the same time that the snake hadn't bitten me. She gave praise to God and said that he was with us to protect us from this war.

> For in the day of trouble He will keep me safe in his dwelling; he will hide me in the shelter of his tabernacle and set me high upon a rock. (Ps. 27:5)

> And call on me in the day of trouble; I will deliver you and you will honor me. (Ps. 50:15)

Fear was running high among all of us, so the adults decided to go deeper into the woods. We survived off of raw food because to light a fire for cooking would alert our enemies to our presence. During this time in the woods, my mother gave birth to my brother. Again, my mother gave praise to God despite the fact that she had borne him on a ground covered with banana leaves. My brother cried a lot at night, and we worried that someone would hear and find where we were hiding.

Eventually, rumors began circulating that the war was over. When we finally returned to our home, it was only to see that it was destroyed. Still, that wasn't the worst part. There were dead bodies on the ground everywhere. I remember people walking among them, checking to see if they were anyone they knew or were related to. The time spent in the woods was like a blur to me; I don't recall how long we were there for, but the dead bodies that were found were skeletons, perhaps from decay or maybe from birds and animals picking at them. In the midst of this horror was a joy—joy that we had not died. We all had to start life over with nothing but our will to live on. It was all so confusing. I remember seeing the dead in the street, and yet around them, I also remember people celebrating. There were also those that were angry and others overcome with grief. Thinking back on it now, I am so relieved that I was a child then; I can't imagine having to see that now.

Time passed, and my father was still unaccounted for. Some of our old neighbors were missing also. When my mother was able, she gathered up some people to help her uncover the hole we had dug in our backyard to protect our things. I was right there watching, and I remember the overwhelming disappointment when we saw what had happened to our things. Our clothes had been eaten by ants. The furniture was destroyed beyond repair. Our suitcases were torn to bits. There was only one thing in that hole that was salvageable. That thing was my mother's Bible. Everyone was speechless. That was when I first realized that there must be a God. He was present always. He was there when we escaped with our lives. He was there when that snake almost bit me. He was there when my mother gave birth to my brother in the woods. My mother still has that Bible to this day, and *that* day, there was much praising of God in the streets. In Uganda as a whole, there was a great revival.

> Give thanks to the Lord, for he is good; his love endures forever (1 Chron. 16:34)

> Give thanks to the Lord for he is good; his love endures forever. Let the redeemed of the Lord say this—those he redeemed from the hand of the foe, those he gathered from the lands, from the east and the west, from the north and the south. (Ps. 107:1-3)

Back in Africa, during those times where I lived, there were no phones, actual addresses, and certainly no mailboxes. People communicated by travelling from place to place to see their loved ones. Locating people was nearly impossible, and our father was missing. A few months had gone by, and my mother told us that someone had seen our father. We never stayed in one spot since our home was destroyed; instead, we moved from place to place looking for a better environment to live. Eventually, our father joined up with us. Things were good for a few months until another war broke out.

This time we had no warning, and I lost my mother in the crowd. I remember hearing this big bang, and then there was a lot of smoke. I saw my mother's hand and reached out for it, but still ended up getting separated. I was in the woods alone that night and was almost shot. Luckily, the bullet hit the tree I had been leaning on. Somewhere in the distance, I heard some people, and I joined up with them. There was a woman among them who recognized me and helped me look for my mother. My father was again lost in the fray. Imagine my poor mother with three small children to care for in these circumstances. We did not blame our father for being gone. It was for his own safety that he would leave us. During the wars, the enemies would round up all the men and boys they could find and force them to fight in the war. God was with us again during that time, and eventually, my father caught up with us again.

When that war was finally over, my mother would read to me from her Bible. Mostly she read to me about the Ten Commandments. She also taught me how to pray, and I did it regularly before bedtime. My parents were Protestants, so that was the church that we attended. There were churches all around that were breaking up. This had a lot to do with other people whom they were calling born agains, who were being mocked by my mother and others. They laughed at them and talked bad about people who worshiped as they did. For myself, I remember sneaking into one such church one day and seeing people who had joy despite what was going on. They talked about healing. They were different from what I was used to.

When I told my mom what I had seen, she got really mad at me. She shouted at me, telling me that if she ever caught me sneaking like that again, she would beat me. She said that I was a Protestant and that I would stay a Protestant. Still, I was intrigued by what was going on in this different church. I would still sneak to go see, but I would stay outside and not join them in the service. I was still obeying, right? Another Sunday came, and my mother dropped us off at the Protestant church. I sat there for a while, and I was bored to tears. There were people around me sleeping, so I left. I decided to go to the born-again church. When I got back home, my mother had already gotten the news that I had gone there. She shouted at me and told me that she had warned me not to go. She whipped me good, but this did not deter me. I decided that since both churches were close to each other, I could attend them both!

When my mother would drop me off, I would stay for about half the service so that my mother's friends would see me there if they were asked. I would leave my brother and sister there with a stern warning not to move until I got back. I would then run all the way to the born-again church and see what was happening there. Oh, how I loved their music. I would dance and dance. At this church, they would talk about Jesus a lot. There was always praise for

Jesus and what he had done in their lives. My mother always thanked God, but what was the difference? It didn't matter. Before they ended the service, I would run all the way back to the Protestant church to pick up my brother and sister. I did this time and time again until my mother found out. She whipped me again.

Later, my mom came to me and said that if I didn't want to be a Protestant, then why not be a Catholic instead? She sent me to a Catholic boarding school. I did everything that I was told, everything they said would bring me closer to God, and yet I didn't feel the joy I had experienced at the born-again church. I was very confused by it all. Then a day came when I was wandering in the city, and I saw a big tent. There were people going in the tent, and I could hear music. I heard from some passing people that they had free food there too, and it was being served by white people. When I got there, I saw this American man singing. He sang with so much joy, and afterward, he talked about Jesus and how he could give us unspeakable joy. He also talked about Jesus healing diseases and asked these simple questions: "Would you like Jesus to come into your heart? Would you like him to come into your life? Come forward." So I did, and he told me that I was born again.

> He was pierced for our sins, he was crushed for our transgressions,
> but the punishment that brought us peace was upon him, and by
> his wounds we were healed. (Isa. 53:5)

When I got home, I told my mom what had happened. I told her the good news about Jesus and how I was born again. She was beyond mad this time, but I got away from her before she could grab me to whip me again.

I believe truly that children can get saved. I remember how I felt at that time, and it is almost indescribable the happiness I had inside. Even when I was struck down with malaria and my mother had gathered all the herbs with which to fight it and still I didn't recover, I remembered the words that man had said inside that tent. He had said that Jesus was a healer, and I believed him. I prayed to Jesus to heal me, and he did that instant! I went to my mother, and she was so shocked to see me up and about. I told her that Jesus had healed me. She checked my forehead and said that indeed I was no longer hot but that I was not to speak the language of those born-again people. However, she didn't whip me this time.

Next, my mother was struck down with malaria, and she wasn't getting well. I asked her if she would like me to pray for her, and she allowed me to. Again, she was instantly healed. She told people in the village what had happened and encouraged people to come to me if they were sick with malaria. My relationship with Jesus started from there, but even with this proof before her, my mother still didn't want me to go to that church; and since I was still enrolled in that Catholic school, I felt I had to keep Jesus in my heart. My mom felt so strongly against me being born again that when we were vacationing at my aunt's house one day, she mentioned to her how I had switched from being a Protestant to being a Catholic. My aunt didn't believe in either and suggested to my mother that perhaps I should be Muslim. Anything was better than being a born again according to my mother, so she put me in these classes where this Muslim guy came to preach, and hence, I then became a Muslim. I was told how many times a day to pray and how to fast. When it was time for fasting, I had a hard time. I was about nine years old at the time and had never gone long without eating, even during the war, but I was willing to do anything to praise God since I had been told this was the only way to be rewarded. So I did what was expected of me by praying when I should and avoiding eating anything that was unclean, and I believed that I must be on the right road. I was a Muslim for six months.

In the Muslim religion, I was taught that you would get a black spot on your forehead if God was pleased with you. This happened to me, but not in the way you would expect. Whenever I would kneel and pray, I would rub my forehead in the dirt, and thus, a black spot appeared on me. My aunt saw it and was overjoyed and explained to me that I was being rewarded by God. Everyone was so happy, but I was so *hungry*. There was this mango tree in her yard, and I thought that I would just eat one to ease my hunger from the fasting. A cousin of mine saw me and told my aunt. She was so mad at me, you would think that I had been stealing. She said I wasn't a true Muslim to have done such a thing and that all the teachings and things I had learned were for nothing. She said I was a shameless girl and that she was sending me back to my mother. My cousins all laughed at me, and I was so hurt.

I was so upset in my heart after all this. I didn't want anything to do with any kind of religion at all. I felt that God was so hard to please. I had done everything I could, and I was repaid by my mother whipping me, my aunt rejecting me, and my cousins laughing at me. I was so confused and disappointed that I couldn't get the joy I had been searching for. In fact, I decided that I agreed with the other nonbelievers that there was no God at all, that it was just in people's heads. So that was the end of me and God and religion as a whole.

How I Met My Best Friend

Rosie and I met at a volleyball court. I used to play volleyball, and so did Rosie. I didn't know much about her, only that all of a sudden she stopped coming to school. I remember one day I was walking in the street and Rosie saw me and called out my name. She started the conversation by asking if I remembered her from volleyball, and I told her that I did. We chatted, and I asked her what she was doing with her life, and she told me that she had dropped out of school. She explained that she hadn't liked school, and that was why she had dropped out. She had a job now. I thought that she was very young to have a job, but I didn't really care that she did.

> A righteous man is wise in his friendship, but the way of the wicked leads them astray. (Prov. 12:26)

The fact that Rosie had stopped going to school because she didn't like it and not because she was in great need of money should have been a sign of things to come for me, but it wasn't. Hindsight sure is twenty-twenty.

How Close We Were

Rosie and I connected immediately. She was always making jokes, and I found out that she liked doing a lot of the same things that I liked to do—watching movies, walking the streets late at night, and dancing. We didn't live too far away from each other, so when I was finished with my duties at home, I would go and visit her. At the time, she had a single-room place that she shared with her nephew. She didn't make lots of money, but with the money that she had left over, she would share some of it with me, buying food and taking us to the movies and stuff. We really enjoyed each other's company and were together often, so much so that people started calling us sisters. It was to the point that when people saw us without each other, they would ask where our "sister" was.

Plans and Dreams We Shared

One of the dreams I had was to travel. I really wanted to see what the world had to offer. I wished to have money that I had earned myself, preferably from my own business. It was important to me that I get my mom a new house. Our house was in disrepair. Any time it rained, the roof would leak in several places. We would scurry about, trying to find pots, cups, basins, or whatever we could find to catch the water. Most of all, I wanted to live by the beach. I loved gazing out at the sea and viewing the sun set over the ocean. It looked to me as if the two were touching.

Rosie also wanted to travel. She wanted to work in a hotel in another country. I am not sure what kind of job she wanted there, but it didn't matter.

> In his heart a man plans his course, but the Lord determines his steps. (Prov. 16:9)

It is God who can bring our plans to fruition. For me, that meant an education. Rosie's plan was to work hard and save money. At the time, Rosie told me that she was working at the university in Makere. She was a professor's assistant.

Rosie's Family Background

Rosie's mother and father had both remarried. She only had one sibling, a brother, with whom she shared the same parents. The rest were from her parents' remarriages. This brother with whom she shared full blood was her favorite. She spoke of him often. It didn't seem to me that she had much of a connection with her stepsiblings.

She had lots of other relatives, so many in fact that we would see them everywhere, and she would point them out and tell me who was who and how they were related to her. Her mother lived close enough to her that she would still go over there often to eat dinner.

Rosie told me lots of things about her family. One thing was the fact that she didn't get along with her mom. The cause of that in particular, she said, was because of something that had happened a long time ago. One day a woman came by her mom's house, claiming that the baby she had borne was her father's illegitimate child. The woman claimed that she had been trying to contact Rosie's father, but without success. Rosie's mom and the woman got into an argument, and it ended with the woman running away and leaving the baby behind. Rosie's mom took the baby and threw it in the latrine and fled, leaving Rosie and her brother, who were little at the time. Rosie didn't like her mom because of this, but not as much as her brother hated her. Her brother vowed to never see her again, but Rosie did seek her out sometime after the war. I wondered why Rosie's mom didn't end up in jail. She said it was because it was a long time ago during the Idi Amin regime. When the war was over, Rosie's mom came back because it was a new government. After all, if you had lived through it and did not get killed by Amin, you were considered a living miracle.

Another reason that Rosie didn't like her mom much was because her mother treated her stepsiblings better than Rosie. For this reason, she also had animosity toward them. It didn't help that her stepsister was very beautiful and that she and her brother were going to the university. She told me how her mother gave them money and stuff. The thing is, though, Rosie's mom was paying for Rosie's small room. When she dropped out of school, her mom got her the job Rosie was now working.

After finding out about her siblings, I realized that Rosie must be much older than I originally thought she was. I mean, she had to be a lot older than me to have younger siblings in the university. I asked her how old she was, and she became very angry, asking why did it matter how old she was. So I left it alone, knowing that she was definitely older than I was even though she didn't look like it. It didn't matter to me, and after hearing all about her family, I just felt sorry for her.

A friend loves at all time, and a brother is born for adversity. (Prov. 17:17)

What Others Thought about My Best Friend

My mother met Rosie for the first time one day when I brought her over for lunch. When Rosie left, my mother sat me down and told me that Rosie was not a nice girl and that I mustn't hang out with her anymore. She said that that day should be the last time that I saw her.

> Understanding is the fountain of life to those who have it, but folly brings punishment to fools. (Prov. 16:22)

My mother discerned something in Rosie, but I didn't want to hear it. I told her that she just didn't like Rosie and that nothing I did pleased her.

There came a day when Rosie and I were walking in the streets, and these German tourists stopped us and asked us for directions to the king's palace. Rosie and I offered to take them ourselves, and they were so grateful that we did that they offered to take us out to dinner. While there, one of the guys asked to speak to me outside, so I went. When were out there, he asked me why I was hanging out with Rosie and said that she was not a good person. I said I didn't know what he meant. I was shocked to hear this from him and my mother because to me, she hadn't done anything wrong.

> For wisdom will enter your heart and knowledge will be pleasant to your soul. Discretion will guard you. Wisdom will save you from the ways of wicked men from men whose words are perverse. (Prov. 2:10-13)

At that time in my life, I lacked so much wisdom. They weren't telling me these things about Rosie because of something they saw her do; they were sensing her spirit. I truly believe that God was warning me at that time about Rosie, but I was too naive to see it.

Still another time came when there were two girls who also talked to me about Rosie. In my mind, I just thought that no one liked her. There was even a lady that met Rosie and me in the street, and she told me to my face that Rosie had a bad heart. I refused to believe it, I guess, but maybe more than that, I just despised correction.

> When you walk your steps will not be hampered; when you run you
> will not stumble. Hold on to instruction, do not let it go; guard it
> well for it is your life. (Prov. 5:12-13)

To anyone reading my words, I say this: Listen to the people in your life who are correcting you and giving you instruction, even if it doesn't make sense at the time. If these are your loved ones speaking to you, value their judgment and their wisdom from past experiences. Even if it seems like they are wrong with opposite opinions of the friend you laugh with or the love interest you have been spending time with, heed their words. Even if that person hasn't done anything wrong in your eyes (like it happened with me and Rosie), don't harden your heart against those loved ones and, in this case, perfect strangers as well and end up blind to the truth.

There Were Some Things I Didn't Like about Rosie . . .

I went looking for Rosie one day at the university, only I couldn't find her where I thought she would be. I asked somebody where she was, and they told me that they knew who she was but that she wasn't working as an assistant to any professor there. When I found her, she was cleaning up a classroom. I was twelve years old and naive, and I didn't think to question the fact that she was an assistant to a professor even though she had dropped out of school and didn't have the education for a job like that. When I confronted her about it, she said that she didn't want to tell anybody her job was cleaning classrooms and toilets because they would laugh at her. I understood how she felt, so I left her alone about it.

Rosie introduced me to some girls she knew, one of which was a girl named Sarah. Sarah was a pretty, well-mannered girl. Rosie told me that Sarah only talked to boys from rich families and that she had a boyfriend, that she would point him out to me one day. There was another girl whom she didn't like and mentioned that she had AIDS. I wondered how she knew this, and she told me that if I saw the girl during the day, then I would see that she had the symptoms of HIV; at that time, it was late afternoon. When we were walking, we saw this guy ride by on a bike, and Rosie told me that he was Sarah's boyfriend. I was surprised because he was a lot older than Sarah, but Rosie said that he had money and that was what Sarah was after. I asked if Sarah's parents knew, but Rosie replied that Sarah was an orphan who lived with a sister that took care of her.

I finally saw the girl whom Rosie said had HIV, and in the daytime, it looked as if it was true. She did display the symptoms for all eyes to see, and I could recognize it myself because at that time, Uganda was the leading country with AIDS. Later on, I saw Sarah talking with that guy that was her boyfriend on a hill. When he was gone, I talked to Sarah, and she told me that she loved him and his family and, of course, all the money he would give her. I was happy for her until I saw this same guy talking to the girl that had AIDS. I told Rosie what I had seen, and she wasn't surprised; she had known this was going on! I was so worried, and I went and told Sarah what I had seen. Sarah was so disappointed that she cried. On the other hand, she was thankful that she hadn't slept with him. She and I vowed to wait until we were married before having sex.

A few days later, a girl named Betty told me that she had heard that I had wanted Sarah's boyfriend for myself so badly that I had made up this story about him and the sick girl just so I could have him for myself! I was so shocked to hear that, so I went to Sarah's house to talk to her about it. When I got there, Sarah didn't want to see me or talk to me at all. It was very distressing to hear that other girls were talking about me badly when what I had said was the truth. I received a message from Betty later on, telling me that she wanted to talk to me. When I went to see her, she told me that it was Rosie who was spreading the rumors about me! She told me that Sarah had been chatting with Rosie and told her what I had said about her boyfriend. In turn, Rosie had told her that I had told her the same story, but that it wasn't true and that I only said it so I could steal her boyfriend away and that Sarah shouldn't let go of her boyfriend. I couldn't believe what Betty was telling me about Rosie Why had she done this? Betty told me that I should end my relationship with Rosie.

I went to Rosie and demanded that she answer for what she had done. She didn't deny any of it, and in fact, she said to me, "Let them die, what do you care?" I told her that I didn't want to be her friend anymore, and then I left. Warning: Be careful what your friends do to others because they will do the same to you. A year and a half later, I found out that Sarah's boyfriend had died. I went to his house and saw him in the coffin. Later, Sarah died too; I don't think she was even in her twenties. My reputation was then cleared. I told myself that I would never again tell anyone something like that, but in my heart, I knew that I could never have been happy had I not told Sarah, and then she had died. Through this, my friend had been exposed, and I finally believed what people had told me about her, but that was just the beginning.

My Arranged Marriage

I was thirteen years old and had already begun secondary school. I was so happy and full of life. I shared my dreams with my mother early on in life, and she told me that I needed to have any education if I wanted to travel and accomplish the other goals for my life. My father never had an education, and he would always tell us that we were lucky to receive an education where he could not and that we should go out and make him proud. I really tried my best to make them happy, and when I would come home with good grades, I was praised and it felt so good. So it came as a shock to me one day when my mother came up to me and said that she wanted to talk to me privately.

She took me aside and told me that my father could no longer afford to send to me to school, that because I could read, count, and speak English, that was all I needed, and he needed to now spend money for my brother and sister to do the same. Instead of school, she told me that my father had found a man to marry me. This man was someone my father knew, and he also knew his family. She said I needed to get ready and prepare because this man and his family were going to come and take me. I refused, and she slapped me. I couldn't believe what I was hearing. It was like a dream or something happening to someone else.

After the holiday passed and my parents weren't preparing me for school, I asked my mother why not, and she told me not to ask stupid questions. That was when it really hit me; my old life was no longer. I was destined to be some man's wife. I cried and cried. Early in the morning, I would see other children going to school outside my window, and I would cry some more. My dreams crashed like glass on the pavement. It was so painful to live with the fact that my parents would do this to me. I would rather have been doing anything else than be married to some man I had never met or spoken to. All I knew was that he was thirty years old. They sent me to marriage classes to prepare for my impending nuptials. The things I learned there were so hard for me to handle and understand.

This Is How I Viewed Marriage at Thirteen

I have lived with some of my relatives who had three wives. There were always quarrels, fights, and competitions. I have also lived with my uncle who had two wives living together in one house; it was just the same. They would quarrel over saucepans, food—you name it! In addition to that, I lived with some relatives who only had one wife and that wife would tell me how her husband was out cheating.

Looking at my mother's marriage, I didn't like the fact that my mother had to have permission from my dad to do anything. He never wanted my mother to work, and yet we lacked so much in our house. They did my siblings and I a favor though; they never quarreled in front of us. My mother treated my dad like he was a king. She would heat hot water and take it to him in the bathroom. After he was finished, he wouldn't remove anything from the bathroom. She would have to go and collect the soap, brush, and basin for him. When we had very little to no sugar, she would give the last spoonful to him for his tea. It was my father who had eggs with his breakfast in the morning, and we kids would eat what was left. She would always make sure he had the freshest or best food and cook it for him, even at our expense.

All this bothered me, but more than that was the fact that he gave her nothing in return. I would hear her beg him for perfume, and he would ask her what she needed perfume for. The other side of this was the fact that we didn't even have enough money for the whole family to eat eggs. This, and other things, added up to the fact that in a marriage, the women were treated badly. They had no say in anything; meanwhile, they had to slave in the garden coaxing food to grow. Some days I would look at the young wives and feel sorry for them, yet knowing this would be my fate also.

One Saturday, my mother joyfully told me that I would be getting married the next Saturday. She then went to buy me a dress. Panicked, I thought to myself that maybe I could go through with the marriage and then run away the next day. Then I remembered all the money, the goats, and the cows that would be given to my father from my future husband. If I left, that would be a problem. Plus, money had already been exchanged between them, of which I would never get to spend a penny. Still, I thought that maybe I could start a new life, but I had no money. I wished that I could just run to the woods and live off of fruit until I figured out what to do, but I was scared of the animals that came out at night.

Friday came, and there was a lot of cooking going on in preparation for the wedding. I didn't sleep that night; instead, I thought of lots of things. I thought of the fact that my future husband already had a wife and that I was destined to be wife number two. She was a lot older than me, so one day, I would be the senior wife when she died and he decided to wed again, but that would be awhile down the road. I turned things around in my mind but couldn't see a way out of this lifestyle. Desperate, I got up at five o'clock Saturday morning, packed my clothes in a trash bag, opened the door very carefully, and ran away!

> For this reason a man will leave his father and mother and be united
> to his wife, and they will become one flesh. (Gen. 2:24)

> And the two shall become one flesh. So they are no longer two, but
> one. (Mark 10:8)

I Ran Away from Home

With only my clothes in the trash bag, I walked away from home, not knowing where I was going. I went to my aunt's house and stayed for a few days. She came to me one day and told me that I could no longer stay there because my mother was looking for me, and she didn't want to be blamed for my rebelliousness. I also found out that my mother had sent letters to my relatives, telling them that I had run away and for them not to accommodate me in their houses. I couldn't go anywhere because of this, and everyone was talking bad about me.

Next, I went to my friend Betty's house and stayed all day with her, sharing what was going on. When night fell, she asked where I planned to sleep; I had no answer for her. She suggested that I go and spend the night at the club and then come back to her house for breakfast. So that's what I did. I snuck in there and hid my things in the corner because I didn't have any money to pay. Betty's mom found out what I did and told Betty to send me away. That morning, I walked eight miles to the city.

There was a park in the city. That park and the clubs were my night houses, my sleeping places. Still, I felt good every day! I was free from that arranged marriage, but at the same time, my relationship with my family was destroyed. I felt like they didn't love me. At a young age, you can't understand why people who are supposed to love and protect you would get a man to marry you, someone whom they haven't even checked to see if he had AIDS. This was especially disheartening because at that time in Uganda, people were dying of AIDS left and right.

One day I was in the club, and guess who came up and talked to me? Rosie! Rosie said that Betty told her what was going on between my family and me. She said she was very sorry about the situation, but that she thinks I made the right decision. I told her thanks, and she went on to say that she was there to ask for my forgiveness. She wanted me to forgive her for what she had done and that she didn't want it to separate our friendship any longer and that she hoped that I would find it in my heart to forgive her. Rosie also said that she felt so bad after hearing about my predicament that she came to find me so she could help. She said that I could come and hide at her place as long as no one saw me. So I told her that I did forgive her, and then we went to Rosie's house.

Rosie had a small single room that she was renting. It was separated from other rooms in the building, but there was only one bathroom and one toilet that she and others shared. During this time, Rosie and I became friends again. During the day, she would lock me in so that people would see the padlock and not know that I was living there. It was so hot in there, but I had a small window and a basin that I used as a toilet. She went to work at 7:00 a.m. and came home at 5:00 p.m., so I was isolated from everything. I would drink a cup of tea in the morning, and that was it until she came back. She would stop at her mother's and get a plate of food that we would share. She took care of me as best she could. Rosie would also go to my sister to get news about what was going on, and from her, I found out that they were still looking for me. My father had also threatened my mother, saying that if she didn't find me, he was going to leave her! I felt bad for my mother because in our culture, anything bad that children do is blamed on the mother.

Then one day out of nowhere, my mother broke into Rosie's house. It was so fast that one minute there was nothing, and the next thing I knew was that I was in my mother's hands. She dragged me outside and started fighting me. I fell down, and she sat on me and started shouting for help. Some guys came, and she told them that I was a runaway and asked them to help her take me to the police. She told my friend to stay away from me. On the way to the police, she told me that she was going to pay them to keep me in jail for three days to punish me for the trouble I had put her through. Something good happened though. She told the men that were holding me that she had no money on her and that she was going home to get the money to take me to jail.

I was dirty and bleeding, and while my mom was away, they asked me why I had run away. I told them, and they said that I should listen to what my parents had told me to do. I agreed with them. I told them I needed to use the bathroom, so we went to find one. They let me go, and I managed to escape from them. This time around, I changed towns and started looking for stuff to do. I would ask people if they had work, and people would give me small things to do, like getting water from the well and running errands and stuff. I didn't get paid money, but I was given food. Things weren't great, but good enough. Time passed and I turned fourteen with no word from my family. One day I did hear an announcement on the radio, but I wasn't worried about it because I went by a different name when I was on my own.

Rosie and I still saw each other at the club. I got myself a small room and was homeless no longer. It felt so good to wake up and just do what I wanted to do without fear. I could sleep a deep sleep without nightmares about being found. Sometimes I would just sit outside my place and relax; it just felt so good.

There came a day when I was riding on the bus, and I saw one of my mother's neighbors. She recognized me and exclaimed her surprise about me living on that side of town. She told me that my mother was still looking for me and that my father had left my mom. She also said that she had heard the announcement about me on the radio. I didn't know what to think about my father, and to avoid being found, I decided to leave the country. I started collecting money, and when I had what I thought was enough to leave, I got ready to leave for Kenya. I told Rosie about what I planned to do, and she said she had heard good things about Mombasa. She said they had lots of hotels and beaches there. I was so happy to hear about the beaches because I loved to sit at the beach and watch the sun go down. She asked me when I was going, and I told her. To my surprise, she came over one day and told me that she had withdrawn all her money from her savings and that she was coming too! I asked her if she had told anyone what she planned to do, and she said no. Again I asked her if she was sure she was going, and she said that she had the money and that she wasn't joking.

To me it was such a big deal, and I felt like our friendship really meant a lot to her. She had even told me I was like a sister to her. Rosie said we should both leave this place where no one loves us and find a better life somewhere else. She pointed out the fact that we both knew some English and that should help us so we don't get stuck. All things decided, the next morning we got up and bought bus tickets.

It took us two days of traveling to get to Mombasa, and when we arrived, we were very tired. However, we both really only wanted one thing, and that was to go to the beach. We asked someone for directions, and then we went straight there with all our belongings. I told her that one of my dreams was to live on the beach, and now I had it! We wandered around and talked to some locals and asked if they knew of any places to rent. There was one guy who knew of a girl that could help us, but that she wasn't due to come back until the evening. We decided to wait for her to come, and when she did, she confirmed that there was a place that she knew of. She offered to take us there, but when we got there, she said the landlord was nowhere to be seen. So she took us back to her house, and we slept there.

The next day, we left our belongings at her house and went to the city to see how the place she showed us looked during the day. When we came back in the evening, we found that she had thrown out our things! Someone came up to us and gave us a message saying that the girl said we had to leave her place because we had no money. We were very surprised. We asked the messenger if she knew of a place we could rent, and she said no. After that, we started to be very careful. We went to the city with our little bit of money. We soon found a place, but we didn't have money to buy a mattress, so we slept on our clothes on the floor.

Soon I started to miss my family, and I wondered if there was a God and why he would let my parents do this to me. My dreams were gone, and I didn't know what even the next day had in store for me. I wanted answers. Many people had told me that God was powerful and that he could do anything, and I wondered to myself why God wasn't stopping what was happening to me. I was so angry with God that my heart became sour against him. I asked him why he put me on this earth.

Life was hard for Rosie and me. The people whom we were living with spoke a different dialect than ours, and we didn't know it. We had paid for three months in advance on our rent, but time was going to run out if Rosie and I didn't find any work. Things got better though. We eventually found work in the beach area. We didn't get paid much, but it was enough to pay the rent, do our hair, and other basic things. We had to save our money though for the low season when there weren't many tourists around. It was hard to survive.

During this, there would be times when I was alone, and I would think of my mom and start crying. I used to be so close to my mom. She would give up stuff for herself and instead buy stuff for me for school. I guess that's why it hurt so badly when she changed. I couldn't understand it, but something in my heart told me I should forgive her. I felt that I couldn't, but this voice inside me wouldn't subside, so I forgave her in my heart.

> Do not judge, and you will not be judged. Do not condemn, and you will not be condemned. Forgive, and you will be forgiven. (Luke 6:37)

> Then Peter came up to Jesus asking, "Lord how many times shall I forgive my brother when he sins against me, up to seven times?" Jesus answered, "I tell you not seven times, but seventy-seven times." (Matt. 18:21-22)

We have to forgive them that harm us. When I forgave her in my heart, the nightmares I had about her coming after me stopped, and all the bad thoughts I had about her disappeared. I was so relieved.

Rosie and I went on with our lives. Deep inside of me, I always kept dreaming. Although my circumstances didn't show me anything promising, I couldn't stop dreaming about some great achievement. Just the thought of it kept me going every day.

Unfortunately, Rosie became sick. We took her to the hospital, and the doctor diagnosed her as having syphilis and gonorrhea. He said that she needed to be treated right away. We didn't have all the money that he wanted in order to treat her, and he said that he wouldn't help her until we did. I had some money and got more after working for a week. I gathered all that and took her back to the hospital to be treated. After all, she had helped me before, and this was a way that I could pay her back. I didn't know at the time what syphilis or gonorrhea were. I asked her, and she told me that they were caused by some infections. I was concerned because I was afraid that I would catch them from living with her. I also wondered if they were something she caught from the country we were now living in.

We went back to the hospital to see the doctor again. After he checked on her, he sat us down and explained to us how we needed to use condoms when we sleep with someone. He explained how sexual diseases were dangerous and how people go around with them and don't get treated, leaving them contagious to other people. I was curious about all these sexually transmitted diseases and asked the doctor a bunch of questions that he obligingly answered. When I asked Rosie about whom she had slept with, she told me that it was a bouncer at this club that we went often. I told her that she needed to be careful.

Strangely, I started having this dream, about twice a week, about a snake chasing me. I told Rosie about it, but she didn't have anything to say about it. I didn't know what the dream meant and eventually gave up trying to figure it out.

Sometime later, I purchased these really nice earrings. I showed them to Rosie, and she said she thought they were pretty. Well, that evening, I wanted to wear them, but I couldn't find them. I asked Rosie about it, but she said she didn't know where they were. Finally, I gave up looking for them. One Saturday after that, I wasn't feeling too well and told Rosie that I didn't want to go out. She really wanted to go out anyway, so I insisted that she go without me. I felt better a couple of hours after she left, so I decided to go out after all. When I got to the place where I knew Rosie would be, I saw that Rosie was wearing my earrings that I thought had been lost! I asked Rosie why she stole them and told her that she should have just asked me if she wanted to borrow them. She looked very guiltily at me, took them off, and walked away. The next day we barely spoke to each other, but that didn't last for long, and we started talking again.

Rosie Meets a Swiss Guy

There was this Swiss guy who saw Rosie and decided he liked her. He sent someone to Rosie to ask her if she wanted to go out with him. Rosie told me about it and asked me what I thought about it. I figured she should give him a shot and asked her what the problem was. She said that she was scared of him because he was white. She also confided in me that she was curious about his skin because she had heard that white people's skin was soft like bananas, and she thought that was weird. The truth is that I had heard the same thing, but I brushed her comments aside and told her that she can't believe everything she hears from people and that she needed to just go ahead and experience it for herself. She was still too frightened to go by herself and asked me to go with her on the date. She introduced me to him as her sister.

The restaurant that we went to was on the beach. It was familiar to me, but I had never eaten there. We laughed a lot at ourselves while we were there. The first thing was the fact that we couldn't understand what the menus were. We joked to ourselves that the waiter had brought books instead of food! Where was the good food? The second, we didn't know how to eat with the forks and knives. The Swiss guy wondered what we were laughing and talking about, and we told him that we didn't know what was going on. He was very nice about it and explained to us that the books were in fact menus. He made us open the menus and asked us what we wanted to eat. We had no idea and said so, so he suggested that we have the lobster. Dumbfounded, we had to tell him that we didn't know what that was either! He told us that it was fish, so we agreed to order them.

To our horror, the waiter came back later and placed what looked like large insects in front of us! Rosie and I jumped up from the table in fright. Everyone around us was staring in our direction, and we were so embarrassed. I didn't care; I was not going to sit down by those insects. The Swiss guy thought the whole thing was very funny, and he laughed and laughed. He begged us to come back to the table, assuring us that the lobsters were cooked and that they were very good. We went back to the table, but we couldn't bring ourselves to eat the lobster, so they took them away. We felt so bad, but the Swiss guy was in good spirits and asked the waiter to bring the menus back again so we could order something else. We insisted that we didn't need anything else as we had eaten all the bread there, thinking that it was the dish. We assured him that we were okay and that we would be fine eating our local dishes outside of that restaurant—thus ended Rosie's first date with a white guy.

Rosie's white guy, surprisingly, was not put off by the fiasco that was their first date and asked for us to dine again with him on another night. This time he took us to an Italian restaurant that was near the hotel. He ordered pizza and told us to relax because pizza was something we could eat with our fingers. When it came, it looked very appetizing. The Swiss guy cut his into big slices with his knife, so I told Rosie to cut hers. She started cutting it, and somehow, it slid off her plate onto the floor! She picked it up really quickly and put it back on her plate. The Swiss guy and I thought it was so funny, and we laughed and laughed, nearly in tears. Not missing a beat, the Swiss guy ordered another pizza for Rosie and asked the waiter to have it precut for her. After that night, I decided that I would eat before going out with them because I was determined not to look like a fool anymore.

There came a day when Rosie said that she was falling for the Swiss guy. She told me that she was going to quit her job and go live with him at the hotel. I was very happy for her and joked that she had been worried for nothing. She invited me to come to dinner with them, and after that, I would occasionally go and visit them to hang out or have dinner with them at the hotel. I would just eat the bread, and when he would ask me about it, I would just say that I wasn't really hungry. Meanwhile, Rosie was learning how to eat with a fork and knife.

For about four times, when it was time for me to leave after visiting them, the Swiss guy always gave me money for a taxi home. The thing was, the money was always a lot more than I needed. It would be enough money to feed me for a month! I couldn't insult him by not taking the money, so I would take it, and they would go back into the hotel. I had never before met someone as nice as him. The Swiss guy would take Rosie shopping and buy her clothes and jewelries.

One time when I was visiting and Rosie was showing me her things, the Swiss guy told me that he loved Rosie and wanted to marry her and take her to Switzerland. Rosie's dreams were about to come true. That night we went out to celebrate. We went out dancing, and when the night was over, he took out his wallet and gave me twice what he had given me before! This guy was so generous. The problem was, while he would give me money, he would only buy Rosie stuff. Rosie was confused by it and asked me in our language why he did that. I told her not to worry since he gives her whatever she wants, and hello, he was taking her to Switzerland! I figured he was just being nice to me because he thought we were sisters.

I thought that would be the end of it, but it wasn't. When I went to visit them at the hotel the next time, right away the Swiss guy started yelling at me! He told me that Rosie had told him everything. He accused me of being a prostitute and that I didn't deserve what he had given me and that I should leave. Rosie had told him that I was just a prostitute that she hung out with sometimes. He was yelling so loud that the guard heard him. I couldn't believe what I was hearing. I was so hurt that Rosie would tell him that about me. I went home and cried for hours.

> Do not accuse a man for no reason—when he has done you no harm. (Prov. 3:30)

> If it is possible, as far as it depends on you, live at peace with everyone. (Rom. 12:18)

Rosie lived there at the hotel for two weeks, and during that time, in my heart, I knew that our friendship was over. I decided not to wait for her to come back and get her stuff; instead, I was going to go back to Uganda to get my passport. I had a lot of money left over from what her boyfriend had given me, and I combined that with the money I had saved on my own. Rosie came over, and it was apparent that she had been shopping. She showed me her things but added that she had been shopping for me also. She gave me some shoes and underthings, all the while acting as if nothing had happened, but I could see through her now. I recognized her for who she truly was. I hardly spoke to her while she was there. Deep inside, I knew that I had to disconnect myself from Rosie. After she showed me the presents, I went down to the beach. It was a favorite place of mine to relax and forget about my problems. When I came back, I told her that I was leaving for Uganda and asked if she wanted to still keep the room. She had been thinking about the same thing. She showed me the money her boyfriend had given her to go get her passport and visa to leave. She went on to say that when she got to Uganda, she was going to open a bank account for him to put money in for her. She wanted us to put our differences aside and speak to the landlord together about what we planned to do.

I packed up all my valuable things and left them with the landlord. Rosie did the same, for we did not want to make the two-day trip by bus to Uganda carrying a lot of stuff since we planned to be back.

> Do not take revenge, my friends, but leave room for God's wrath, for it is written: "It is mine to avenge: I will repay," says the Lord. (Rom.12:19)

When we got to Uganda, we were both on our own. I got my own hotel. I arrived in Uganda with a sense of split responsibility to myself and to my family. It had been two years since I had run away, and I hadn't seen any of my family since. I was torn about going home; I was afraid that they would try and stop me from living my life, so I decided not to visit. I spoke to a guy who worked at the passport office. He told me that it would take three weeks to get my passport ready. I didn't want to have to wait that long because I feared that someone might see me and tell my parents.

Rosie, on the other hand, had found someone who could do her passport in one week. She also asked me to help her open her bank account. She had trouble reading and wanted me to help her fill out the forms. I agreed to help her.

> Do not be overcome with evil, but overcome evil with good.
> (Rom. 12:21)

Rosie then had to call the Swiss guy up and give him all the information about the bank. She did this, and he said that he transferred the money. I accompanied Rosie back to the bank, at her request, to see if the money was there. At the bank, they asked us for a transfer number, which we didn't have. Rosie had to call the Swiss guy back to get the transfer number. She was on the phone with him, and apparently, there was some problem because she asked me to speak to him for her because she was having trouble understanding what he was saying. So we went back and forth for a while on the telephone, them talking and me talking to him. I am sure he was wondering why Rosie was with me at all since I was allegedly such a bad person and a prostitute. Rosie got the information that she needed, but she drew the line at that. She did not want me to be at the bank with her when she picked up the money. I let it go.

> If your enemy is hungry, feed him; if he is thirsty, give him something
> to drink. In doing this, you will heap burning coals on his head.
> (Rom. 12:20)

I don't know exactly what had happened, but when Rosie went to pick up her money, she couldn't get it for some reason. The bank said the Swiss guy would get it back. She decided she would go back to Kenya and open an account there and try again. When she went to pick up her passport, the place where the guy had been was empty. It turned out that he was a con man! Rosie was very distraught because she was running out of money. She had been spending it in expensive stores in anticipation of the money the Swiss guy was going to send her, which now had fallen through along with her passport. She decided to leave and go back to Kenya. I stayed in Uganda and waited for my passport, which thankfully came on time.

> In his heart a man plans his course, but the Lord determines his steps. (Prov. 16:9)

I travelled back to Kenya. I really didn't want to see Rosie, so I decided to stay in Nairobi, whereas she was in Mombasa. I did go to Mombasa for one day to get my things that I had left with the landlord. When I got there, he told me that Rosie was no longer there. She had been gone from there for about a month. I figured she must already be in Switzerland. He said something about that she had been suffering. I asked him about my stuff, and he went to get my suitcase. The way he was carrying it when he came back made me realize that it was not heavy. Sure enough, when I opened it, it was empty! I asked the landlord where my things were, and he told me that Rosie had asked to get something from my suitcase. He did not know what it was that she had removed from there. He went on to say that he hadn't been there at the time, that it had been his wife that she had asked. Rosie had taken my jewelry and my clothes! I asked if Rosie had left anything of hers, and he said a suitcase. I asked to see inside it, but he wanted money from me first. I gave him some money, and I was able to get her suitcase. In it was a gold necklace and the watch the Swiss guy had given her. I took those things and left her a note telling her what the landlord had told me and how I was now taking her things in exchange. I mentioned to her that I knew she had taken my necklace and pretended it was hers (someone had seen her), so she could sell it. I also told her that we just needed to go our separate ways from then on.

From there, I left and went back to Nairobi by bus, which took all day. I went on with my life, and things got better, and I began to enjoy life again.

What Life Meant to Me at that Time

I thought life was about having a lot of material things. I would see people driving nice cars, and I wished I could have one also. I thought that having more money to buy whatever you wanted was the same as living life to the fullest. I used to hear songs on the radio encouraging people to enjoy life before we die. I remember this particular song where this woman was saying that down in the grave, there is no partying or drinking. There is no mom or dad or friends. She said when you die, you die for good. To myself, I mentally nodded that this was true. I had met men who dated lots of women, changing them like you would clothes. On the other hand, there were women whose only search was for a rich man because they believed their troubles would then be over. For my part, I started enjoying life the way I thought it should be.

I went dancing every day, and it was fun, but the next day I would feel real empty. I didn't like that emptiness. I didn't like that feeling, but everyone around me acknowledged and accepted that emptiness inside them like it was supposed to be that way. They would say things like, "You can't have everything. Be happy with what you have." To myself, I wondered how I could be happy when I dreamed of big things that never seemed to come to pass. Some people I also knew said that religion was the way to happiness, but my past experiences told me otherwise. All I knew of religion was the sacrifices I had to make in order to please God and the religious people I knew did not seem happy; there was nothing attractive about them, and they seemed to have just as many problems as the next person who wasn't religious.

I really couldn't see how I could fit in with the religious crowd. It seemed that lots of things I did and liked were unreligious. For example, some religious people didn't believe in having money; I sure did! For some, wearing makeup was a sin; I certainly did that, and so on and so forth. To me, those restrictions didn't add up to living life to the fullest and certainly didn't seem joyful. I wanted that joy that didn't stop. I wanted it when I woke up, when I went to bed, and every moment in between. Having that, to me, was living life to the fullest. No one around me had that. I realized that I had been trying to find it in dancing and drinking and other things, but it wasn't there.

I soon found myself doing things for others. I used to walk the streets and give money to the poor that would be there begging. That made me feel happy, so I continued doing it. I would help my neighbors when I could. Sometimes it was just little things, like giving sugar to someone who needed it. A little joy would enter my heart, just a little, but surely that was better than nothing. I remember seeing people who were poor and dirty, and yet they seemed happy. That would always make me wonder, *Was it joy that made them feel that way?*

> Better a poor man whose walk is blameless than a rich man whose ways are perverse. (Prov. 28:6)

> He who gives to the poor will lack nothing, but he who closes his eyes to them receives many curses.(Prov. 28:27)

What I Thought about God at That Time in My Life

At that time in my life, there were so many unanswered questions about God. There were times when I knew deep inside that God was real, and then there were other times that I wasn't so sure he was even there. I didn't understand why we have to die. More than that, I was really fearful of death. Anytime I saw a dead person or heard that someone had died, I became scared. I didn't want to die. I will go so far as to say it was my greatest fear in life at that time. It got to the point where I had stopped even going to burials because the imagery of seeing that person being put in that hole would stay with me for weeks.

It was all so confusing to me. People would always say that God loved us, yet when someone would die, I would remember my mom saying stuff like, "God has taken them," or "It was God's will that they died." If God loved us, why would he let death take us away from our loved ones? If God was real, why was there all this suffering? On the radio I would constantly hear about bad things happening. I would hear people say that if you are a good person, then good things will happen to you, and yet bad things happened to good people all the time. I considered myself a good person—I have never killed anyone, never robbed a bank. I lied a few times, but who didn't? All my lies were small ones anyway. I had caught my parents lying all the time, so no big deal. I considered myself kind; I helped people whenever I could. I didn't think I was a fornicator. I never cheated on anyone. My relationships were ended because of things that weren't my fault. So if God was real, then, I thought, he should've been able to see that I was an all right person, right?

Still further, I couldn't believe that a god who was real would let a man walk away from his kids and his wife who has no job to support them. A god that was all powerful could fix this man's mind to not want to do that. Of course, in this case, I am referring to my mom and dad. He left her, saying that it was her fault that I ran away. Was my running away really an act of rebellion? The Bible does say, "Honor thy mother and thy father." I can't claim ignorance of this commandment, for my mother did read it to me time and time again, and yet they were basically selling me to this man for some cows and goats. So who is wrong and who is right? Certainly God wasn't going to judge me for that action since what was being done against me was so unfair, right?

In my mind, there were crystal-clear times when I thought that there must be something greater than us in existence—times like when we peered down into that hole my parents had dug to see everything but our Bible destroyed. The sheer fact is that there were all these wild animals around us living free and them *choosing* to stay away from us and not harm us. These animals weren't in some reserve, locked up behind gates or something; they were living free like us. I couldn't explain the fact that people inherently knew which herbs to use for healing. My mother had taken me into the forest when I was a child to show me what herbs were for healing various ailments. Being a doctor was not something that was common where I was from. Everyone took care of themselves. If a certain herb didn't work like it should, then you would go to a native doctor to find out some other herb to use. To me, this knowledge must come from God who, after all, created the herbs in the first place.

> He makes grass grow for the cattle and plants for man to cultivate
> and bring forth food from the earth. (Ps. 104:14)

The sun, what causes the sun to shine in the day and the moon to glow at night? How did fires start in the mountains where no one lived?

> The moon marks off the seasons, and the sun knows when to go down.
> You bring the darkness, and it becomes night. (Ps. 104:19-20)

> God said, "Let there be light in the expanse of the sky to separate the
> day from the night and let them serve as signs to mark the seasons
> and days and years, and let them be lights in the expanse of the sky
> to give light on earth." (Gen. 1:14-15)

> He who looks at the earth and it trembles, who touches the mountains
> and they smoke. (Ps. 104:32)

There were other things I couldn't explain, like the multitude of languages there were in my own country and all over the earth. If there was no God, then how did it happen?

Now the whole world had one language and a common speech. (Gen. 11:1)

Then they said, "Come let us build for ourselves a new city, with a tower that reaches to the heavens . . . but the Lord came down to see the city and the tower the men were building. The Lord said, "If as one people speaking the same language they have begun to do this prideful thing, then there is nothing they won't do. Come Let us go down and confuse their language so they will not understand each other." So the Lord scattered them from there over all the Earth and they stopped building the city. (Gen. 11:4-8)

Other things, like skin color differences, were a wonder to me. I had heard that God created people, but I had also heard that people came from monkeys. I love monkeys by the way! Once I had a pet monkey, and it was so clever. It kind of looked humanesque; in fact, I knew someone who looked like a monkey! Still, I asked myself, "How many monkeys were there to have had so many people with all these different skin colors?" There just had to be a creator; something would have had to create the monkeys in the first place, right?

Through Him all things were made; without him nothing was made that has been made. (John 1:3)

So God created the great creatures of the sea and every living and moving thing with which the water teems, according to their kinds, and every winged bird according to its kind. (Gen. 1:21)

God made the wild animals according to their kinds, the livestock according to their kinds, and all the creatures that move upon the ground according to their kinds. (Gen. 1:25)

So God created mankind in his own image . . . male and female, he created them. (Gen. 1:27)

I guess, in my heart, I always knew there was a god. Yet I was still confused how there were so many religions that believed so many different things. Individually, they believed that they had the *true* religion, that they were worshipping the *true* god. Still, others believed that religion didn't really matter in and of itself, that we were all worshipping the same God anyway. I couldn't believe that though. How could Muslims be worshipping the same god? The god I was familiar with would not be pleased if you killed some Christians so that you could be rewarded with some virgins! Even Catholicism seemed a little off to some extent. I remember when I attended Catholic school, we had to pray and essentially worship the Virgin Mary. There was an image of her carrying the baby Jesus with Joseph by her side that we had to bow and pray to before school started and before we left at the end of the day. That didn't sit comfortably with me even back then as a child. When we had to do it, I would remember my mother reading to me from the Bible.

> You shall not make for yourself an idol in the form of anything in heaven above or on the earth beneath or in the waters below. You shall not bow down to them or worship them; for I, the Lord your God am a jealous God, punishing the children for the sins of the fathers to the third and fourth generation of those who hate me. (Exod. 20:4)

It's funny the things that stick in your mind, and the Ten Commandments are one of the things my mother drilled in my head. To me it didn't make sense to do this if the Bible specifically said not to, but I was a child and not wise enough to trust my own understanding.

How I Found Rosie

The friendship that Rosie and I shared had long passed. We both moved on in our lives. I didn't know exactly where she was, but I knew what city she was in, and I suspect that she knew the same of me. I had pretty much ceased thinking of her until one night I had this dream. In the dream, she kept calling me and asking me why I gave up on our friendship. She would then ask me to look for her, and I would see her. At first I ignored the dream, but it would still pop up every now and again.

There came a day after having the dream that I couldn't stop thinking about her. Unable to let it go, I made a decision to go and look for her. I rode all day to the city where I had left her. I visited all the places where we used to hang out, and I asked people about her. No one knew where she was. I even went back to our old landlord and asked after her, but he said that he hadn't seen her since she had come for her suitcase. As long as I live, I will never be able to explain, but something told me to take a taxi to a certain village; I forget the name right now. Anyway, I got there, and I had a sense of where to stop, and I had the taxi stop there. I got out and visited some shops, asking people if they knew a girl living around there who was from Uganda. Everyone said no until one person said they knew someone who knew a girl from Uganda, but he wasn't going to be available until the evening. It was morning at the time, so I decided to get my hair done at the salon across the street while I waited. When I was done, I waited until it was time to meet the guy. When I met him, he said that he knew a girl who was from Uganda who is married to a friend of his who was a Kenyan. Together we went to see them.

At this point, you can guess that it turned out to be Rosie. When she saw me, she welcomed me but didn't seem surprised to see me. She was surprised at how I came to find her though. It turned out that she married the guy who had given her those diseases all that time ago. Of course, this surprised me; what happened to the Swiss guy? When we entered the house, I saw a baby sleeping. She told me that it was her baby and that she had gotten pregnant right before we went to get our passports. She said that she didn't tell me because I wasn't really talking to her at the time. As I looked around, I could see that her living conditions were very poor. The man she had married was still a bouncer, and he didn't make much money. Certainly not enough, for the baby had no diapers, and Rosie's clothes didn't look too good either. She told me all about what she had gone through. I apologized for having taken her gold necklace, and she apologized for taking my stuff. She wanted us to start over.

She seemed very happy to see me, and we talked and talked for a long time, often laughing over stupid things we had done in the past. When I was about to leave, Rosie stopped me and said she wasn't sure what I had planned, but why not stay with her. She offered to have her husband see if he could find me a job at the hotel that he worked at. The hotel was very large and had a club, two restaurants, and a crocodile village. I figured that it wouldn't hurt to ask. When her husband came home, Rosie again introduced me as her sister and asked him about finding a job for me. He agreed.

The next day, the husband came home and said that he had found two possible positions for me and that the manager wanted to meet with me for an interview the following week on Wednesday at 2:00 p.m. I was very happy, and the next day I decided to give Rosie some money for her and the baby for clothes and food. We bought some food first and brought it home. Later we went to a flea market, and I gave her 500 KSh. That was a lot considering that her rent was 350 KSh a month. I bought some shoes and a handbag. She wanted to split up and said for us to meet back in an hour.

When an hour had passed, she came back all upset. She told me that her money had been stolen! She showed me her bag where it had been cut by someone on the bottom where the money could come out. I asked her how that could happen, and she said that she had been looking at baby clothes and that when she went to pay, she reached in her bag and found that this had happened. All the money was gone. I had a little money left and offered it to her so she could buy some clothes. When we got home, I told her that if I got the job, I would travel back there. I went for the interview and got the job. Having done this, I traveled back to Nairobi to get my things. When I arrived back, Rosie said that she had found a place for me to rent. I went there and paid up front for three months.

I was supposed to work at the hotel from 2:00 p.m. to 11:00 p.m. When I got there the first day, they told me to wait for the manager. The manager came and told me that they had given the job to someone else! I was so disappointed. Rosie's husband was optimistic and told me not to worry. Unfortunately, time went by—first one month, then two! Rosie suggested that I move with them before I get evicted; I thought that her place was too small. She insisted that they could make room for me until I figured out what to do next. Once again, life wasn't going so well. Things weren't horrible; after all, I had my friend back, and she was helping me out.

I Gave My Life to Jesus

I was walking the streets one day, and this man asked if he could speak to me for a few minutes about Jesus. He was very polite and said that it wouldn't take long. So we moved out of the way of the main flow of people to a street with a quiet corner. He started talking to me and telling me that Jesus was everything and that Jesus could change my life. He told me that in Jesus, I could have the joy that the world couldn't offer me. He said that I needed to be born again and receive him. When he said that, I remembered back to all those years ago when I had seen that white man in that tent who had said the same things that this man was now saying. I remembered how my mom didn't want me to be one of those born-again people. I asked him how I could be born again when I thought I had done this all those years ago, but when I was seven, I didn't have the same understanding. He told me that it was simple and to just repeat after him. He said, "Lord Jesus, come into my heart. I give you my life, take control of it. Forgive me my sins and make me a new creature from this day forward. I will serve you. Satan, I renounce you, for you are not my god. Jesus, fill me with your Holy Spirit. Amen." The man then commanded me to find a church and go there, and then he left.

> Now there was a man of the Pharisees named Nicodemus, a member of the Jewish ruling council. He came to Jesus at night and said, "Rabbi, we know you are a teacher who has come from God. For no one could perform the miraculous signs you are doing if God were not with him." In reply Jesus declared, "I tell you the truth, no one can see the kingdom of God unless he is born again." "How can a man be born when he is old?" Nicodemus asked. "Surely he cannot enter again into his mother's womb and be born!" Jesus answered. "I tell you the truth, no one can enter the kingdom of God unless he is born of water and the Spirit. Flesh gives birth to flesh, but the Spirit gives birth to Spirit." (John 3:1-6)

After I had that prayer, I felt as if a heavy blanket had been removed from me. I could now see clearly, almost as if I had been blind before! The joy I had been looking for filled my heart; the empty place was now filled! I cried and I asked myself how is it that I didn't know of this before. I looked in the mirror, and I could see myself clearly there. I woke up with joy the next day also, and I knew that Jesus was in my heart.

> Whoever believes in me, as scripture has said, streams of living water shall flow from within him. (John 7:38)

> Then Jesus declared, "I am the bread of life. He who comes to me will never go hungry, and he who believes in me will never be thirsty. (John 6:35)

Notice that it doesn't say that you have to worship Buddha, Mary, Joseph, a cow, or anything else. You also don't have to pray five times a day facing a certain direction or bow before an image either. You just have to believe in him.

Before this, I was a living person, but I was dead inside. I was happy when I was dancing, but when I stopped, there was nothing. I felt good when I was drunk, but when the alcohol left me, there was nothing. I would cry for no reason; there was an ongoing sadness and an emptiness that couldn't be filled with whatever I was doing. I still had my dreams and wished for accomplishments, but at the same time, there was no realistic way of achieving them. It was as if my spirit was dead.

> Jesus said to them, "I tell you the truth, unless you eat of the flesh of the Son of Man and drink his blood, you will have no life in you. Whoever eats my flesh and drinks my blood has eternal life, and I will raise him up at the last day. For my flesh is real food and my blood is real drink. Whoever eats my flesh and drinks my blood remains in me, and I in him. Just as the living Father sent me, and I am in him, so the one who feed on me will live because of me. This is the bread that came down from heaven. Your forefathers ate manna and died, but he who feeds on this bread will live forever." (John 6:53-58)

I used to think that if a person was rich, then that meant that they were happy and lacked nothing. I met a girl in the club one night who proved me wrong. This girl had everything. She had two kids, her husband was rich, she was driving an expensive car, and she even had a maid to clean for her. What was strange was that when she came to the club, she would sit in the corner by herself. We eventually became friends, and after that, she started to open up to me. She told me how unhappy she was even though she had all these things. She seemed to think that I was happy, but that was after I had had a few beers! I realized that having money was not enough. Having money doesn't stop lots of rich people from committing suicide, as ridiculous as that seems to some people. I am sure that I am not the only one who hears people around them saying that once they get married, they'll be happy. Then it becomes once they have kids, they'll be happy. People all over the world are looking for joy, to feel good on the inside all the time, but they don't know what can do that, what can fill that void. We all look for it in the wrong places—relationships, drugs, alcohol, shopping, power, and so on—but it's not there. I didn't know either, but I do now! In the book of John, it speaks of when Jesus met a Samaritan woman, who had gone through several husbands, at a well.

> He told her, "Go call your husband and come back." "I have no husband," she replied. Jesus said to her, "You are right when you say you have no husband. The fact is that you have had five husbands, and the man you now have is not your husband. What you have said is quite true." (John 4:16-18)

This woman was looking for joy and happiness from men. Jesus offered her joy "like a spring of water welling up to eternal life." When the Spirit of God comes and fills the empty places in our lives, it gives us joy every day, whether you are rich or poor, whether things are going well in our lives or not. The Spirit of God gives peace that springs up every day, regardless of how people treat you or how they are acting around you.

When I think of joy, I think of babies. I personally believe that babies have the Spirit of God in them because babies are so filled with love and peace. Have you ever really just watched a baby from afar? If you leave a baby by itself and it has been fed and all that, that baby will lie or sit there and talk and look at something you can't see and smile and laugh, so full of life and joy. Babies are always smiling at people, and when they do, people can't help but feel a piece of that joy and smile back.

I Fell in Love with Jesus

I fell in love with Jesus, and he gave me what I had been looking for—peace, love, and joy; truly these are gifts from God. I was a new creation; my sins were forgiven and washed away by the blood of the cross. Salvation. Salvation is not a religion. Salvation is a relationship with God, and in fact, religion separates us from God. I know that when I was seven years old and I met that American man who was preaching in that tent, I became a new creation, and the Spirit of God was upon me. That Spirit drew me to other born-again people at that church. Spirit led me in prayer that healed me and my mother of malaria. My mother, still an unbeliever of my born-again status, forced me to go to that Catholic school and then had me become a Muslim, though I was neither in my heart. Those experiences disconnected, separated, me from God. By the grace of God, I was drawn back into the fold, and I was not going to let that happen again.

I told Rosie about what had happened to me and expressed my great happiness and hope for the future. At that time, all my dreams seemed possible again. I told her that my finding God again was proof that through him, my dreams can come true. Rosie was silent. I found a new church in the area, and I urged her to come with me so that she also might find Jesus. She finally came one day, but afterward, she was unhappy and said that she had felt nothing. Since I didn't have a job, as a new member now, I was able to attend the church whenever it was in session, whether it was on Sunday or during the week, day or night. If there was praying going on, I was there. When you give your life to Jesus, God gives you his Spirit, which will start to work in your life.

> We have not received the Spirit of the world but the Spirit that who
> is from God, that we may understand what God has freely given us.
> (1 Cor. 2:12)

> Don't you know that you yourselves are God's temple and that God's
> Spirit lives in you? (1 Cor. 3:16)

That empty place inside of us is not an accident. God created us in his image, and he wanted to have a place in our lives. That emptiness can only be filled by him through Jesus so that he might fellowship with us. Religion in and of itself won't do it, only Jesus.

This is something that Satan knows. He knows this, and he will do whatever he can to keep us from getting what is right and true. He used my mother against me when I was a child. She lectured me and whipped me for going to the born-again church. Instead, she preferred me to be a Catholic or a Muslim. Even being a Protestant at the time in Uganda was not the same because they were not teaching about being born again and receiving Jesus and the Holy Spirit within us. There is only one way, and if anyone says they received the Holy Spirit and it was not through Christ (people have said this to me), then they are believing falsely.

> Dear friends, do not believe every spirit, but test the spirits to see whether they are from God, because there are many false prophets that have gone out into the world. This is how you can recognize the Spirit of God: Every spirit that acknowledges that Jesus Christ has come in the flesh is from God, but every spirit that does not acknowledge Jesus is not from God. This is the spirit of the antichrist, which you have heard is coming and is already in the world. (1 John 4:1-3)

> And many false prophets will appear and deceive many people. (Matt. 24:11)

I Had a Dream from God

As I mentioned before, I moved in with Rosie and her husband and child. A few days after regiving my life over to Jesus, I made friends with a woman at the church I had found. She was a deacon there. She and I exchanged life stories, and she suggested that I could move in with her instead of staying with Rosie. This woman had a two-bedroom flat, and it was near the church. This was very generous of her, as I still had not found a job at this time. I left all my stuff with Rosie and only took my clothes with me.

This lady treated me like a sister. We went together to the church nightly for prayer. I started volunteering at the church, and I helped in every way that I could, even by cleaning it. Everything was going well. However, there were some strange things going on at this church. The lady I was staying with was connected to the pastor. She would go to the pastor's house sometimes, but she never took me. One day, my friend told me that the pastor had been invited to do some preaching in Norway and that he was going to make the announcement that Sunday coming up, which he did.

The Monday after the announcement, my friend came home from work at 4:00 p.m. She told me that she was going to go over to the pastor's house. I was confused; I thought that the pastor had left that morning to travel to Norway. She told me that he did travel there and that he was back. She laughed and said that I obviously didn't know much about God. The pastor, she said, was able to do this because God gave him power so that he could travel through water, not airplanes! She said that she had also travelled through water with the pastor to Tanzania, where she talked to a witch there! I was in total shock. I told her to please just stop telling me those things, and she realized that I didn't believe her. I didn't know what to say or think, so I just had to walk away.

After this had happened, I had a dream. In this dream, an angel of the Lord came to me. He told me that he was a messenger from God and that he had a message for me. He told me that God was going to take me to America. He said that I was going to have a profitable business doing hair and that I would use this business to minister to both men and woman from all nations and walks of life. He then went on to name some of the nationalities of the people I would minister to and thusly be serving God. The angel also told me that I would find a church in America and that I would sing in the choir there. This angel sang a song to me that I would sing in this choir. He also told me about the services of that church and the community I would be involved in. He warned me that I would be persecuted by the devil in this church but said that I should not be fearful, for God would be with me. This angel told me how much God loved me, but I couldn't believe that was true. The angel noticed this and reemphasized that God truly did love me and told me to receive his love then, and I did. He warned me that the devil was going to try and stop all these things from happening and that he would shift me. Just before he disappeared, he said, "Peace be with you." When I woke up, the room was filled with peace, and the atmosphere was so sweet. In wonder, I kept repeating to myself that an angel had been there. The next morning, I was so excited to tell everyone I knew about this angel that had visited me.

The first person that I told was my roommate. After I told her, she didn't say anything; she just walked away and went into her room. Next I went to Rosie's house and told her everything the angel had said to me. I spent the whole day there. Rosie was helping me take the braids out of my hair. While she was doing that, I heard something suspiciously like my hair being cut and not just the braids. I asked her about it, and she said it was just a mistake. She said it was only a small part of my hair that was gone. It was late when she finished my hair, so she suggested that I stay there at her house for the night. I agreed, and while I was there, I kept talking about that angel. Rosie wanted to know how this was all going to come about since I didn't have a job. How was God going to get me to America, she wanted to know. I couldn't answer her because I truly had no idea, but I believed it would happen because the angel told me.

I don't believe you have to be special to have dreams from God, and in fact, I believe that at some time or another, we can all dream these types of dreams from God and even from the devil himself. There is no specific formula to these dreams, and they might not make sense at the time that they are dreamed. They may simply be a solution to a problem we are having or a warning against something that is happening or about to happen. Not everyone can accept a dream as something true or will even act upon them, but that doesn't diminish the power or accuracy of these dreams. Telling people about them can bring scorn or awe of God's power.

> Joseph had a dream, and when he told his brothers, they hated him
> all the more. (Gen. 37:5)

An angel of the Lord appeared to him in a dream and said, "Joseph son of David, do not be afraid to take Mary home as your wife, because what is conceived in her is from the Holy Spirit." (Matt. 1:20)

An angel of the Lord appeared to Joseph in a dream. "Get up," he said, "take the child and his mother and escape to Egypt." (Matt. 2:13)

Speaking to Rosie made me wonder why God had chosen me. Why had he given such a dream to me, and more than that, why was he going to bless me in this way? I wasn't anyone special. I was a runaway who was poor and had nothing of credit to my name, no degree, no nothing. I tried to think of how God was going to make these things come to pass. Perhaps he was going to make a way for me to go back to school so that I could hold my own against the people in America who were so much more advanced than me. Then I though that God had sent that angel to me, so maybe somehow, he was going to use that angel to make these things come to pass. Possibilities whirled around in my head with no conclusion forthcoming.

When I went back home, my roommate seemed very displeased with me and demanded that I speak with her after dinner. It was definitely more of a command than a request, so I said okay. After dinner, she said that she could not believe for a moment that God had spoken to me or sent an angel to tell me anything. Why should he, she asked, since she had been saved for several years and this had never happened. I, on the other hand, had only been born-again for six months. She continued explaining why this could not have happened to me, and then she told me to pack all my clothes and to leave her house. After saying that, she went to her room and slammed the door shut. I went into my room and cried. I couldn't believe this had happened. How could she do this to me? I thought she was a good person. To myself, I then said that she was just upset and that it would blow over. I didn't pack anything, and instead, I went to Rosie's house to tell her what had happened.

Rosie laughed when I told her. It seemed to delight her to tell me how these born-again people call themselves servants of God, and yet this happened. She reminded me that she had invited me to stay with her and that I decided to leave and go to that church, but I could return and stay with her. She told me to go back and get my stuff. I decided to wait until lunchtime, when I knew my roommate would be home. I wanted her to see me get my things and know that I hadn't taken anything else. When I got there and tried to use my key, it didn't work! She opened the door and showed me that she had already packed my things. I picked them up and left. All the joy I had from this message from the angel was gone. I felt so deflated as I went back to once again live with Rosie.

While I was living there, I became sick. I took some herbs, but they didn't help me. I thought perhaps I had malaria, so I took some malaria tablets, but that made me worse. Then I decided to pray about my illness and I got better! I decided to go walking, but I didn't know where to go. Due to the circumstances, I didn't want to go back to that church. As I was walking, I was thinking. Rosie had told me that it was okay for me to stay at her house, but no longer at nighttime. Her husband had been complaining to her that they no longer had any privacy with me there. I was basically homeless again. I would go and spend nights at the bus station park because there was always someone working and walking through there. Sometimes, I would spend some time at a little kiosk by the hotel that was on the beach. This kiosk would sell food to the staff that worked there at the hotel. I got some sleep at night, but mostly I would sleep during the day at Rosie's. During this time, I wasn't sad. I had joy and peace, and nobody who saw me would think that I was going through anything.

Do not grieve for the joy of the Lord is your strength. (Neh. 8:10)

I was eating lunch at Rosie's one day, and I looked down at my plate and saw a lizard and something else entering my body! They both disappeared into my body, and the next thing I knew, I was jumping up and shouting and making all kinds of noises. It was like I was insane! I heard all sorts of music in my ears, and I was dancing. Rosie somehow snapped me out of it, and I heard a woman telling her to take me to the hospital because I must have cerebral malaria that was affecting my brain. The next day came, and I was still not back to my normal self. I was quiet now, but I was still seeing things. We went to the clinic and had to wait for a while because there were so many patients. When the doctor finally got to me, he looked me over, and then they took my blood. We had to wait for the results, and when they came, the doctor said that there was no trace of cerebral malaria, no HIV, or any kind of sickness in my blood, so we went home.

The noise in my head had not abated. It was so painful. At times, I could hear voices in my head. There were two distinct groups, and they were fighting over me. They would argue over which side had rights to my soul. At times, it would sound like things were landing on the roof of the house, coming and going like in an airport. At nighttime, I would see these beings of which I had never seen in my life. They were half human and half animal, and I would beg them not to kill me. In the midst of things, I could see Rosie, but I didn't know who she was. I remember a woman telling her to take me to the church I had been attending so that they could pray for me because it was obvious that I was crazy.

Rosie brought me there and dropped me off. While there, things became worse. I started to see other things. I remember these two chickens would come, and they tormented me by picking at my feet. I would scream and scream for mercy, but that didn't stop them. There was also this woman who looked like a mermaid, with the upper body of a woman and the lower part like a fish. When she came near me, the pain was even worse than that of the chickens. She would just look at me, and an overwhelming fear would come upon me. I would call for help, but no one came. Sometimes I would be aware enough to see actual people, but this mermaid would come and stand next to them, and they, of course, didn't see her. I would try to tell them and ask them to help me get rid of her. One day, this mermaid seemed to enter my body; I don't remember what happened after that, but when she left me, I saw her go to the ocean.

Next there was another creature that had the body of a woman, but the head of what looked like a cow that had a bigger nose and bigger ears. This creature looked so angry, and when it was there, the pain it brought was worse than that of the mermaid. It tormented me without mercy. This creature would whip me and abuse me; it would also talk to me and mock me. I tried to get these people at the church to help me, but they couldn't see what I was talking about, so they ignored me. Sometimes it seemed as if they couldn't even hear me. All these creatures—the chickens, the mermaid, and that half human-half beast—were demons. They were tormenting me because I was born again, but they couldn't possess me or truly inhabit my body because I still had the Holy Spirit inside of me. Had I not given my life to Jesus, I know that things would have been much worse for me. Demons are real and can posses people.

> Many who were demon-possessed were brought to Him(Jesus) and he drove out the spirits with a word and healed the sick. (Matt. 8:16)

> A man who was demon-possessed and could not talk was brought to Jesus and when the demon was driven out, the man who had been mute, spoke. (Matt. 9:32-33)

Matthew 17:14-20 tells of Jesus rebuking a demon out of a boy who had been suffering from seizures. Demons are presently on this earth tormenting people, influencing them, and causing diseases. I never knew of this until it had happened to me. None of the biblical teachings I encountered had come upon these passages in the Bible. This experience made me wonder at people who are in mental hospitals all over the world suffering as I did. Were they truly insane, or were they being tormented by demons and unable to break through? Thank God that that preacher had found me when he did and thus spared me a fate like that.

I can't tell you how many days went by that I was tortured by these demons, but one day, they were just gone as if they had never been there. In a daze of sorts, I got on the bus and left that church. I went back to my so-called best friend's house, and when she saw me, she couldn't believe it. She took me to the mental hospital and told them what had been happening. The doctor there checked me over and said there was nothing wrong with me, that he could see no sign of insanity at all. The doctor told her that she could take a walk with him to one of the wards there and see some actual insane people for herself, and they left. I didn't follow them, and they left me lying down in the hallway.

Through this ordeal, I guess I hadn't eaten much. I was as thin as a stick, and I had no energy. Even in the doctor's office, I couldn't stand but, instead, was lying down. I couldn't even talk. While they were gone, I heard a voice, and it told me to stand up and go home. How I managed this, I could not tell you because I was so weak with no energy to eat, let alone walk, but I did. As I was walking, the voice told me to go to the butcher and ask for money for the bus. The mental hospital was far from where Rosie's house was. I made my way to this butcher shop, and I spoke to a human there, and he responded and gave me money for the bus. I say "human" because before this, the only interaction I had was with the demons; no humans ever responded to me. I took the bus and made it home to Rosie's. When Rosie finally saw me, I could tell she was shocked to see me. She didn't say a word, and I walked into the house. There were no more voices in my head and no more noises. I was truly healed from the demonic-induced mental illness. It was God that delivered me from these demons that tortured me, allowing me to be here at this moment, writing this book.

> He reached down from on high and took hold of me; he drew me out of deep waters. He rescued me from my powerful enemy, from my foes, who were too strong for me. They confronted me in the day of my disaster, but the Lord was my support. He brought me out into a spacious place; he rescued me because he delighted in me. (Ps. 18:16-19)

There is a story in the Bible about a man who had been possessed by demons and was released from them that touched me deeply.

> When Jesus stepped ashore, he was met by a demon-possessed man from the town. For a long time this man had not worn clothes or lived in a house, but had lived in the tombs. (Luke 8:27)

Imagine how this man must have felt with these demons tormenting his mind and having him live naked in tombs.

> When he saw Jesus, he cried out and fell at his feet, shouting at the top of his voice, "What do you want with me, Jesus, Son of the Most High God? I beg you, don't torture me!" (Luke 8:28)

I find this interesting. This man was possessed, and it was the demon speaking through him. Demons know Jesus for who he is and knew he had the power to do them harm.

> For Jesus had commanded the evil spirit to come out of the man. Many times it had seized him, and though he was chained hand and foot and kept under guard, he had broken his chains and had been driven by the demon into solitary places. Jesus asked him, "What is your name?" "Legion," he said, "for we are many." (Luke 8:29-30)

Jesus asked the man his name, but it was the demons who answered him, showing Jesus that they were in control.

> And they begged him repeatedly not to order them to go into the Abyss. (Luke 8:31)

The abyss is a place of confinement for evil spirits and for Satan. To know more about this, you may read Revelations 9:1.

> A large herd of Pigs was feeding there on the hillside. The demons begged Jesus to let them go into them, and he gave them permission. When the demons came out of the man, they went into the pigs, and the herd rushed down the steep bank into the lake and was drowned . . . The man from whom the demons had gone out begged to go with Jesus, but he sent him away saying, "Return home and tell how much God has done for you." So the man went away and told all over town how much Jesus had done for him. (Luke 8:32-38)

There are doctors all over the world that are dealing with people with mental conditions. Statistically, I wonder how many are battling demons. How radical it would be if we treated people with prayer, with Jesus, so that they might be set free. There are people all over the world who celebrate Christmas and stop at that not knowing, not realizing, not truly understanding the power of Jesus and how powerful he could be in their lives.

There are demons that are wandering around in the spirit, who are no more powerful than you or I. They know Jesus is the Son of God, and they know the power he possesses; they fear him for that and rightly so. This experience I had was not a dream or vision. It truly lasted for days and days. At the time, I didn't know what was going on; it was only afterward, as time passed, that God revealed it to me, revealed himself to me, and gave me these scriptures to prove what he was revealing to me was true. How did he do this? After I was delivered by the Lord from the demons that had tormented me, I had another experience. It wasn't a dream or a vision, but rather, this time, I was caught up in the spirit by God. My human eyes were open, but in addition to that, God enabled me so that I could see in the spirit world. There was a noticeable difference between this experience and the one I had with the demons. God was in control, and throughout, there was nothing but peace. At first I wasn't sure what was going on, but then God started revealing and teaching things to me. This revelation commenced at a pace that I could handle. He told me he wanted me to understand, and we handled it like a Q&A session. He first told me that there are many demons in this world and that they want to live in human bodies. I asked why were there not more people running around mad. He told me that they are working on people in different ways. He told me that they are invisible to human eyes but that you can see them in the spirit, and then he opened my eyes to see. He pointed out a man to me, and I could see from a distance that there were demons inside of him. The Lord asked me how many there were, but I could only tell that there was more than one; yet he looked normal from the outside. As if reading my mind, the Lord said that he was not normal, and these demons were controlling this man's life and causing him to make bad decisions, and he can't sleep at night.

Next he showed me a woman, and I could see the demons inside of her. He explained to me that these demons caused her to overeat, and she also could not sleep at night. I was in Rosie's house as the Lord was revealing this all to me. I could see so far, it was astonishing. I could see the roads and into different houses, and there were demons everywhere. There was a particular man that the Lord showed me; he was in the road and a demon was just standing there, talking in his ear. The Lord said that this is something that commonly happens in people's lives: demons whispering in people's ears. As I watched, the Lord opened my ears to hear what the demon was saying and what the man was thinking. The man had had an argument with his wife and was very upset. He felt that he was tired of his wife. The demon asked the man why doesn't he just kill her. I could visibly see the man receiving these words. To himself, he said that no one would know it was him. The demon heard this thought and, even louder, said that he should kill his wife and added that no one would know that it was him and that this was the only way out of his marriage. The man received those words also and was convinced to think about it further.

The Lord said that the man didn't have the Word in him, and thusly, "Thou shall not kill" was not written in his heart, and because of this, he would continue to listen to the demon. The Lord went on to say that he had given people his Word and that it is in bibles in houses all over the world, and still people do not read or heed them and that his Word has power and is the only way to defeat these demons. Jesus himself was tempted by Satan and used the Word to fight him.

> Then Jesus was led by the Sprit into the desert to be tempted by the devil. After fasting for 40 days and 40 nights, he was hungry. The tempter came to him and said, "If you are the Son of God, tell those stones to become bread. Jesus answered, "It is written: 'Man does not live on bread alone, but on every word that comes out of the mouth of God.'" Then the devil took him to the holy city and had him stand on the highest point of the temple. "If you are the Son of God," he said, "throw yourself down for it is written: 'He will command his angels concerning you, and they will lift you up in their hands, so that you do not strike your foot against a stone.'" Jesus answered him, "It is also written, 'Do not put the Lord your God to the test.'" Again, the devil took him to a very high mountain and showed him all the kingdoms of the world and their splendor. "All this I will give to you," he said, "if you will bow down and worship me." Jesus said to him, "Away from me, Satan! For it is written: 'Worship the Lord your God, and serve Him only.'" Then the devil left him, and the angels came and tended him. (Matt. 4:1-11)

So the Lord said that if this man could say God's Word in his mind against those murderous thoughts, the demon would leave him alone. However, if he does not, he will continue to listen to this demon and kill his wife and be caught. How can you know God's Word if you don't read it? The devil knows this, and that is why he fights so hard against bibles being in schools and stuff like that. He knows that if children read the Bible and have this information, he will lose power over them. Instead, he encourages them to watch TV and get on the Internet so he can feed them whatever he wants.

The Lord showed me some men in a house that were smoking marijuana, and then he showed me a demon in a tree and indicated that he was the controller of the whole village. I could draw you a picture of what this demon looked like. It was so big it could look over the whole village. It had a body of a human from its head to where the wings started. Under its wings, it had hands with fingers on it and the legs of an animal with fur on it. The Lord told me to look at what the demon does to them after they smoke. This is what happened: This demon was on the tree far from where the men were smoking. It reached its finger across the way, and while the men were smoking, he commanded the first man to go steal. The man didn't hesitate and left immediately. He told the next man to go beat his wife up and to then go hide in the bushes and wait for another woman to beat. Again, this guy didn't hesitate either. The third guy in the house was Rosie's husband. The demon stretched his hand to him and commanded him to commit adultery with another woman, and off he went. This demon was watching them and was laughing and enjoying himself. The Lord showed me these men doing these things and explained to me that when these men smoked, they gave their minds up and were no longer in control of themselves. The demon waited until they were smoking and getting high and used that as an opening to use his power on them.

Demons That Rule Over Towns

God told me that big demon ruled over that village and that every sin that was committed was caused by him in one way or another—either by demons suggesting and prompting people, like the man and his wife, or by direct control over people's minds, like what happened when those men were getting high and leaving themselves vulnerable. These men could not be directly controlled when they were sober because they weren't possessed. The demon in charge had lesser demons that reported to him and carried out his instructions. This kind of activity is not uncommon and is in fact very common in cities and countries all over the world. You can observe for yourself certain cities where certain types of crimes happen with regularity. For example, there are cities with high murder or robbery rates, whereas another city might have a severe drug problem, or still even another city, where sex crimes are committed on regularly. That is why it is very important to find out about an area before moving to it.

Believe it or not, I was attacked by the demon of gluttony when I lived in Ohio. It started one day with me just eating and eating. I was compelled to do it. At first I just thought that I was adjusting to being in America after recently coming from Africa, but it was more than that. I would even wake up in the night and just eat and eat. We are not just talking about snacking. I was overeating for no reason. After a few days, the Holy Spirit revealed to me that it was the demon of gluttony attacking me, and I prayed about it, and the demon left me. Suffering from the demon of gluttony might sound unimportant in a world where there are people starving, but here in America especially, people are dying because of problems caused by overeating. People get diabetes, have heart attacks, and have other issues that stem from the fact that they are compelled to overeat even when they know it's bad for them. They know and can't or won't stop; sounds like the demon of gluttony to me.

> When you sit down with a ruler, note well what is in front of you, and
> put a knife to your throat if you are given to gluttony. Do not crave
> his delicacies, for that food is deceptive. (Prov. 23:2-3)

That proverb sounds innocuous, but think of it in the context of how overeating makes you feel. Invigorated? No. Tired, sluggish, more apt to make wrong decisions or not make decisions or act at all because of the fact that you are not operating at full capacity. Sometimes people even use food to bribe you or make you more open to their plans. Ever heard of a business lunch? How about some drinks first, business later? These tried-and-true tactics are used by people all over the world. Plying people with lots of food, and drinks make people let their guards down and leave themselves open to plotting and deceit.

Demons That Rule through People in Authority

It is very important for us to choose leaders that will not give in to the demons that are running around. We need people in charge that are of good character. People who are honest, disciplined, and have a healthy fear of the Lord.

> The fear of the Lord is the beginning of wisdom, and knowledge of the Holy One is understanding. (Prov. 9:10)

A God-fearing person is not going to give in to these demons. A man who is of God will recognize the demons for what they are and resist and rebuke. It is a shame that the world doesn't seem to care if a person has a godly background or outlook on life. Yet having people of not just moral character (even Satan can say what is right and wrong) but godly character plays a big role in the spiritual realm of things. It is not enough to see that such and such leader has a Christian name and calls themselves a Christian or goes to church on Sundays. What kind of things are they doing in their life, in their career, and for others under their leadership?

We had a president called Idi Amin in my country. This man did unspeakably horrid things to the people in my country. He killed so many people, but so did Hitler. However, this man took it beyond that. He even killed a woman that he had slept with. He cut her body up, cooked it, and ate it. He didn't stop there. The demons he was serving—and there is no doubt in my mind that he was being influenced or controlled by demons—had him kill and eat his own son! Some people might try to just say he was just crazy, but no, this is beyond that. This was a man in control of an army, of a country, who gave himself over to demons. This man had no fear of anything or anyone, and thus he did whatever he wanted, or rather, whatever the demons wanted. He killed and killed and killed people like they were insects.

A biblical example of a man in power who killed indiscriminately, out of what can only be seen as being prompted by Satan or his demons, is King Herod. King Herod was minding his own business and running his piece of the world as he always did; he was definitely no Solomon. Some magi came to him, asking for Jesus whom they called the one who has been born the king of the Jews. Of course, Herod considered himself the king of the Jews and was troubled that someone else could stake such a claim. More than likely, that troubling came from demons that were whispering to him that his power could be thwarted by someone with such a claim. However, Herod told the magi to find this baby and report back to him so that he might worship this child also. The magi did find him and bestowed gifts upon him but didn't report back because they were warned in a dream that Herod's true purpose was to kill Jesus. When Herod realized what had happened, he had his army go out and kill all the newborn male children in Bethlehem and the surrounding areas in an attempt to make sure Jesus was dead. Unknowingly, he failed because an angel of the Lord warned Joseph in a dream of the danger, and they escaped. (Matt. 2:1-23)

In reality, Herod shouldn't have been worried at all. He knew the prophecy that the magi spoke of, and it didn't even allude to the type of power that Herod possessed or the actual position that he held.

> But you Bethlehem, in the land of Judah, are by no means least among the rulers of Judah; for out of you will come a ruler who will be the shepherd of my people of Israel. (Matt. 2:6)

However, Satan knew what the real deal was, and he was worried. He knew what it all meant, and he tried to prevent Jesus from doing what he came to do. So he himself, or the demons in his control, influenced Herod to do what he did. Even today, we have things like this going on. The president of Iran wants to wipe Israel off the face of the earth. Why in reality should he really want to do that? He really is calling for the destruction of another place. We are not just talking about invasion of property for resources or the kidnapping of women because their population is declining. He is being influenced by demons, and in turn, he is influencing his nation to do this horrible thing.

The Hatred That Demons Have for Human Beings and How They Came to Be on Earth

God created us in his own image and likeness and has a plan for our lives.

> Then God said, "Let us make man in our own image, in our likeness, and let them rule over the fish of the sea and the birds of the air, over the livestock, over all the earth, and over all the creatures that move along the ground." So God created man in his own image, in the image of God he created him; male and female he created them. (Gen. 1:26-27)

He blessed and tasked us to be fruitful and multiply. God does not force himself on us; he gave us a mind of our own and freedom to do as we want. He created this beautiful earth full of everything we could possibly need. Unlike angels, God calls us his children. He loves us so much even though we sin against him. More than that, *despite* the fact that we sin against him, he provided a way through Jesus that we might be redeemed from our sins.

The devil knows how God feels about us; after all, he used to be an angel of God himself. When he turned his back on God, he turned his back on us. He tries to hurt God through us, and he will do it with any means at his disposal, demons included. Satan's first act against us occurred in the Garden of Eden (he sure wasted no time, eh?). We all know the devil, who was disguised as a serpent, tempted Eve into eating the fruit from the tree in the middle of the garden. She then gave some of it to her husband. The serpent lied to Eve and convinced her that God's edict, that they not eat from that tree, was due to selfishness on God's part and that by eating it, she would be as knowledgeable as God, as well as live forever. The devil knew that God didn't lie and that they would die if they ate of it, and he wanted them to die, but why? They had done nothing to him.

The devil, once an angel serving God, became jealous of God and wanted God's power for his own. He rebelled against God and was tossed out of heaven.

> You were the model of perfection, full of wisdom and perfect in beauty . . . you were anointed as a guardian cherub, for I so ordained you. You were on the holy mount of God . . . you were blameless in your ways from the day you were created till wickedness was found in you . . . you were filled with violence, and you sinned. So I drove you in disgrace from the mount of God . . . Your heart became proud on account of your beauty, and you corrupted your wisdom because of your splendor. So I threw you to earth . . . you have come to a horrible end and will be no more. (Ezek. 28:12-19)

> How you have fallen from heaven, O morning star, son of the dawn! You have been cast down to the earth, . . . you said in your heart . . . I will raise my throne above the stars of God . . . I will ascend above the tops of the clouds; I will make myself like the Most High, but you are brought down to the grave, to the depths of the pit. (Isa. 14:12-14)

As if that wasn't bad enough, to Satan's perspective, he was forgotten and then replaced with humans, and he could not, cannot, get over it, and thus he causes havoc here on earth. The thing is, he has help from his demons and from us. We have free will; he can't *make* us do stuff. He and his demons can't just possess people whenever and however they want to; there has to be an open door in our minds and hearts. He didn't shove that fruit into Eve's mouth; he lied to her and convinced her that it was in her best interest to eat that fruit. This is why we must be ever vigilant and aware of his tactics, and more so than that, we must know the character of God. If you ever are compelled to do something that is against the Word or find people reasoning things in a way that is not consistent with the character of God, then you know it is not from God, but from Satan.

How Demons Enter Your Life through Sin

The devil had to trick Eve into sinning. When God gave Moses the commandments, he didn't do it so he could have control over us; if he had wanted that, then he wouldn't have given us free will. Those commandments were given to us as protection against Satan and his demons, because sinning gives Satan power in our lives. Sinning brings us farther and farther away from God, and that is exactly what Satan wants! He uses our weaknesses against us. No one is safe from his machinations. Even Judas, a disciple of Jesus who had witnessed Jesus in all his splendor who had seen him work miracles firsthand, still betrayed Jesus because of his love of money.

> And Judas went to the chief priests and the officers of the temple guard and discussed with them how he might betray Jesus. They were delighted and agreed to give him money. He consented and watched for an opportunity to hand Jesus over to them when no crowd was present. (Luke 22:4-6)

> While he was still speaking, Judas one of the Twelve, arrived. With him was a large crowd armed with swords and clubs, sent from the chief priests and the elders of the people. Now the betrayer had arranged a signal with them. "The one I kiss is the man; arrest him." Going at once to Jesus, Judas said, "Greetings, Rabbi!" and kissed him. (Matt. 26:47-49)

> When Judas, who had betrayed him, saw that Jesus was condemned, he was seized with remorse and returned the thirty silver coins to the chief priests and elders. "I have sinned," he said, "for I have betrayed innocent blood." "What is that to us?" they replied. "That

is your responsibility." So Judas threw the money into the temple and left. Then he went away and hung himself. (Matt. 27:3-5)

Why would Judas do this? Both John 13:27 and Luke 22:3 say that Satan entered Judas, and then he betrayed Jesus's whereabouts to the priests who wanted to arrest him. Then instead of repenting when he realized the consequence of his actions and getting forgiveness from God, he then turned around and made it worse and hung himself. Certainly the devil rubbed his hands in glee. The devil could not have entered Judas if he wasn't beset with the love of money.

The same goes for us. If we are actively sinning in our lives, it leaves the spiritual door open for Satan to come in and cause our demise. Like Judas, we want that immediate satisfaction of doing something wrong but thinking it will still be for our good. For Judas, he saw that money as a means to buy who-knows-what for himself. He figured he would get the money and deal with the rest later. Certainly he must have thought that Jesus would find a way out of the mess Judas had got him in, for he was the Son of God. However, that's not what happened. He couldn't undo what he had done since the priests wouldn't take back the money they had given him and release Jesus. Why would they? They had already been plotting to arrest Jesus anyway.

And they plotted to arrest Jesus in some sly way and kill him. (Matt. 26:4)

I met this gentleman while I was at a restaurant, waiting to be seated. Our conversation started by me asking him for the time. He then wanted to know why I was eating dinner alone, and I told him that I was single. He was also alone, but I noted that he was wearing a wedding ring. When I asked him about it, he said that he was on a business trip. I don't know how we changed the subject, but the next thing I knew, he was telling me how much he loved his wife and children, but despite that, he had hired himself a prostitute one day out of the blue. He explained to me how badly he had felt after the episode, and yet he did it again and again in the future. He told me that his wife had no idea of his actions. He started crying and saying how he felt like he couldn't control himself, that he felt like he had to keep doing it. I could see the pain this man was going through, and I felt that I knew what the problem was, but I felt that I couldn't tell him because I didn't know what his beliefs were as far as God was concerned. Still, I told him that I would pray for him.

To myself, I thought about how the man had thought that his hiring of the prostitute was his own idea out of the blue and that going would be a onetime thing. Yet his acting on that thought opened the door for demons to continually influence him to do it over and over. This is nothing new in the world. It is a tried-and-true method, demons suggesting things that seem to have little or no consequences that end up turning into addictions and lifestyle changes. Satan and demons alike have a standard mode of operation: they try to persuade. They tempt us in order to bring about our eventual destruction. You can resist them like Jesus did, or you can give in like Judas. Satan and demons are a problem, no doubt about it, but worse than that is the fact that people don't recognize certain thoughts to be from the enemy in the first place. They say stuff like, "I don't know why I did this/that," or "Something just came over me." Satan wants us to think these things because it keeps the focus off him and his minions. He wants us to think it is just us and our human deficiencies when we are really involved in an equation that is spiritually designed to bring us to ruin.

Every time we listen to the enemy's prompting and act on it, every time we sin—whether it is adultery, stealing, lying, or submitting to addiction—we are giving these demons a foothold in our lives that they can use to control us. Remember, if we don't have things like greed and lust in our hearts in the first place, we wouldn't be susceptible to those types of temptation from the devil. Think of it like this: There can be one person that would never even entertain the idea of sleeping with a woman other than his wife, no matter how many demons are whispering to him; however, this same man could justify to himself the reasons why he was stealing from his employer. Simply put, different strokes for different folks.

There was another man that I met who was forty-six years old. We started talking, and he told me that he was going through a divorce. I expressed my sympathy, but he told me not to be sorry because he wasn't. He, in fact, was very happy about the impending divorce because he had plans to marry a younger woman. He had children with his current wife and had been married to her for ten years; however, he felt that ten years was too long, and he wanted to start over fresh. He had the thought that he was missing out on something in life by staying married to his wife, so he decided to divorce her. He said that he couldn't wait until the divorce was finalized so that he could do what he wanted. The thing that I thought made this situation even worse was that he didn't even have a specific woman in mind. He just specified that she had to be between twenty-six and twenty-eight years of age. I was astonished that he would give up his wife and kids for a woman that he hadn't even met yet. He replied that he was certain that he would meet her eventually. What about his wife and kids? I wondered. He said that they would be okay because he had given his wife everything she wanted—the house and so on. There really was nothing that I could say to him anymore; he wasn't listening to me, so I just excused myself and left his presence.

Where is God in all this? God's kindness is apparent in this situation and in other similar situations. I didn't just meet this man by accident and God used me to speak wisdom to this man, but the man did not want to listen. It doesn't matter if this man believes in God or not; God offers wisdom to us all for we are all his children, but we have to choose to listen to him. Where do you think the errant thought about missing out on something in life came from? Certainly not God! The enemy put that idea there with plans to destroy this man's marriage and his finances. Instead of rejecting the idea or recognizing that it was from the enemy, he embraced it, thought about it over and over until he was convinced that it was a good idea to leave his wife and children. So this man will go ahead with what he plans to do, signing the papers and all that. The demon that planted the thought will move on after this man finds the young wife he thinks he needs, or perhaps it will stick around to depress the man when he realizes what he did was wrong, that this new woman was no better or was worse than the wife he previously had.

The problem this man had started with a thought. People who betray their friends, sell drugs, kill others, molest children, and so on all started behaving that way based on an initial thought. We have to hold our thoughts captive, analyze where they are coming from—God or Satan? If our thoughts are not of God, then we have to fight them off with the Word of God like Jesus did. If we don't do that or if we end up sinning, don't blame God, and don't say, "The devil made me do that" because that isn't true.

> Blessed is the man who perseveres under trial, because when he has stood the test, he will receive the crown of life that God has promised to those that love him. When tempted, no one should say, "God is tempting me." For God cannot be tempted by evil, nor does he tempt anyone; but each one is tempted when, by his own evil desires, he is dragged away and enticed. Then, after desire has conceived, it gives birth to sin; and sin, when it is full grown, gives birth to death. (James 1:12-15)

Note that it says that first you are tempted because of *your own evil desires* (greed, lust, and so on), and then the enemy entices us. That enticement would be when the errant thoughts first arrive. Then there is the conception stage—for example, finding the prostitute and paying for services or, in that man's case, finding and contacting a lawyer for divorce. Then the sin/birth occurs—the act of adultery or the disillusion of the marriage. After that comes the consequences of those actions—death. Nowhere in that scripture does it say that the devil *made* anyone do anything. He can't make us sin; he can only point the way.

That said, what can we do so that we don't fall into sin?

> Wash and make yourselves clean. Take your evil deeds out of my sight! Stop doing wrong, learn to do right. (Isa. 1:16)

> Wash the evil from your heart and be saved. How long will you
> harbor wicked thoughts? (Jer. 4:14)

God asks that we make ourselves clean inside and put aside our wicked ways and thoughts so that when the devil comes to us, there is nothing for him to use to lead us to sin. There are things that we do that we don't even recognize as wrong behavior—for instance, take relationships and marriage. Many people are walking around, being hypocrites without realizing it or sometimes without even caring. They decide to get in a relationship or love someone because of the money or power they possess. Some people even marry for sex, thinking that at least they won't be fornicators. The thing is that if you don't love someone 100 percent and for the right reasons, your "love" is hypocrisy and sinful in God's eyes.

> Love must be sincere. Hate what is evil; cling to what is good.
> (Rom. 12:9)

God recognizes hypocrisy, and so does the devil, and he will use this information to take away that money, that power, and so on to make you miserable and to keep your focus on your problems and not on God. What else can we do to safeguard ourselves from the enemy?

Prayer

Thus far, I have spoken of the demons that God had shown me. He also showed me his angels. There was a man that the Lord showed me who was in his house and was praying. This man prayed and asked that God would bless his day, his family, and give him safety on his upcoming journey. When he was done, an angel immediately arrived to protect him. The man then left his house and got in his truck and drove away. In this particular instance, the Lord told me that had this man not prayed, he wouldn't have had a safe journey. Angels are at God's disposal and are protecting and comforting the faithful every day. How else do you explain people who have been in terrible car wrecks where the damage to the car is such that no one should have been able to walk away alive, and yet they escape with just cuts and bruises?

Despite this, some people still don't believe in angels being with them or even demons being around. However, I think we as people know more than we realize. We are aware of more things in the spirit than we realize. I believe it is a defense mechanism of sorts to protect us, more or less like a warning system. For example, I have met people who seem to have a kind of peace surrounding them. I recall a cashier that I met while shopping at a Dollar General who was surrounded by such a beautiful atmosphere of peace; I thought to myself that there was something special about her. The same goes with some people's houses. I am certain all of us have gone to some people's houses that radiate peace from the moment you step in the door. In contrast, I visited this mansion in California once that was so beautiful on the outside, like a photo, but when I went inside, I couldn't wait to leave. There was heaviness, a depressing, oppressing atmosphere in that house, so much so that I was getting a headache! From this and other similar experiences, I have learned to pray before I enter places because I don't want to feel that negative energy that demons and such leave in their wake.

God then told me that his children don't pray, that he could intercede more in their lives, but they don't pray and ask him to.

> In all your ways acknowledge him and he will make your paths straight. (Prov. 3:6)

Is there a relationship between bad things happening to good people and good things happening to bad people? Is prayer, or the lack thereof, at the root of it? Not necessarily.

> He causes his sun to rise on the evil and on the good, and sends rain on the righteous and unrighteous. (Matt. 5:45)

However, we are told in the Bible to pray.

> Be joyful always; pray continually; give thanks in all circumstances, for this is God's will for you in Jesus Christ. (1 Thess. 5:16-18)

What for? Everything—your children, your job, your spouse, your family, your finances, your needs, and even your wants.

> Do not be anxious about anything, but in everything, by prayer and petition, with thanksgiving, present your requests to God. (Phil. 4:6)

We are to pray for protection for ourselves and others.

> And pray that we may be delivered from wicked and evil men, for not everyone has faith. But the Lord is faithful, and he will strengthen and protect you from the evil one. (2 Thess. 3:2-3)

We should pray that we can resist temptation.

> Watch and pray so that you will not fall into temptation. The spirit is willing, but the body is weak. (Mark 14:38)

We should pray for healing.

> And prayer offered in faith will make the sick person well, the Lord will lift him up. If he has sinned, he will be forgiven. (James 5:15)

Most of all we should be praying for God's will in our lives. Even Jesus did this.

Going a little farther, he fell with his face to the ground and prayed, "My Father, if it is possible, may this cup be taken from me. Yet not as I will, but as you will." (Matt. 26:39)

Still don't know what to pray for? God has that covered as well.

In the same way, the Spirit helps us in our weakness. We do not know what we ought to pray for, but the Spirit himself intercedes for us with groans that words cannot express. And he who searches our hearts knows the mind of the Spirit, because the Spirit intercedes for the saints in accordance with God's will. (Rom. 8:26-27)

Prayer is a form of communication between us and God. Prayer can move mountains.

Why Is It that Some People Pray and Seem to Receive No Response from God?

The first question should be, to whom are people really praying? Are they praying to Allah? Perhaps some are imploring Mary, the mother of Jesus, to help them. Still, today there are people who believe that they should pray to people who were martyred, thinking that their particular death circumstances makes them powerful or special, but this is not so. The Bible says in John 14:13-14, "And I will do whatever you ask in my name, so that the Son may bring glory to the Father. You may ask me for anything in my name and I will do it." It also states in John 15:7-8, "If you remain in me and my words remain in you, ask whatever you wish, and it will be given to you. This is to be to my Father's glory, that you may bear fruit, showing yourselves to be my disciples." We are to pray to God through Jesus's name. However, this doesn't mean you should pray, "God, give me a new car, in Jesus's name, amen." If we are fellowshipping with God and immersing ourselves in the Word, we can become aware of what God's will is for our life and be led to pray things according to his will.

Another thing that can hinder our prayers is the existence of unconfessed sin in our lives. Sin in our lives acts like a barrier between God and us; it separates us from him. The more and more sin there is, the thicker that barrier becomes. Our prayers are essentially bouncing off this obstruction. That doesn't mean that God can't hear us, because he can. It also doesn't mean he can't help us, because he can; he is all-powerful. However, we are told to confess and repent for our sins so that we may be forgiven. When we do this, that wall crumbles, and there is nothing between us and God, leaving the way clear for prayers and blessing alike.

I remember a time in my life when I felt that none of my prayers were being heard by God. I became so unhappy, and finally, I broke down and asked God why he wasn't answering me anymore. He showed me that I had unconfessed sin in my life. The important thing about that was the fact that he showed me things that I wasn't aware of as sin in my life. I confessed and asked to be delivered from these things, and after that, I could see God acting again in my life. God wasn't ignoring my prayers; he was waiting for me to become aware of this barrier between us so that we could tear it down. Had he continued to act in the way that I had wanted him to, I never would have become desperate enough to seek him out for the one thing that really mattered: my connection to him.

I can't reiterate enough the importance of unconfessed sin in our lives and the consequences thereof. I met a woman who was going through a divorce. She didn't want to go through with the divorce, but her husband was already doing the paperwork. During our conversation, she revealed that her husband had acquired or was suffering from a mental problem. Neither she nor her husband had a history of it in their families. Of course, this raised red flags in my mind because of my own personal experience. I told her that I wasn't positive what was going on, but I would pray for her and her husband. I asked God to reveal to me what was going on in their situation, and the Lord showed me in a vision that the husband had been cheating on his wife. He told me that he had convicted the man in the spirit about it, but that the man had hardened his heart against him. Because the man refused to correct his ways or confess and repent for them, he left the door open for an evil spirit to enter his mind, and that was the cause of the mental problems he was experiencing.

The Lord told me that he was not going to work in the way that I was asking him to at that time. Another thing was that the wife herself was not honest with me. I had initially asked her about adultery, and she had said no. Honesty is important. We must be honest with ourselves and with each other and in front of God, for he sees everything anyway. Why did she waste her time telling me that neither she nor her husband had committed adultery and still turn around and ask for help? We have to take responsibilities for our actions; confess our sins; own up to playing ball in the house, resulting in that broken vase; and then we can move on.

> Therefore confess your sins to each other and pray for each other that you may be healed. The prayer of a righteous man is powerful and effective. (James 5:16)

Another thing that is important in the answering of prayer is faith. Some would say that if they didn't believe in God's power, then they wouldn't be praying in the first place. However, I think we all know that is not entirely true because we all doubt God from time to time. Some believe in God for the small things, but not the big stuff and vice versa. So unbelief can hinder our prayers as well.

> I tell you the truth, if anyone says to this mountain, "Go throw yourself into the sea," and does not doubt in his heart but believes that what he says will happen, it will be done for him. Therefore I tell you, whatever you ask for in prayer, believe that you have received it, and it will be yours. (Mark 11:23-24)

> Everything is possible for him who believes. (Mark 9:23)

The Angels

So far, we have established that there are both angels and demons among us. One thing you should know is that the demons are afraid of the angels. In the spirit, the Lord revealed this to me, and I could see them deliberately staying away from the angels because they know that the angels have the power to destroy them. That means that *we* have the ability to destroy them through the power given to the angels from God. After seeing this, I was confused. Why then, if these angels were so powerful, why didn't they always stop bad things from happening? One thing is that these angels are ours to command. They are like an army that is awaiting instruction or a powerfully strong dog on a leash. If that is your dog that is bound to you, you can tell it to attack someone, and it will. A really good dog will only attack on command regardless of what is going on around it. Yeah, it may growl at people or other animals that are a danger to you to let them know that it is capable of protecting you, or in the case of angels, let their power shine that the demons may see and then choose stay away from you. Regardless, when they are there, they are always protecting you even if you don't recognize it as such.

You might have a different idea of what protection means in a particular situation that is not the same as what God feels it means to protect you. Protection doesn't necessarily mean that nothing bad is ever going to happen to you. If nothing ever went wrong, how would you grow or learn to rely and trust in God? Conversely, a situation might call for physical protection, and God can provide it as he did for Daniel.

> My God sent his angels and he shut the mouths of the lions. They have not hurt me. (Dan. 6:22)

> For he will command his angels concerning you to guard you in all your ways; they will lift you up in their hands, so that you will not strike your foot against a stone. (Ps. 91:11)

Another thing that God showed me was what could be referred to as limited resources, as in that there aren't that many of his angels just wandering around. Again that goes back to us requesting them or, in other cases, being in a place to receive them. There is only a place at our side for either. You can't have a demon on one side and an angel on the other. They cannot coexist this way. As a believer, you can have angels at your side.

> Are not all angels ministering spirits sent to serve those who will
> inherit salvation? (Heb. 1:14)

Angels come into believers' lives from God. He will send them to us for one reason or another. But what of those who don't believe? It is actually more of a question of those that *won't* believe. There are those that are currently not believers but will become believers in the future. Remember, God is omnipotent; he knows who his children in Christ are ultimately going to be, so he can protect and send angels to minister to those who aren't his yet. He also sends people in our lives to minister to us or arranges circumstances to do the same. Remember that American man with the blue eyes that I met when I was a child? How about that man I talked to on the street corner? This is a way that he will show his faithfulness to us even when we weren't being faithful to him. He loves us. For those who are not his and have turned away from him and won't ever believe in the future, no, he will not command his angels on their behalf.

The Bible is full of instances where angels just show up without warning. How they appear varies also. They may arrive in all their angel splendor, or they might look like a human. Sometimes they are messengers to tell of something that is going to happen, like that angel that told Mary about Jesus before he was born, or with Abraham and his wife, Sarah, who was barren.

> I will surely return to you about this time next year, and Sarah your
> wife will have a child. (Gen. 2:10)

Sometimes they will be sent in our dreams, like when Joseph was warned about the danger to Jesus when he was a baby. Lot was awake when he saw some angels arrive.

> The two angels arrived at Sodom in the evening, and Lot was sitting
> in the gateway of the city. When he saw them, he got up to meet them
> and bowed down with his face to the ground. (Gen. 19:1)

Some people have told me that they have seen angels, and I don't disbelieve them; however, I am sure to ask if they are born again. Why? People need to realize that not all demons are ugly or dull-looking. Satan himself was beautiful. Earlier on, I talked to you about testing spirits to see if they are from God or not; this applies even if you see something that looks like an angel. Satan and his cohorts are in the business of deception. We can't forget that.

Let's go back to our power to command the angels. We also have power *within* us, although we may not realize it. The disciples had it, and so do we. A believer is empowered supernaturally through the Holy Spirit that is inside of us.

> But you will receive power when the Holy Spirit comes on you; and you will be my witnesses in Jerusalem, and in all Judea and Samaria, and to the ends of the earth. (Acts 1:8)

God explained to me how believers have this power and how we can utilize it to stop demons from operating in our lives or in the lives of others. With this power, there is also responsibility; we are not to just sit around talking about it.

> He gave them power and authority to drive out all demons and to cure diseases and he sent them out to preach the kingdom of God and to heal the sick. (Luke 9:1-2)

> I tell you the truth, anyone who has faith in me will do what I have been doing. (John 14:12)

We don't just have power, but we have authority—authority to act in Jesus's name against the enemy and to heal the sick as well. We don't have to stop and ask if it is all right to fight the good fight. It's like being a joint user on a credit card.

> In my name they will drive out demons; they will speak in new tongues; . . . they will place their hands on sick people and they will get well. (Mark 16:17-18)

> I have given you authority to trample on snakes and scorpions and to overcome all the power of the enemy. (Luke 10:19)

All right, so the power is there; then why aren't all born-again Christians acting as the disciples did? First, a lot of people just don't believe they can, just like a lot of people don't wholly believe in the power of prayer. Other people don't know how to access the power that is inside them. The majority of people, however, don't even know that they have the power at all. That is why it is important to be reading your Bible. The knowledge is there for those who seek it. I know I have that power, and I use it.

Before I was saved, I was beset with the spirit of depression. Personally, I hate this spirit! This is a spirit that fills you with such sadness and negative thoughts. It is a pain that you can feel deep in your soul. It will remind you of all the people who said they loved you and still hurt you. There were days when I would just cry and cry. When I was saved, the Lord used the Holy Spirit to reveal this spirit of depression to me in a dream. I could see it come and just sit on my shoulder. It looked like half of it was money, and the other part was some other creature. I was also given a verse: Matthew 18:18. When I woke up, I read it and it said, "I tell you the truth, whatever you bind on earth will be bound in heaven and whatever you loose on earth will be loosed in heaven." I took that to mean to recognize that spirit for what it was and to put it away from me. I read these verses to this evil spirit, and I felt it leave me, and I have not been afflicted with it in many years. God's Word is the sword we are to use to fight these spirits that trouble us.

> Take the helmet of salvation and the sword of the Spirit which is the word of God. (Eph. 6:17)

Fellowshipping with God and reading the Word is what equips us to do battle against the enemy. What good is power if you don't know how to use it? Paul says in Ephesians 6:11-12 that we must "put on the full armor of God so that you can take your stand against the devil's schemes. For our struggle is not against flesh and blood, but against the rulers, against the authorities, against the powers of this dark world and against the spiritual forces of evil in the heavenly realms."

Listening to people like myself may not convince all people of the reality of what is going on in the world. There will be doubters, maybe some that are reading this book now that say, "I don't believe in this. I don't believe in the Bible. I don't believe in demons attacking or angels protecting because I don't see them. If God exists, he doesn't love or respect us." God can reveal himself to you. You should ask him to, but you need to be sincere in your asking and not just like someone waiting to see a rabbit pop out of a hat.

Here is an example. In my life before I was saved, there was a time when I couldn't sleep. I felt like there was something in my bedroom. This is a fear that started when I was a child and continued throughout my teenage years. It was especially when I was a teen that it affected me. I remember a particular day when this fear weighed heavily upon me. I went to a religious preacher and told him what I felt was going on. He told me to put a Bible under my pillow and the fear would go away, so I did. That night I waited and waited, and of course, nothing happened; and I still felt like there was something in my room, and I was terrified to close my eyes and sleep. Someone else told me to sleep with the light on. I did that also, and there was no change. Still another person told me to drink a beer before going to bed. Well, that helped, but only because it made me go to sleep. It didn't take away the fear, and I would wake up hours later and be terrified. So I drank another and another when I woke up again. I became drunk, which took away the fear, but then eventually, I just couldn't go back to sleep at all.

Sometime after I was saved, the Lord showed me a vision of my room. In it, there was a spirit just standing there, looking at me in bed. With that information, I was able to get my Bible out and read from the scripture that God had pointed me and command that spirit to leave. That night, I was able to fall asleep, and I slept peacefully the whole night through. As I said before, we have the ability to sense things in the spirit, believers or not, but the power to banish evil spirits from us comes from the authority of Christ in us when we receive him in our hearts, coupled with the Word of God on our tongues. Just having a Bible in your house is not enough nor is sticking it under your pillow or in the area where you are sensing a problem. You have to open it and read it. You have to meditate on God's Word and then apply it in your life.

People all over the world are suffering from lack of sleep. Some of them might have the same problem that I did, and they also drink beer or another alcoholic beverage or sleeping pill to get them to sleep. Perhaps they should be calling on the Lord and reading his Word to help them. If we do this, we can be on the offense instead of on the defense all the time.

> No weapon forged against you will prevail, and you will refute every tongue that accuses you. This is the inheritance of the servants of the Lord, and this is their vindication from me. (Isa. 54:17)

> Submit yourselves, then, to God. Resist the devil, and he will flee from you. Come near to God and he will come near to you. (James 4:7-8)

Healing and How Sin and Demons Afflict Man with Diseases

When I was in the Spirit with the Lord, he revealed to me how demons afflict us with diseases. You would be surprised to know how many diseases are caused by demons. By "caused," I don't mean certain or specific diseases are from demons but rather how many, as in quantity. Diseases that are caused by demons need spiritual healing; they are harbored by demons and need to be cast out for they can't be healed by doctors. If you are suffering from something that doctors with their knowledge cannot cure by their painkillers and medicines, perhaps you need a prayer intervention.

Our Lord God has the cure for every disease known to man, big or small. He told me that he created our bodies, and of course, he knows their every function. He demonstrated this to me, and would you believe my ears started hurting and then he healed me of it? He told me that part of the power of the cross was that Jesus also freed us from disease. We can call on the Lord about sickness because of Jesus's sacrifice. Sure, we will get aches and pains in our bodies that are natural due to age, and then of course, there are other things that we do to ourselves, but God has the power to heal it all.

> But he was pierced for our transgression; he was crushed for our
> iniquities; the punishment that brought us peace was upon him, and
> by his wounds we are healed. (Isa. 53-5)

Some might translate that to mean only that we are forgiven, but I believe it means that we are made whole, healed by the cross. As in we can tap into Jesus, and through the power of the cross, be healed. Jesus suffered on the cross for us to be free from addiction, diseases, and every other human suffering that we have in this world today. I believe a lot of people remain sick because they don't know or believe that Jesus can heal them.

Whenever I get sick or have pain in my body, I shout that verse in my head, and I get well! I also pray it over my friends and family if they are ailing. Don't take this the wrong way. I am not saying that you shouldn't go to the doctor. I believe that doctors and researchers have been given knowledge by God to make medicines for healing and to suggest certain treatments for different illnesses, for they are diligently seeking to make people well. However, if I go to the doctor, I will pray over the doctor so that he/she will be able to ascertain exactly what is wrong with me so that the correct and quickest action might be taken. It is not God's will that we stay sick; even Jesus went around healing people.

> Jesus went through all the towns and villages, teaching in their synagogues, preaching the good news of the kingdom and healing every disease and sickness. (Matt. 9:24)

What sicknesses?

> News about him spread all over Syria, and people brought him all who were ill with various diseases, those who were suffering severe pain, the demon-possessed, those having seizures, and the paralyzed; and he healed them. (Matt. 4:24)

> Great crowds came to him, bringing the lame, the blind, the crippled, the mute and many others, and laid them at his feet; and he healed them. (Matt. 15:30)

It is such a shame that people don't believe that Jesus's healing is for now; they think that it was all for the past and that we are not entitled to healing anymore, but that is so untrue. I have witnessed Jesus's healing in my own life. I told you of what happened to me as a child when my mother and I had malaria, but maybe you don't believe me; perhaps you think it was my imagination as a child and that it didn't happen quite like that. Here is another example. Back in Africa, I rented a house. When I first moved in this new house, I started to have head pains every afternoon. This pain would last for the duration of the day until I went to bed. At first, I didn't think much about it, but then they started to become worse, and I noted that the time was the same every day at 2:00 p.m. Realizing this, I knew that I had a serious problem that wasn't just the pain alone, so I began to pray, and the next day there was no pain!

Sometimes our sins stand in the way of healing. Imagine again the barrier of sin that separates us from God. How is that related to healing?

> And he preached the word to them. Some men came, bringing him a paralytic, carried by four of them. Since they could not get him to

Jesus because of the crowd, they made an opening in the roof above
Jesus and, after digging through it, lowered the mat the paralyzed
man was lying on. When Jesus saw their faith, he said to the
paralytic, "Son, your sins are forgiven . . . ." He said to the paralytic,
"I tell you, get up, take your mat and go home." He got up, took his
mat and walked out in full view of them all. (Mark 2:1-12)

Our sicknesses are a problem for sure, but the bigger problem is that
we be free of sin, free of that barrier between us and God. Jesus addressed
the man's sins first and then healed him. I know of a similar situation with a
Christian couple.

There was this Christian couple who loved God. Everything with them was
going wonderfully until one day, the husband got sick. He eventually went
to the hospital, and they told him that he had cancer and had only months to
live. This wasn't some small little cluster or anything; it had spread through
his body, and there was no hope. The wife went to her pastor and told everyone
else she knew so that they might pray for him. They prayed and prayed, and he
did not get well. The wife was so distraught and could be found crying often.
She kept asking God why he wouldn't heal her husband. The husband finally
heard from God that he needed to tell his wife of the sin he had committed
against her. This man was so ashamed, for he had committed adultery with a
prostitute he had picked up from the streets. He told his wife what he had done,
and she had a nervous breakdown; it was so bad. The husband later asked his
wife to forgive him; she did, and he got healed from his cancer.

I don't believe every man who has cancer has cheated on his spouse;
however, this was an example of a disease that was brought on by sin. It is
important that you have a relationship with God because he can reveal to
you the cause of your ailments, whether it is caused by sin, a demon, a direct
action you are doing (like overeating, which is gluttony anyway), a natural
cause, or even a generational disease. Yes, there are generational diseases
and curses on families. Healing is available for everyone. Natural causes
and attacks by the enemy are actually easier to deal with than those from
sin because those caused by sin, by their nature, need to be confessed and
repented for, and some people can't or won't do so out of shame or possible
embarrassment or other tangible consequences. However, the Bible tells us
to speak of it.

And the prayer offered in faith will make the sick person well;
the Lord will raise him up. If he has sinned, he will be forgiven.
Therefore, confess your sins to each other and pray for each other
that you may be healed. The prayer of a righteous man is powerful
and effective. (James 5:15-16)

Something else that can stand in the way of healing is lack of faith. Noticing a trend yet? We talked earlier about how lack of faith results in lack of power. The same thing applies to healing. Some people will believe God for other things, but not healing. Why? I guess because it is so personal that they think that God wouldn't do something so small as to heal them when there are other more important things. Some people don't have faith in God at all and you can pray and pray for them, and they might not get healed until they have faith that God can heal. For this reason, I am never afraid to tell people how God has healed me or someone in my life. I want people to hear these testimonials so they might start believing God for their own healing. God can use their situation to bring them closer to him, that he might work more in their lives. God can heal anyone; he doesn't play favorites, but faith acts like a key that unlocks the door to healing.

But what is faith?

> Now faith is being sure of what we hope for and certain of what we do not see. (Heb. 11:1)

Okay, so where do we get faith from?

> Consequently, faith comes from hearing the message, and the message is heard from the word of Christ. (Rom. 10:17)

So when people hear or read the word of Jesus, it produces faith. God then acts on that faith and can cause healing. From that healing comes belief. Remember in Matthew 2:1-12, it said that Jesus saw their faith, and then the healing came. Conversely, Hebrews 11:6 says, "And without faith it is impossible to please God, because anyone who comes to him must believe that he exists and that he rewards those who earnestly seek him."

I remember one day I was at the salon, and I was talking about healing. While I was talking, my coworker was disbelieving me and jokingly asked me how I was feeling because the day before, I had been suffering from the flu. I told her that I was well and that I had prayed and God had healed me. There was a customer there who had heard our conversation, and when she was leaving, she told me about her father who was in the hospital in a coma. She asked me to pray for him. I asked her what his name was, and when I was driving home, I prayed for him. Two months later when she came in the salon to get her hair done again, she thanked me for praying for her father. She told me that her father had come out of the coma that very day I had been praying! God was truly at work at that salon, for I had another coworker there who was

Muslim, and after hearing this woman's story, she asked me to pray for some pain that she was in, and God honored my prayers for her as well. It was a cycle of me resting in God's Word on healing, people hearing it and having faith, which brought about God's healing and their belief. Now they will tell others of God's work in their lives as well.

How Demons Can Enter Your Life and Body through Sex

I was quite speechless when the Lord spoke with me about how demons can enter people's lives and bodies because of sex. People don't often see it this way, but sex is a very spiritual thing. When you sleep with someone, two become one, not just physically, but spiritually as well.

> For this reason a man will leave his father and mother and be united to his wife and the two will become one flesh. So they are no longer two, but one. (Mark 10:7-8)

In the world today, people think that if they have not married or exchanged vows or rings, they are not joined together; they are just dating or whatever, but in the spiritual world, it is not the exchanging of rings or the signing of papers that join people together. It has to do with the intimacy, the sexual doings, that join people.

> Do you not know that he who unites himself with a prostitute is one with her in body? For it is said, "The two will become one flesh." But he who unites himself with the Lord is one with him in spirit. (1 Cor. 6:16)

The same concept applies for us.

(It is important to note that Jesus used the example using a prostitute because back then, women who slept around with different men other than their husbands were called harlots or prostitutes. Today, people sleep around, and it just falls under the category of dating unless there is no kind of relationship going on; then a girl is called a slut, and a guy is called a player.)

What spirits are with you become part of them and theirs with you when you engage in sex. Imagine how that could add up if you have slept with several people. Think of all the times you have said or have heard other people say, "I was never like this before I met so-and-so." Sometimes, there are certain problems that never happened before you were involved with a certain person. The spirits that are attached to the person you are in a relationship with are not happy to just trouble that person; they can trouble you also. They can cause arguments and sadness, they rob couples of true intimacy and growth, and they control emotions and can suck love up until the well is dry. The interesting thing is that people know and are aware of what is happening, but they put another label on it called baggage. They talk about people bringing "baggage" with them into the current relationship; and in truth, that is a correct statement, but it simplifies things to be all about the person without realizing that the direct cause is the bad spirits hanging on to a person, and they try to treat the symptom and not the problem.

The Lord showed me a spiritual manifestation of the uniting of two people. He showed me in the spirit of this man and woman that were married to each other, and between them was a spiritual tie. It looked like an electrified wire connecting them together. I could see this couple, but I could also see other people connected to them both; they were unclear, but there. They were called soulties (pronounced soul-ties). These soulties were joined to this couple because the couple had slept with other people other than just each other. Soulties are also part of the baggage that people can bring into future relationships. These soulties stay a part of you until you get rid of them. Think of the times when you or someone you know can't stop thinking about or dreaming of an ex, even when the relationship is long over. Soulties are not bad unto themselves when between a husband and wife. However, there should only be one between them if they want to avoid having certain problems.

After I learned about this soultie concept, I did some research into it. I talked to different couples and polled how long they had been married, if they had slept with anyone else before they got married, and so on. There were couples that I met that had been married for a long time, like thirty-five years or so; and I asked them how they met and stuff like that, and I commonly heard that they were school sweethearts or that they had met when they were fourteen and they were still together and in love. I could see that love in their eyes and how they acted around each other. The important thing is that they were never with anyone else before they got married or after, so they have no other interference that comes from having uncut soulties with other people.

You may be wondering how important it is to disconnect yourself from other soulties other than the one with the person you are in a relationship with or how the devil can play a role in all this. Let me start by saying that the devil is very happy if you sleep with lots of people. So that tells you to be wary because whatever the devil really likes is certainly not good for you! As I said before, people bring their baggage and their soulties with them, so that gives the devil opportunity to spread more of his spirits around. The devil has us tricked into believing that we need more sexual experience before we get married and settle down. People think they are just enjoying life. They tell themselves that they are searching for Mr. or Mrs. Right, that they are just going to experience and experiment until they get married. Most people are earnestly seeking happiness, but they are going about it the wrong way, and there will not be true happiness in their relationship until they have repented for this type of behavior.

I had an uncle back in Africa who, at the time, was a real quiet guy in his twenties. My mother sent me and my sister to visit him for a few days. Even though I was young, I saw what my uncle was doing, and it was shameful. My uncle would go to work at seven in the morning, and then at ten o'clock he would come home with a woman and stay home for about an hour with her and then go back to work. At four o'clock, he would bring another woman and do the same. At nine o'clock, it was the same thing again, and this happened every day! He got married eventually to one of these women that I remembered from back then. She was one of the ones that he had over the house more frequently than some of the others. Well, when he married her, things were fine; but then he went back to his old habits, only he used a hotel instead. His wife found out about it, and she left and then married someone else. Will this teach my uncle a lesson? I don't think he will learn and will continue in his ways until he repents and asks God for deliverance.

He can't stop because he is tied to this lifestyle. It is no longer a habit, but rather bondage to sin, but he can be freed from this and all the various soulties he has acquired over the years and have a successful relationship in the future. How? He can do this by praying, fasting, and repenting. Before the Lord opened my eyes to this soultie concept, I could never believe the sincerity of a person who cheated on their spouse and then cried about it and asked for forgiveness, received it, and then turned around and did it again. They would say they loved the person they cheated on, but I thought that it was untrue and that they didn't know what love is or that they never really loved the person to begin with, but it happens because people have these soulties and the devil has his hooks in them. A person can love you all they want, you could be perfect for each other, but both of your pasts will eventually get in the way of a happy relationship.

I have broken soulties in my own life, and my husband has done it also before we were intimate with each other. My marriage would not be ultimately successful and enjoyable if we had not been delivered before we were married and had intercourse. Don't despair if you are already married and are reading this; it is not too late! You too can begin now and do as I have instructed. It would be best if you did this with your spouse, but if you can't, you can still pray for your spouse. You can start by praying a prayer similar to this:

Dear heavenly God, I come to you as a sinner, and through my Lord Christ Jesus, I repent for all the people I joined with before I got married (and if applicable, any after I was married). Please forgive me and wash me with the blood of Jesus and cleanse me of all unrighteousness. I stand on God's Word in Matthew 18:18 that says, "Whatever is bound on earth will be bound in heaven and anything that is loosed on earth will be loosed in heaven." To any soulties that are attached to me right now, I bind you off my life! I bind the soulties off the life of my spouse in the name of Jesus! I loose the power of God to break the power of soulties in my life and that of my spouse. In the name of Jesus I pray. Amen.

When a person repents, they send a message out into the spiritual world. These soulties will hear this prayer in the spirit. You have the regal right to use God's words and the power of Jesus's intervention in your life. If you are struggling with lust, pray that prayer to break the spirit of lust. If you are struggling with pornography, pray that prayer, inserting the word *pornography* there where applicable. Whatever sins you have active in your life that you know of, pray that prayer and repent. You will see a difference in your life. If you are single, do this before you get married. If your intended doesn't know anything about it, let them know and pray with them too. There are no perfect people in this world, so if you are searching for them, you can forget about that for we have all sinned, but you can ask God to bring the person that is right for you into your life. He can do this. He can bring the person that you need, and together with them, you can grow and be closer to God together.

Marriage

God's purpose for marriage was that it be a mirror representation of his love and desire for fellowship with us. We are to unite with our spouse and become one flesh with two purposes: to love each other and be fruitful. The physical manifestations of that are sexual intercourse (expressing love) and reproduction (being fruitful in the spirit).

> For this reason a man will leave his father and mother and be united
> to his wife, and they will become one flesh. (Gen. 2:24)

We leave our parents (who are spiritually represented by sin) and become united with our spouses (who, in the spiritual sense, are represented by God) and become one flesh. Having sex and being married is a very serious symbol and should be treated with respect; however, that is not being done today. The idea and true purpose of marriage has been diluted and misused over time and continues to be in a serious decline, more so today than it ever was in the past. The devil is delighted of course, for he knows that Hebrews 13:4 says, "Marriage should be honored by all, and the marriage bed kept pure, for God will judge the adulterer and all the sexually immoral."

It is important that people understand that being married has nothing to do with signing papers, wearing a white dress, or exchanging rings. Marriage is about the spiritual joining of two people, which happens when you have sex. Dating is not marriage; sleeping with someone you are dating is fornication. So technically speaking, if you are living together with someone and having sex with them only, you are spiritually married to them and not fornicating. The problem is the insincerity, the noncommittment, the mentality associated with just living together and not being married on paper. With that comes the future possibility of sleeping with other people other than your spiritual spouse and the acquisition again of soulties and spirits.

Some people think that if they are only sleeping with one person at a time within a devoted relationship, they are not being promiscuous or that they are not fornicating; but if they aren't living together, they are. You are only supposed to be joined to one person, period—not one person at a time. The Bible tells us in Matthew 6:24, "No one can serve two masters." You can't be spiritually married, living with someone and sleeping with them (serving God) but still leave yourself the option or the freedom of stopping and finding and sleeping with someone else (serving the devil) when you feel like it or if things become too hard. It doesn't work that way; it is all or nothing. 1 Corinthians 6:18-20 says, "Flee from sexual immorality. All other sins are outside the body, but he who sins sexually sins against his own body. Do you not know that your body is a temple of the Holy Spirit, who is in you, who you have received from God? You are not your own; you were bought at a price. Therefore honor God with your body." God is not out there looking to punish people. He loves us and wants to bless us and deliver us from our sinful lifestyles. He wants nothing more from us than that we repent and turn from our sinful behavior that we may have relationship with him.

God's Will for Our Lives Here on Earth

We have been talking a lot about what not to do. The next question, what should we be doing, what is God's will for our lives? For those who do not know, let me tell you that above all else, it is God's will that we have a relationship with him. What's great is that we don't even have to figure out how to do that.

> For it is by grace that you have been saved, through faith—and this is not from yourselves-it is the gift from God—not by works, so that no one can boast. (Eph. 2:8-9)

> For through him we both have access to the Father by one Spirit. (Eph. 2:18)

God has made himself available to us through Jesus Christ, and the Bible lays out everything we need to do to bring us closer to him. If that wasn't good enough, there are benefits other than the obvious one of salvation and the indwelling of the Holy Spirit.

> But the fruit of the Spirit is love, joy, peace, patience, kindness, goodness, faithfulness, gentleness, and self-control. (Gal. 5:22-23)

Innately, we are seeking these things. The world cannot give us these things; it can only give superficial substitutions for these things. We think that if we amass possessions like houses and cars and clothes, it will bring us these things. We think money or power and even religion will give us what we are constantly searching for, but that is untrue.

Religion is a big thing that masquerades as a substitution for true intimacy in Christ. What do I mean by that? The definition of *religion* is this: "A set of beliefs concerning the cause, nature, and purpose of the universe, especially when considered as the creation of a superhuman agency or agencies, usually involving devotional and ritual observances, and often containing a moral code governing the conduct of human affairs. A specific fundamental set of beliefs and practices generally agreed upon by a number of persons or sects (e.g., the Christian religion, the Buddhist religion)." There is nothing wrong with going to church and fellowshipping with other Christians. There is nothing wrong with being on the church committee and serving in the child-care area on Sundays and doing worship on Wednesday nights, but if you think that doing that will give those true fruits of the spirit, you are wrong; it's not enough. The biblical law isn't going to do it, as in just following the Ten Commandments won't give you those things.

What you have to do is walk in the Spirit. It's not something hard to do or something you have to make yourself do or force it, but if you do, it will be beneficial.

> So I say, live by the Spirit, and you will not gratify the desires of the sinful nature. For the sinful nature desires what is contrary to the Spirit and the Spirit what is contrary to the sinful nature. They are in conflict with each other, so that you do not do what you want. But if you are led by the Spirit, you are not under the law. (Gal. 5:16-18)

That is very good news, for that means it is not on our own strength that we walk by the Spirit. Certainly that makes it easier. Romans 6:14 says, "For sin shall not be your master, because you are not under the law, but grace." Don't we all want to be free from sin's rule in our lives?

How can the indwelling of the Spirit help you in everyday life? Let's touch on decision making. Every day, we are faced with making seemingly simple decisions that can have serious ramifications. Take for instance, you are married, and a single coworker asked you to go to lunch with them. Do you go or not? It seems innocent enough. One side of you says you shouldn't go alone and that you should bring another coworker as well, but the other side says, "Hey it's not that big a deal, for it is only your coworker." If you are walking in the Spirit, you will have the courage and the conviction to say no. It is commonplace to hear of people having affairs with their coworkers, and it stems from spending more time than necessary with them in inappropriate situations. It doesn't just happen overnight. That is why it is important for you to receive the Holy Spirit.

It is God's will that we receive his blessings. We are his children, and he wants the very best for us. He wants to bless us in every area in our lives. We can't earn grace, for it is freely given through Christ's death, but we will receive blessings by honoring God in our lives. Do you want to honor God in your marriage? Your job or business? In general? Advice is given to us in the Bible concerning everything.

> Wives, submit to your husband as to the Lord. (Eph. 5:22)

> In this same way, husband ought to love their wives as their own bodies. He who loves his wife loves himself. (Eph. 5:28)

> All of you live in harmony with one another; be sympathetic, love as brothers, be compassionate and humble. Do not repay evil with evil or insult with insult, but with blessing, because to this you were called so that you may inherit a blessing. (1 Pet. 3:8)

Another thing we are called to do is to tithe. God asks that we give a percentage of our earnings. It is a sign of faith. It shows that we are trusting God with our finances. He doesn't need our money; however, when we tithe, we show that we are trusting God to provide for us. That little bit we give to him could very well be used for something else, but God is not going to ask us to tithe so that he can bankrupt us or cause us to struggle. He will take that offering and return it to us with even more than what we gave up to begin with.

> Honor the Lord with your wealth, with the first fruits of all your crops; then your horns will be filled to overflowing, and your vats will brim with new wine. (Prov. 3:9-10)

> Bring the whole tithe into the storehouse, that there may be food in my house. "Test me in this," says the Lord, "and see if I will not throw open the floodgates of heaven and pour out so much blessing that you will not have room enough for it."(Mal. 3:10)

The first fruits mentioned in that scripture means that you take 10 percent of your earnings right off the top. That should be the first thing you do, and then you spend the rest of your money how you see fit. The "storehouse" means *church*. The church is then obligated to spend the money taking care of the poor, the widows, and to use this money as means to preach the Gospel, whether that means to fund mission trips or whatever. So we should do our part, and God will do his part and reward us for our faithful behavior. God has certainly rewarded my business. He has brought me customers and provided me adequate space to take care of them all. This also gives me an opportunity to spread his word to all that I meet. Another great benefit of tithing is this: "'I will prevent pests from devouring your crops, and the vines in your fields will not cast their fruit,' says the Lord almighty" (Mal. 3:11). That is my favorite part. God isn't going to just leave you out there like a sitting duck. He will provide protection for your job or place of business. Have you been tithing and then got laid off? Don't lose hope, because God has something different for you. He is always faithful. If you lost your job, there is a reason for it; seek him and find out what. I am not just saying this to be saying it; I have had experience of this in my own life.

A few months after we bought a home, my husband received an email informing him that he was losing his job. This was a big deal because we had just gotten a new house. Before this had happened, my husband wasn't happy in his job, and he had to drive pretty far to get there. Still, he went to work faithfully and did his job like he should. When he told me what had happened, I wasn't worried about it because I know what the Bible says and what God has promised. We had been tithing faithfully, so I knew God would come through. I told my husband to seek diligently for a job and something would come up. Well, it did. He ended up only being out of work for one week. My husband was able to find a job that was close to home and only about a mile from where I worked, which allowed us to have lunch together. He didn't have to work weekends either, unlike his other job.

We have talked about how to conduct ourselves in two specific things like marriage and business, but let's talk about in general. There are general expectations God has for us and how we should act in our everyday lives and to each other. God wants to bless us, and we can honor him and be ready to receive his blessings by staying true to the Word.

> Above all, love each other deeply, because love covers a multitude
> of sins. Offer hospitality to one another without grumbling. Each one
> should use whatever gift he has received to help others, faithfully
> administering God's grace in various forms. (1 Pet. 4:8-10)

That last part is very important. What gift has God given you? God has given us each something different. It doesn't have to be something huge. Some people think if they are not evangelizing from a pulpit to thousands of people that God can't use them, but that isn't true. God can use ordinary gifts in extraordinary ways. Sometimes even the smallest thing can be used to help others. Have you been told that you have beautiful smile or an infectious laugh? Don't belittle how encouraging a smile or a touch of humor can be when someone is down. Can you sing? You don't have to be a pop star. Sing at your church or even around your house and to your children. Singing can be soothing or uplifting to others. Maybe you are very good at encouraging people or motivating people to act. Use that gift to further God's cause.

We also have the greatest gift of the Holy Spirit dwelling in us. It is definitely there for people to see when you are walking in the Spirit. Conversely, when we are not walking in the Spirit, it is noticeable. People are always watching other people, waiting to make judgments on them. That is why gossip columns, magazines, and sensation news are so popular. People in your everyday life are watching you. Be aware of this. Nonbelievers especially are looking at believers to see how we behave. They will look at how we treat one another or what we do in our everyday life. They are also going to see how you handle yourself through adversity.

> Be self-controlled and alert. Your enemy the devil prowls around like a roaring lion looking for someone to devour. Resist him, standing firm in the faith, because you know that your brothers throughout the world are undergoing the same kind of sufferings. (1 Pet. 5:8)

If you are not walking in the Spirit and are doing things contrary to what God's Word says, people pick up on that and think that what you say about God or Christianity isn't true. However, when you are treating those around you with love and your behavior honors God, then they want to draw closer to you and are willing to hear more of what you may say about God and Jesus.

> For you were once in darkness, but now you are light in the lord. Live as children of light (for the fruit of light consists in all goodness, righteousness and truth) and find out what pleases the Lord. (Eph. 5:8)

Look again at 1 Peter 5:8. God wants us to be healthy and lack nothing. He doesn't give diseases; he heals them. He doesn't want people to be poor but, instead, wants to deliver people from poverty. This said, we need to be alert and always on the lookout for the devil dressed in sheperd's clothing. God can bless you with a good career, and the devil can get you one too, but you need to think about what that job entails and if it is something that God would have you do. Is it a quick fix, a fast-track-to-money-type thing? Children in low-income areas can be drawn to the easy money gained from selling drugs, prostituting, or even stripping. I remember this girl that came to me to get her hair done. We were talking, and I asked about her parents and whatnot. She told me that she was in school but that she also had a job stripping. She then told me that I should come with her to her job, and she could talk to her boss for me.

She felt sorry for me that I was doing hair, which is so much work and making so little in comparison to what she made as a stripper. She said she makes three to five thousand dollars a week. I asked her if she was ever scared that someone might follow her home or hurt her in some way, and she said yes, but that they have guards there. I told her that I was happy with the money I was making and the fact that I don't have to worry about my safety. She went on to say that she wasn't going to do it forever but that it was helping her get through school. Right there is the devil's trick. He tempts you to do something morally wrong with the promise of good things in the future. He fails to mention how doing that demoralizing thing might affect you or even put you in harm's way.

> The blessing of the Lord brings wealth, and he adds no trouble to it. (Prov. 10:22)

> Better a little with the fear of the Lord than great wealth and turmoil. (Prov. 15:16)

> Don't be deceived, my dear brothers. Every good and perfect gift is from above, coming down from the Father of the heavenly lights, who does not change like shifting shadows. (James 1:16-17)

God's riches are enjoyable. Some religions teach people that being poor is a blessing. The truth is that God can bless you even if you are poor, and it doesn't have to be monetarily. God doesn't want us to lack for anything. God can bless you with a house that is filled with peace. God can bless you with a spouse that is loving and caring. God can bless you with children that will bring joy and honor to you. The other side of this coin is the fact that just as God blesses us, the devil's main motivation is to steal and destroy.

> The thief comes to steal and kill and destroy; I have come that they may have life, and have it to the full. (John 10:10)

It is also God's will that we read the Bible. There is so much that God wants us to know, and we can know it through the Word, and if there is one book the devil doesn't want us to read, it is the Bible! God communicates to us through the Bible. People throughout the world are lost because they don't immerse themselves in the Word. Letting your pastor read a small section to you on Sunday is not enough, especially because oftentimes, it can be taken out of context. However, if you are not reading the Bible for yourself, how will you know that? We have so many false prophets, preachers, and religious sects that have led people astray from the truth, for the simple fact that people lack understanding of what God's Word actually says. How ridiculous is that when people have bibles in their hands and in their houses?

There are people opening churches just to make money—yes, it's true. They go around using Jesus's name and talk about God. They put on a good show, and people fall for it. Meanwhile, they are sleeping with fellow church members, favoring members that donate large amounts of money, staging miracles or healing sessions in order to draw people in, knowing that they are lying. Remember, the devil knows what we want to see and hear. He knows the Word of God, and that gives him the knowledge he needs to twist and turn it for his own ends, but that only works against people who don't know the truth for themselves. I once attended a church, a false church, if you will. Remember I told you about when I felt like there was a presence in my room and I went to the church I was attending and told the preacher, who instructed me to put my Bible under my bed? Nowhere in the Bible does it say that when you have fear, you should put a Bible under your pillow . . . but I digress. This wasn't the only thing that he did. Once, we had some foreign visitors to the church. They donated so many bibles to us. Do you know that my preacher took those bibles and sold them to a Christian bookstore? I helped them load the books into a van because one of the guys with the pastor had offered me a ride to my house. I had no idea what they planned to do. The bookstore was on the way to my house, so we stopped there first. I couldn't believe what happened. That was the last time I had anything to do with that church. God's Word shows us how to know the difference between his servants and false prophets or teachers.

> Watch out for false prophets. They will come to you in sheep's clothing, but inwardly they are ferocious wolves. By their fruit you will recognize them. Do people pick grapes from thorn bushes, or figs from thistles? Likewise every good tree bears good fruit, but a bad tree bears bad fruit. A good tree cannot bear bad fruit and a bad tree cannot bear good fruit. Every tree that does not bear good fruit is cut down and thrown into the fire. Thus by their fruit you will recognize them. (Matt. 7:15-20)

It doesn't get any clearer than that. Remember we talked about the fruit of the Spirit? That applies here as well. Pay attention to what people are really doing and saying. Do they practice what they preach? We all know that phrase, but it is true. People mess up; we all sin, but are there patterns of sin and disregard for the Lord? Are they justifying or covering up bad behavior with no remorse? Are they taking verses out of context to suit their own purposes?

Some of these false prophets take things even further. They embrace the devil, maybe unknowingly, and by doing this, they use the power of darkness on people. What does that mean? When I was in Africa, someone told me of a powerful man of God who was performing miracles. She told me that when you go to the church, there is a pumpkin that you put money in. After that, you talk to the pastor, and he gives you some water to take home and bathe in. That water is supposed to possess the power of God. When she told me that, I laughed and laughed. I asked her if she believed this, and she said yes. When I questioned her about where this man got the water, she said that he goes down to the sea and God gives it him. I told her that he was a false prophet and not to go back there. I convinced her that God would not be involved in something like that. Still, I was curious, and as I drove past this church one day, to my surprise, I saw a lot of people going in and out with bottles. I was so shocked and sad.

My mother didn't live far from this church, and I went to her house and asked her about it. She told me that people go there all the time and give cloth, goats, cows, and land to this man also. I told her that I didn't believe what this man was doing and how I hated it when people use God in this manner. Don't shake your head and think this kind of thing only happens in Africa; it happens all over the world. Think of all the cults out there. Remember Waco? People are searching for God. They want love and healing. They want salvation, and they are willing to believe lies; they are willing to give up a part of themselves or things in their lives for falsehoods that seem easy or are quick fixes. Some of you reading don't want to believe this could happen to you or anyone you know or anywhere in your town, but the Bible warns us about this kind of thing happening.

> The Spirit clearly says that in later times some will abandon the faith and follow deceiving spirits and things taught by demons. Such teachings come through hypocritical liars, whose consciences have been seared with hot iron. (1 Tim. 4:1-2)

> But there were also false prophets among the people, just as there will be false teachers among you. They will secretly introduce destructive heresies, even denying the sovereign Lord who bought them—bringing swift destruction on themselves. Many will follow their shameful ways and will bring the way of truth into disrepute. In their greed these teachers will exploit you with stories they have made up. (2 Pet. 2:1-3)

Just as dangerous are people that try push their disbelief on you and make you question God's truth or sovereignty.

> First of all, you must understand that in the last days scoffers will come, scoffing and following their own selfish desires. (2 Pet. 3:3)

Right now, I am telling you this. You are reading this. However, if I didn't tell you this, how would you know? How does anyone know this? It is in the Bible. We must seek out God's truths for ourselves that we may be made aware. Forewarned is forearmed. The devil knows this, which is why he goes to great lengths to keep people from reading the Bible. He strives to keep Christianity out of the mainstream and the Bible out of schools. He knows how malleable children are and how they will suck up the Word and keep it with them if it is constantly reinforced. Instead, they are inundated with things, ideas, and concepts of the world instead. Read the Bible to your children. People don't realize how important this is, how important it is to get the foundational knowledge into your children before the enemy substitutes something else.

Let's not lose hope. God has his servants here on earth who serve him with their hearts, who love his people. Some people have been blessed by God with the power of healing. I remember a preacher from my childhood. This was during the time when I was sneaking away to the born-again churches that I had heard of. He was a preacher who opened up a small church made of grass. God gifted him with the power of healing, and I saw for myself that healing at work. People would bring the sick, and they would be healed. I remember a boy that was crippled due to polio who was healed by this man. Yes, it is true. I saw with my own eyes his legs stretch out and him walk out of there with no help. He healed people with demonic problems and people who had severe mental problems that had been tied up by their family members; they were delivered. I sat there and listened to them as they received the Word and Jesus into their lives. They weren't just listening to a man speak; they listened to this man reading out of the Bible. These things I am speaking of didn't just happen in one day like an exhibition of power. This happened constantly. I snuck over there as often as I could.

One time I was there, he talked about a dream that he had. In that dream, he saw himself preaching the Word of God outside Uganda, and he saw that one day, they would not worship God in this grass building but that the Lord would bless them with a big concrete church. There was another time when I came that it started raining while he was preaching, and he didn't stop. He kept preaching as the water fell upon him. Years later when I was in the United States, I was flipping through the channels, and I saw that preacher on TV. He was in China, speaking English, and there was someone translating for him there. He laid hands on a blind Chinese man, and God opened this blind man's eyes so he could see! When I went back to Uganda to visit, I asked my mother where this man's church was, and she gave me the directions. I was late to church that day because I got lost, but when I got there, I saw that God had truly blessed him with a big church. I found out how God had blessed him and how they acquired this and that for the church, and I heard his testimony about the church he had dreamed about. That evening, there came the time when he offered healing to the people there. I saw him lay hands on this woman who was covered in sores that her doctor had told her was from skin cancer. He asked us to all pray, and we did. He laid hands on her, and the sores disappeared! That was years ago that I saw him there in Uganda, and I saw him here in America in a church doing the same thing. He was anointed when he was younger, and he has continued his service to God by helping the poor, the hungry, and the disadvantaged children, preaching the Word of God, and so on. Do you think I made this up to make a point? Do you think I am just writing this to sell books? God's power is available to us.

> And these signs will accompany those who believe: In my name they will drive out demons; they will speak in new tongues; they will pick up snakes with their hands; and when they drink deadly poison it will not hurt them at all; they will place their hand on sick people and they will get well. (Mark 16:17-18)

God wants us to know that his power is available to us. It is written in the Word, and he will anoint people to use his power through. However, you won't know this to be true if you don't read the Bible, and he can't use you in this way if you don't have a personal relationship with him.

God also wants us to know who our fellow Christians are, the ones who are truly his. There are a lot of people who say they are born-again and that they are filled with the Holy Spirit, and yet their actions say otherwise. Ever known anyone to go to church to find a mate? I am sure we have all heard people say things like, "Churchwomen are good" or "Churchmen are good." These people are not there at church to worship God; they are there to find someone. This is not to say it isn't great if you find someone to be with at your church, but that can't be why you go there or to the church meetings or why you volunteer to help out with this or that. God can bring someone into your life, and maybe you will meet them at church if that is God's will that you do.

A long time ago, after I had given my life to Christ (after talking to that man in the street) and I started attending that church where that pastor who claimed he had travelled to Switzerland and back in spirit seconds or whatever preached at, I remember one day in church that I noticed a man sitting about ten people away from me. I always sat in the same spot every time I attended, and I realized that he kept looking at me. It was a little unnerving, but I thought maybe it was just in my head, so I decided the next time I would sit someplace else. Turned out, he changed the place where he sat too! No matter where I decided to sit, he would sit about ten people away from me. I found this to be very distracting, so I made it a point to be late to church and let everyone else get seated before I did. After that day, I didn't see him again until one time I was walking from church, and he stopped me and asked if he could talk to me. I allowed him to speak, and he told me that the Holy Spirit had told him that I should be his wife, and he demanded that I accept! I told him that the Holy Spirit had not revealed to me that I was supposed to be his wife. He said he was certain that it would. I did not know what to say to that or if I even believed that the Holy Spirit was talking to him or how; what I did know is that I did not like this man or how he was following me, and I wondered what he was up to.

Well, one day the man came up to me again and told me that he knew that the Holy Spirit had talked to me because the Holy Spirit had talked to him and told him so. I explained to him that this was not so, but he wouldn't hear of it. He then told me that he was going to go fast in the woods for forty days and that when he was done, he was going to come for me, and I would become his wife. I declared that I didn't care what he did and that I wouldn't be his wife, and I walked away. That Sunday, the pastor announced that some people were going fasting and asked that anyone who wanted to participate should get themselves ready. This guy went, but he came back in a few days and repeated that the Holy Spirit had spoken to him, but still I told him that the Holy Spirit had not spoken to me, and I asked him to go away again. If I had been in the Word more then or if that guy had been, perhaps we would have had the knowledge that we needed to question/ test whatever was speaking to him and telling this man that stuff and find out if it was from God. Rather, we would have known it wasn't from God because he would have made it clear to me if that man was for me, and we would have been married if it was meant to be, because remember that 1 John 4:1 says, "Dear friends do not believe every spirit, but test the spirits to see whether they are from God, because many false prophets have gone out into the world."

In another case, I know of a woman who was devoted to God, and she was serving God with all her heart. There was this guy who was going to church also and never missed a service that I knew of. They got together and got married, but as soon as that happened, this guy stopped going to church. He didn't want to pray with his wife anymore or anything. She was so disappointed and bewildered as to why he did that, but it was because he got what he came for—her. He was just there to find a good wife. That is why we need to be in a personal relationship with God and question him even about any choices, even if it seems like it is the best choice in the world. Again, we need to be aware of what people are saying and doing, and in this case, even that is not enough; you have to apply to God for wisdom, truth, and clarity in all situations so that you might stay on the right path. Remember there are people out there, just like this man who play church on Sunday and live like the devil during the week. They say they are Christians, and yet they are prejudiced against other races. They say they are Christians, but they don't care about anyone but themselves. They use the church to help themselves instead of helping people in need. They steal from the church. They commit adultery with other members of the church. There are some that do so many things that are the exact opposite of what a Christian should be doing.

Being a Christian means being Christlike. We are to be representatives of Christ on this earth. Ever hear of the saying "What would Jesus do?" It is a question that we should be asking ourselves daily; sometimes it has to be hourly. Every time we are going to do something that could be in any way questionable, we should ask ourselves that question, because there are believers and nonbelievers alike who are watching us and judging our behavior and equating that with the behavior of God. Would you want to serve a god that you can't trust, who is hypocritical, who says one thing and does another? Yeah, it is that serious. People wonder why they should give there lives to Jesus if they are still gonna be no better than someone else who does whatever they want without worrying about consequences or heaven and hell, angels or demons. That is a viable question. There are "Christians" all over the world giving Christianity and God a bad rap. Yet again, there is nothing new under the sun. We have been commanded to love our neighbors, and yet many do not. What did Jesus teach about this?

> In reply Jesus said, "A man was going down from Jerusalem to Jericho, when he fell into the hands of robbers. They stripped him of his clothes, beat him, and went away leaving him half dead. A priest happened to be going down the same road, and when he saw the man, he passed by on the other side. So too, a Levite, when he came to the place and saw him, passed by on the other side. But a Samaritan, as he traveled, came where the man was; and when he saw him, he took pity on him. He went to him and bandaged his wounds, pouring on oil and wine. Then he put the man on his own donkey, took him to an inn and took care of him. The next day he took two silver coins and gave them to the innkeeper. 'Look after him,' he said, 'and when I return, I will reimburse you for any extra expense you may have.' Which of those three do you think was a neighbor to the man who fell into the hands of the robbers?" The expert in the law replied, "The one who had mercy on him." Jesus told him, "Go and do likewise." (Luke 10:30-37)

Certainly we all know someone or know of a person like that priest who is supposed to be a man or woman of God who would have passed by that man rather than be bothered. We must be aware of people like that, and we must take care to not be like that ourselves. Here are some verses that will help us.

Dear friends, let us love one another, for love comes from God. Everyone who loves has been born of God and knows God. Whoever does not love does not know God, because God is love. (1 John 4:7-8)

If anyone says, "I love God," yet hates his brother, he is a liar. For anyone who does not love his brother, who he has seen, cannot love God, who he has not seen. And he has given us this command: Whoever loves God must also love his brother. (1 John 4:20-21)

If you know that he is righteous, you know that everyone who does what is right has been born of him. (1 John 2:29)

If we claim to have fellowship with him yet walk in darkness, we lie and do not live in truth. But if we walk in the light, as he is in the light, we have fellowship with one another, and the blood of Jesus, his son, purifies us from all sin. If we claim to be without sine, we deceive ourselves and the truth is not in us. If we confess our sins, he is faithful and just and will forgive us our sins and purify us from all unrighteousness. If we claim we have no sinned, we make him out to be a liar and his word has no place in our lives. (1 John 1:6-10)

I can't say it enough how important it is to remain in God and live like the Bible stipulates. People will say stuff like, "It is so hard to be a Christian," and "There are too many rules and stuff," but if you are immersing yourself in the Word and letting the Holy Spirit work through you and guide your actions, then it doesn't have to be hard. We must remember that we aren't responsible for our salvation. God is. You can't get into heaven based on good works or righteous behavior; we can only get there through Christ Jesus. It is through God's mercy and Jesus's sacrifice that we have entry into heaven; however, as long as we are on earth, we are emissaries of Christ, and we cannot think to bring others to Christ if we are misrepresenting Christ. Churches have lost members because people turn away and say God or Christianity isn't for them because of the behavior of people in the church or because of inaccurate doctrine being taught by a misguided preacher or, worse than that, because there are members that have been led astray by false prophets.

Jesus gave his life for us. Is it so hard to love your neighbor? Is it so complicated to refrain from committing adultery or murder? How about stealing, do your hands ache to take things that aren't yours? If so, then Christianity really isn't your problem; you have character flaws or demons in your life that can be dealt with God's help. So Christianity is *still* for you.

Don't think because you've backslidden or fell into some old behavior patterns that God is no longer interested in you. Don't think that the behavior of some people in a particular church or churches is indicative of how churches are in general. Come back to God. Start reading your Bible if you have stopped. Start praying again and ask God to lead you to a new church or to bring some true Christians into your life so that you can fellowship with them. It is not God's will that any should be lost to him. This is what God showed me in the Spirit. He told me these things and told me he would write them in my memory, and I have never forgotten.

The Hatred My Best Friend Had for Me

It was about 3:00 p.m. when my best friend walked into the room. There were no preliminaries, no niceties; she just began by saying that she hated me. She asked me who I thought I was and stuff like that. She went on to say that when we used to hang out, it bothered her so much when men would pay me attention, or when I wasn't with her, people would ask her where her "pretty sister" was. She told me that all my stupid dreams were just that, dreams, and that they would never come to pass. She sneered at me and said, "Look at you now, no one can help you." She then went over to the dresser and pulled out a pair of my underwear. "How do you think this got here?" she asked. I was quite surprised about it actually. I thought that pair of underwear, my favorite, had been lost, but no, she said that she had taken them along with some of my hair she had cut (remember when she was doing my hair?) and took it to the witch doctor. She said she had paid the witch doctor with the money she pretended to lose that time when we had gone shopping. She told me that the witch doctors were all powerful and that the voice I had heard (you know the dreams I had about Rosie?), she said that they were from a demon she had sent out to me to bring me to her. She said she had been consulting the witch doctor from way back when I had left my parents' house. The witch doctor had told her to go with me when I left the city, which is why she had given up her job and decided to come with me when I left Uganda. She had been told that she had to be with me in order to receive my blessings. It doesn't stop there though. She continued spewing all these vile things and even told me that she had practiced voodoo so that I wouldn't acquire that job and would come back looking for her. She mocked my dreams of going to America to do hair and said that I was nothing, but still she didn't stop there.

Next she asked me, "Where is that Jesus so he can save you, huh?" She asked me why Jesus didn't save me from her and her voodoo. She called out,

"Jesus, come and save her!" Laughingly, she said, "So where is he?" She said her plan was for me to become totally mad and be living in the woods somewhere, but that I kept coming back. There was no option left, she said, but for her to kill me! "You are going to die," she said, "and you will never see your family again, and they will never know that you are dead." She said that I didn't deserve anything but death and that she had hated me forever, but I was too stupid to realize it. She ranted on and on about how she hated her life of poverty, but that I was worse off than her, believing in Jesus and talking to her about his powers. She claimed her witch doctor had more powers and that she was going to show me, and then she left the room.

I thought that it was all a dream. I helplessly looked at her, and I couldn't speak at all. I was so surprised that this was happening to me; I cannot explain to you in words how I felt, but I remember thinking of my mother and my siblings and how far I was from them. Everything she said to me was as painful as a knife to the heart. The fact that she practiced voodoo was a total shock to me; I didn't believe that voodoo worked, but the fact that she did and that she had tried to use it on me was just astonishing. I had always thought it ridiculous that people would spend their money on stuff like that, but again, she had. Not only did she use money, but she also stole money from me to do it, the money I lovingly gave for her to use for herself and child . . . How could she? But more than that, did it really work on me? And if so, *how*?

Witchcraft

When I was having those urgent dreams about finding Rosie, I was in a city far away from where she lived. I would say the distance was like between Georgia and Florida. Like I told you earlier, one day I just started thinking about her and couldn't stop doing so. I hadn't seen her in about eighteen months. She said she sent a demon after me; how in the world could a demon come and find me? How did she get my underwear? So many things didn't make sense. The witch doctor had told her I had so many blessings coming to me, and he gave her something to put on me so that my blessings would be hers, but still she had to be with me. How exactly was that supposed to work, and how did she stop that manager from hiring me?

I guess the first thing to understand is how stuff or people—like witch doctors, palm readers, psychics, and magicians—work. Earlier in my life, I never believed anything like this really worked, not really. I just thought it was a matter if you believed in it; then it will work on you or for you specifically. I used to wonder about the people in Africa who claimed that these things worked or that they were these types of people, and also, I would question why they didn't get themselves out of poverty. I figured these people were, at heart, a bunch of liars, and certainly nothing they could do would work on a Christian. Still, what we need to remember is that God has his servants on this earth that he works through and who work for him; likewise, the devil has the same. The difference between them is whereas God uses his power for good, the devil uses his power for bad—to kill, to destroy, and to distract. It sounds like a comic book, but is true. The devil anoints people with his dark power, and they use it for his purposes.

Rosie went and saw such a person, that witch doctor. She told him what she wanted them to do for her. She was asked for a picture to identify me, hair, and underwear. My underwear carries a scent of mine; sounds gross, but true. We as humans all have unique scents, and the demon was able to sniff that out. My hair was used so that when it found me, it could attack me mentally.

Speed and travel are nothing for a demon; distances have no meaning. Different demons have different powers/abilities. This demon filled me with thoughts of Rosie, feelings of missing her, and the compulsion to seek her out. This demon attached itself to me and told me where to go; remember, I had not seen her in eighteen months and had no idea where she was. When I found her, she had another plan. She was the one who cut her bag when I had given her that money to go shopping. She got my money to fund her next plan against me since the original one didn't pan out after we split up that last time. The witch doctor sent a demon to influence that manager's mind against giving me a job. Meanwhile, I had that dream from God, and I told it to Rosie.

That is what truly set her off, and she went to plan C, the one that involved driving me mad. Remember, she had my hair, and this is what is needed to attack someone mentally. The witch doctor released those demons that tortured me—the half woman—half fish, that other creature, and the chickens. Since I had given my life to Jesus, they could only do so much, and God delivered me from it. In Africa, the witch doctors give people love potions to put in someone's food. People think it is something in the potion—the ingredients—that make it work, but it is not that. There is a demon that is released to influence that person and cause them to have false feelings of love. The demons are instructed to do this for a time and then leave. When the afflicted person is released from them, they act on their true feelings, which will then cause the other person to seek out the witch doctor again, pay again for a potion, and the process starts over again.

Palm readers receive powers from the devil to see your future. People don't believe that to be true, but remember, God knows the past, present, and future as well. The Bible says before we were in our mother's wombs, he knew us. Just because our future is known doesn't mean we can't affect it or that we should be fatalists, thinking nothing we do matters. It does matter; it is just known by God what we will do. God has a perfect will for each of our lives, a specific purpose for us. $1 + 2 = 3$, right? However, we have free will, and the devil wants to destroy anything that God has planned, and he has minions at his disposal to wreak havoc in our lives. The thing is, if we surrender ourselves to God, he can get us back on track if we get going in the wrong direction. It might just turn out that $1 + 1 + 5 - 3 + 8 - 9 \times 2 - 3 = 3$. A palm reader is enabled to see what God has planned for us, and thusly, demons are sent out to mess that up, or we are given false information to lead us astray. Perhaps they will tell someone to take a job that they shouldn't take or to get involved with a person that they shouldn't or something like that.

In my case, Rosie went to a palm reader who told her what blessings were in store for me. She was falsely told that she could obtain my blessings for herself. Rosie believed this and attempted to get my blessings by being with me as she was instructed. The thing is, whenever Rosie was with me, things always seemed to go wrong for me. Of course, the devil knew this would be the case, so he was able to essentially kill two birds with one stone. Rosie hated me; it was a rage so deep, and I can't believe that I didn't notice it. Her hatred only increased as time went on, and she didn't get what she thought she would based on what the witch doctor and palm reader told her. I would advise that no one get themselves involved in something like this. A lot of people are skeptical when it comes to witchcraft, but forms of it are out there in the world and have been since time began. We think of things as being myths or just exaggerated stories from the past, but it's not all make-believe. There are grains of truth in all that stuff; add that to lack of understanding and the fact that things weren't written down all the time, and you have plenty of evidence that supports the existence of witchcraft. Still in denial? Even in the Bible, it mentions witchcraft being performed, both good and bad.

> So Moses and Aaron went to pharaoh and did just as the Lord commanded. Aaron threw down his staff in front of Pharaoh and his officials, and it became a snake. Pharaoh then summoned his wise men and sorcerers and the Egyptians magicians also did the same things by their secret arts . . . But Aaron's staff swallowed up their staffs . . . Moses and Aaron did just as the Lord had commanded. He raised his staff in the presence of the Pharaoh and his officials and struck the water of the Nile, and all the water turned to blood . . . But the Egyptian magicians did the same thing with their secret arts . . . so Aaron stretched his hand over the waters of Egypt, and the frogs came up and covered the land. But the Egyptians did the same thing with their secret arts . . . Aaron stretched out his hand with the staff and struck the dust of the ground, gnats came upon men and animals. All the dust throughout the land of Egypt the dust became gnats. But when the magicians tried to produce the gnats by their secret arts, they could not. (Exod. 7:10-8:19)

That is a clear demonstration of witchcraft/sorcery/otherworldly power channeled from both God (Aaron) and the devil (the pharaoh's magicians). Why do people think just because this happened long ago that it ends there? Why was it possible then and not now? I find that European cultures as well as American cultures are more close-minded. People that practice the dark arts don't do it out in the open like they do in Africa and other places. I think that largely has to do with events like the Salem witch trials and the fact that Christianity is more recognized here, which is against such practices. The intolerance for it has led people to believe over time that such things don't exist in this day and age. Back in Uganda, around the city, there were magicians that used to perform. I would notice them on occasion and stop to observe what they were doing. They would pick people out of the crowd and perform stuff, like putting a handkerchief into a passerby's hand and then have them open their hand for a dove to fly out. This was commonplace there, no tricks, no paying to go see a show; this was out in the open.

On TV today, we have shows like *Ghost Whisperer* and *Medium*, and we also have movies like *The Sixth Sense* that show people communicating with the dead. People take this stuff to be fiction or make-believe, but even the Bible accounts for this kind of phenomenon.

> Now Samuel was dead, and all Israel had mourned for him and buried him in his own town of Ramah. Saul had expelled the mediums and spiritualists from the land . . . When Saul saw the Philistine army, he was afraid; terror filled his heart. He inquired of the Lord, but the Lord did not answer him by dreams or Urim or prophets. Saul then said to his attendants, "Find me a woman who is a medium, so that I may go and inquire of her . . . ." Then the woman asked, "Whom shall I bring up for you?" "Bring up Samuel," he said . . . The king said to her, "What do you see?" The woman said, "I see a spirit coming up out of the ground . . . ." Then Saul knew it was Samuel, and he bowed down and prostrated himself with his face to the ground. Samuel said to Saul, "Why have you disturbed me by bringing me up?" . . . "I have called on you to tell me what to do." Samuel said, "Why do you consult me, now that the Lord has turned away from you and become your enemy? The Lord has done what he predicted through me. The Lord has torn the kingdom out of your hands and given it to one of your neighbors—to David. Because you did not obey the Lord or carry out his fierce wrath against the Amalekites, the Lord has done this to you today. The Lord will hand over both Israel and you to the Philistines, and tomorrow you and your sons will be with me. The Lord will also hand over the army of Israel to the Philistines." (1 Sam. 28:1-24)

Again I say that in all myths or things we believe to be just stories or fairy tales or trickery have their beginnings in truth. Mediums and psychics are not new to the earth. The power is there for those who chose to access it through the dark arts. It is not meant that we should dabble in such things, but people do.

In the Bible, there is also a tale of a fortune-teller.

> Once we were going to the place of prayer, we were met by a slave girl who had a spirit by which she predicted the future. She earned a great deal of money for her owners by fortune telling. This girl

followed Paul and the rest of us shouting, "These men are servants of the Most High God, who are telling you the way to be saved." She kept this up for many days. Finally Paul became so troubled that he turned around and said to the spirit, "In the name of Jesus Christ I command you to come out of her!" At that moment the spirit left her. When the owners of the slave girl realized that their hope of making money was gone, they seized Paul and Silas and dragged them into the marketplace to face the authorities. They brought them before the magistrates and said, "These men are Jews, and are throwing our city into an uproar by advocating customs unlawful for us Romans to accept or practice." (Acts 16:16-19)

What is interesting is that the spirit in her knew who God was; it knew who Paul and Silas served. It also knew the customs of the day and knew that Judaism had legal recognition but Christianity did not. It knew that if it kept shouting long enough, someone would realize what was up and that Paul and Silas should be thrown in prison, which they were. This girl had a spirit of divination. When you give your hand to fortune-tellers and such, you are giving these spirits permission to look into your life. The places where people like this reside or offer their services will have other demons about ready to attach themselves to you when you leave that place. This girl was not given the gift of prophecy from God like John had been. There was a spirit/demon in her that needed to be cast out. Paul recognized the difference and did what needed to be done. You also have the authority to command any spirits that you, or someone you know, may have acquired by visiting such a place, and the demons that attached themselves have no choice but to flee.

I had a customer who told me one time to make sure that I never become friends with an African or a Haitian because they practice voodoo. I asked her, "What about Americans? Don't they do the same kind of things?" I told her that I have seen so many psychic and palm-reader shops around and have seen those infomercials on TV about it. I asked her what she thought of that. If she were to go to a palm reader here in America, what kind of power would she think they have and where did they get it from? How does she think these people get information about people they have never met before? Psychics too, how are they able to see the things they see? They are not all fakes. All these powers are from the devil; they are powers of darkness and not from God.

This same woman told me that her boyfriend had left her and that she had been very depressed. A friend of hers took her to a palm reader in New York. She told the man about her boyfriend, and he told her to come back with a picture and some money. I asked her if she went back, and she said yes. I asked her if she allowed witchcraft to be done on her boyfriend, and she said no. Well, the palm reader did something, and the boyfriend came back. He got her pregnant and left her again, and it turned out that he was married! I told her that she had indeed been a party to witchcraft even if she didn't know it, and that it is not just Africans and Haitians that practice this sort of stuff. I have met so many people who say they don't believe in witchcraft, and yet they participate in stuff like this, but it is all the same. It is no different than someone standing over a pot of boiling water, dropping in ingredients, and chanting. It all comes from the same place: the devil.

You can ask God to reveal stuff to you, and you can believe it won't cost you anything. God knows what you should do, where you should go, and so on. You need to just ask, and he will let you know in some way. For some people, it is through dreams; other people will know the truth through circumstance. For example, you can pray that God will close the wrong doors and keep open the right doors for you to go through, and still others will know from other people. Ever wondered if you made the right decision about something or have had a tough time making a decision in the first place? When some people pray and ask for clarity, they will find that loved ones around them will consistently confirm the right decision for them. God can and does use other people to let us know what the right decisions are; we just have to surrender to him and be in constant prayer.

For me, God was constantly showing me and telling me and having other people tell me to stay away from Rosie, but I didn't. Remember, my mother told me early on to stay away from Rosie, but I didn't listen. There was that German tourist that I met that told me that Rosie had a bad heart, that she wasn't a good person, remember? When I was with Rosie, I would have that dream about the snake chasing me. Remember how the snake was the devil in disguise in the Garden of Eden? So too was Rosie, an enemy masquerading as my friend. Of course, there were Rosie's actions that shouted to me loud and clear that I should stay away from her, but I didn't. God knew what would happen if I kept hanging around Rosie, and he warned me to get away from her, but I wasn't paying attention to the signs. God wants to help us; he wants to protect us from harm. We need to be in prayer and be asking that we hear God's voice in our lives. Pray that he puts trustworthy people, God-fearing people, in our lives that can counsel us if we aren't sure we hear what God is trying to tell us.

I had a roommate from Puerto Rico; she was the best roommate I ever had. She felt she was having trouble finding a good man and decided to go see a certain man in New York about it. He told her that she was having trouble because she was cursed. He offered to remove the curse from her for about $7,000! I told her that she needed to pray and fast and ask God to find a good man for her and that I would pray also. I encouraged her and told her that it wasn't easy to find a good man these days, but with God, all things are possible. I urge you to stay away from palm readers and the like, and it is not just me who says this.

> Do not turn to mediums or seek out spiritualists, for you will be defiled by them. I am the Lord your God. (Lev. 19:31)

> The proconsul, an intelligent man, sent for Barnabas and Saul because he wanted to hear the word of God. But Elymas the sorcerer (for that is what his name means) opposed them and tried to turn the proconsul from the faith. Then Saul, who was also called Paul, filled with the Holy Spirit, looked straight at Elymas and said, "You are a child of the devil and an enemy of everything that is right! You are full of all kinds of deceit and trickery. Will you never stop perverting the right ways of the Lord? Now the hand of the Lord is against you. You are going to be blind, and for a time you will be unable to see the light of the sun." Immediately mist and darkness came over him, and he groped about, seeking someone to lead him by the hand. When the proconsul saw what had happened, he believed, for he was amazed at the teaching about the Lord. (Acts 13:7-10)

Again Paul was able to see the difference between someone who is serving God and someone who isn't. It is important to see that he was filled with the Holy Spirit. So too can we be able to tell the difference between those who are for God and who are for the devil.

I Was Killed by My Best Friend

After Rosie finished mocking me and telling me about the hatred she had for me, she left the room and then the house. I couldn't move, I couldn't talk, but I was in my right mind. The things she had told me were heartbreaking. I couldn't believe it, and yet it was true. Rosie came back to the house in the evening around 6:00 p.m., and she started back talking to me again, saying basically the same things. She told me that I was going to die and that she had just come from the voodoo man who had given her something strong to finish me off. I just sat there, listening to her tell me that she was going to kill me, and I felt so helpless, for my biggest fear was death. I had been fearful of death since I was young when a family member of mine had died, and I saw them put him in a hole in the ground. For some reason, I didn't feel like I could talk to her, couldn't even beg for my life. Maybe I just felt that it was inevitable, for there was an atmosphere in the room that reeked of death. Rosie continued ranting on and on and eventually got back to the fact that Jesus wasn't protecting me from her.

The next thing she did was pull a table right up next to me. She sat down and started performing the voodoo right in front of me. As she did this, I saw a lizard come to me and enter my heart. I became dizzy, and then I said one word to her, "Good-bye." Rosie looked at me and left the room. Then I saw two angels in my room, and they said they had come for me and for me to not be afraid. So I did; I left my body (I could see it there), and then I was in another form. Before that, though, the angel asked me what time it was before I left my body, and I noticed that it was 10:00 p.m. As I said, I could see my body, and yet I was in another form that was me also. The two angels had come in a chariot, and they told me to get in it, so I did. I could see us leaving the earth, and when we passed through the first atmosphere, I could feel that it was filled with agony, and one of the angels looked at me and said, "This is the first heaven. We are just passing through it." The first heaven was full of an evil so palpable that I could feel it. People think of heaven as being one place, but there is more than one.

> I must go on boasting. Although there is nothing to be gained, I will go on to visions and revelations from the Lord. I know a man in Christ who fourteen years ago was caught up to the third heaven. Whether it was in the body or out of the body I do not know—God knows. And I know that this man—whether in the body or apart from the body I do not know, but God knows—was caught up to paradise. He heard inexpressible things, things that man is not permitted to tell. I will boast about a man like that, but I will not boast about it myself, except about my weaknesses. (See 2 Cor. 12:1-5)

The first thing to note is that there are three heavens. The first heaven is the earth's immediate atmosphere. This is where Satan's kingdom is. He isn't just sitting in hell all the time waiting for us.

> For our struggle is not against flesh and blood, but against the rulers, against the authorities, against the powers of this dark world and against spiritual forces of evil in the heavenly realms. (Eph. 6:12)

Realms—more than one. The second interesting thing is that Paul talked of a man having an out-of-body experience. Whether he was near death at the time is unclear, but he came back from it and was able to tell something about what he saw and heard.

We then continued on to the next atmosphere, which was filled with stars both big and small—outer space—and it was so quiet. The angel said to me, "This is the second heaven, but we are not stopping here." After we passed through there, I saw the angels open a door; and the next thing I knew, I was sitting in a chair, a judgment seat. It looked like a chair that a judge sits on here on earth. The angels left me sitting there. On my left, I could see a pit full of people of all colors. Some were burning, and some weren't, and they were all screaming and in so much pain. I tried to force myself to look away, but the screams were so loud that I kept looking back. As I observed them, I could see that though the fire was burning fiercely and seemed to be causing much pain, it was not actually burning the people up, as in they weren't then turning into ashes after a time. I was so scared and fearful sitting in this judgment chair, and I didn't know if I was going in this pit, but I knew, just knew, that that was hell. As I was looking, I saw a woman who was burning, and as she was burning, she looked at me. I started calling on Jesus, and she started calling to me, and the other people around her started to look at me also. As I sat there, I realized that I never really believed that there was a hell; I thought that the problems we faced on this earth were hell, but as I sat there, I knew I had been wrong. There was a hell, and I was looking at it. I was terrified that I was going to go there, and the fear I felt was so intense that it was painful.

Life in Hell

What I saw of hell was the epitome of the most suffering, the most painful thing you could imagine. The people were alive, as in they were physical beings in that place, and they were being ever burned by a fire with no relief. Let's see what the Bible says about death and what follows for those who are saved and righteous and those who aren't, as well as characteristics of those unrighteous people.

> When the Son of Man comes in his glory, and all the angels with him, he will sit on the throne in heavenly glory. All the nations will be gathered before him and he will separate the people one from another as a shepherd separates the sheep from the goats. He will put the sheep on his right and the goats on his left. Then the King will say to those on his right, "Come, you who are blessed by my father; take your inheritance, the kingdom prepared for you since the creation of the world." (Matt. 25:31-34)

> Then he will say to those on his left, "Depart from me, you who are cursed, into the eternal fire prepared for the devil and his angels . . . ." Then they will go away to eternal punishment, but the righteous to eternal life. (Matt. 25:41, 46)

> This will happen when the Lord Jesus is revealed from heaven in blazing fire with his powerful angels. He will punish those who do not know God and do not obey the gospel of our Lord Jesus. They will be punished with everlasting destruction and shut out from the presence of the Lord and from the majesty of his power. (2 Thess.1:7-9)

> For, as I have often told you before and now say again with even more tears, many live as enemies of the cross of Christ. Their destiny

is destruction, their god is their stomach, and their glory is in their shame. Their mind is on earthly things. (Phil. 3:18-19)

But for those who are self-seeking and who reject the truth and follow evil, there will be wrath and anger. There will be trouble and distress for every human that does evil. (Rom. 2:8-9)

Hell is a real place, and there is nothing worse than going there. There is no sin or pattern of sin that is worth burning in hell for eternity. Disbelief of the truth about God and Jesus is what is going to send you there. Not believing the truth and holding it to your chest is what is going to have you out in the world doing the wrong things that keep you farther and farther from the truth. Certainly there is no extramarital sex good enough, no amount of money or power worth the punishment of hell. Again, those actions are just a result of not believing the truth and surrendering to God. On top of those things, people believe in false doctrines. Like what? Well, Darwinism for one is a big deal. That is a direct insult to God who has created us in his image. To say that we evolved instead from monkeys is like a slap in God's face. Surely the devil laughed himself silly when he created that lie that so many people started to believe. It is also a lie to believe that just because you are a moral person who does good deeds, you will wind up in heaven. Some people believe in heaven but don't believe in hell, just like I did, but there can't be one without the other. Still, at the end of the day, technically it doesn't matter if you believe in heaven or hell themselves because they exist without your belief; however, if you don't believe that they exist, you can be led astray and that will be to your detriment.

Some people will say that they have had loved ones who have died and then came back and told them there was no heaven or hell and that they are just roaming around or living someplace or whatever, but don't believe that. I remember having a dream where my grandmother appeared to me, saying that she was in the wilderness looking for a place to stay, and she was asking if she could come and live with me. She was wearing the dress I had bought her and we had buried her in. When I woke up, I was in shock; I had led my grandmother to Christ before she died, so I knew she was in heaven. I came home one day after that and I felt a presence in my room, and it was pretending to be my grandmother, but I knew it was not her. It was a demon, and there are demons masquerading as your loved ones to confuse you and lead you astray! There is nowhere in the Bible where it says that when a person dies, they live in someplace where they can come and go as they please or watch over people. Beware of people who go around spreading such lies, no matter how sincere they seem. I am not saying that they are liars but that they are *believing* lies.

Certainly the manifestations were real to them, but those manifestations were not who they were claiming to be; they were demons.

Another example of something like this came up in a conversation I was having with my mother. She told me of a widow she knew who was having a problem finding another man to marry. She told me that her friend's dead husband would come to her at night and have intercourse with her and that any time she would try to have a date with another man, something would happen with the date. I told my mother that what she was experiencing was an attack by a demon that was either attached to the husband before he died or is a manifestation of the guilt the woman feels for trying to move on with her life after her husband's death. I told her to send the woman to a good church where she could receive prayer and ask for deliverance from this demon. I also had another woman tell me of a similar experience. If something like this happens to you, do as I did. I got my Bible, and I started shouting at that demon in my room. I told that demon that it was not my grandmother and that she was in heaven. I commanded it in the name of Jesus to leave my presence. I also quoted Matthew 18:18, and it left. After that, I never had any more dreams like that one or had a visit like that one. This was no longer an area where the devil could reach me, for I knew the truth. It is important to understand that the devil is unceasing in his desire to destroy us. That is why we must be aware of any open doors in our life where the devil or his minions can get in and get a foothold in our lives. We must be in the Word and in fellowship with God so that we can stand on the truth in the face of deceptions for our eternity is at stake.

Jesus talked many times about heaven and hell and the importance of where we are going to spend eternity. The life of a human on earth is little compared to that of eternity; therefore, it is imperative that we know the truth and not let the devil confuse us with inaccuracies. Nowadays, the devil is having a field day with humans because there are so many ways, so many avenues that offer confusion. There are crooked churches, radio, TV, the Internet, and movies. I know of a movie where they portrayed Jesus as being married and actually committing sin! That is not true, but people want to believe it; they want to believe that Jesus is not perfect because they know they can't be perfect, but that is why he *was* the perfect sacrifice—one without sin or blame, the ultimate substitute for a fallen world. I also saw someone on TV saying that the Bible is just a fairy tale. I wonder where he got that idea from. I guess it will be a shock to him when he dies and realizes he is wrong. He will probably try and say he was misinformed, but it won't matter because the truth is out there for those who truly seek it. The devil and his minions know that, and they know that they only have a limited amount of time to wreak havoc on earth, and they are trying to take as many people with them into hell as they can.

> Two demon-possessed men . . . "What do you want with us, Son of
> God?" they shouted. "Have you come here to torture us before the
> appointed time?" (Matt. 8:28-29)

So what can we do in the face of such formidable enemies to make sure
our fate is not linked with theirs?

> If your hand or your foot causes you to sin, cut it off and throw it
> away. It is better for you to enter life maimed or crippled than to
> have two hands and two feet and be thrown into eternal fire. And
> if you eye causes you to sin, gouge it out and throw it away. It is
> better for you to enter life with one eye than to have two eyes and
> be thrown into the fire of hell. (Matt. 18:8-9)

This is good advice straight from Jesus himself. Basically, he is saying that
you have to cut the things out of your life that are causing you to sin. Cut out
the people in your life that are causing you to sin. Quit that job that is causing
you to sin. Whatever it is that is in your life that is causing you to sin, you have
to turn your back on it or you are going to suffer the ultimate consequence,
which is being cast into hell. Do not believe the world and its lies that tell you
certain things are okay because everyone is doing it, like lusting after people
or watching porn or downloading music without paying. Didn't your mom
ever ask you, "If everyone jumped off a bridge, would you do it?" The same
thing applies here; if everyone is going to hell in a handbasket, are you going
there too? You don't have to. Dare to be different. Dare to believe the Bible's
truth over the devil and the world's lies. Times change. People change. What
is considered acceptable changes, but God never changes, and neither does
hell. They are both always there, and the rules that get you into the presence
of God and the rules that will cause you to be cast into hell won't change. It's
time to let go of the world and embrace that which is heaven-sent—Jesus.

I Sat in the Judgment Seat

Time passed as I sat there in the judgment seat, and then an angel appeared before me, carrying a long white sheet of what looked to be paper. When I glanced at it as he passed, I noticed that it was filled with all the sins I had committed. On my left appeared a dark being that was pulsating with anger, and then on my right stood Jesus. The angel took a place in front of me in the middle. Nervously, I called to Jesus in my heart. The angel stepped close to me and showed the paper to me, and oh my goodness, there were so many sins on it. If you had asked me what sins I had committed before I had arrived at that place, I would have only been able to tell you the two—dancing and drinking beer—both of which I had been told were sins by some churches I had attended. Yet that paper was so full of sins that I had committed. The angel then read out the first sin on the list. He said what it was, the date, and time that I had done it. As he said it, I remembered very well that I had done this thing, and I couldn't deny it. The being on my left angrily shouted, "Yes, she did it!" Then Jesus shouted back, "I paid for it on the cross!" The angel then read the second sin on the list, and this too I remembered. Again the being shouted, "Yes, she did it!" And again Jesus replied, "I paid for it on the cross!"

On and on the list continued, but during this a few things came up, and Jesus said, "No, she did not do this, you did, she is not guilty of it." There were also things on there that Jesus said I was not guilty of for I was newly created in him. On that list were sins that I had committed in my heart, and as they were brought up, I remembered each of them. For example, if you hate somebody in your heart but never tell them or show them, but you do something like give them bad advice on purpose even though they don't know that this is what you have done, this is a sin. If you are in relationship with someone because of money or sex or benefits of some kind but you are looking them in the face or acting as if you love them, you are sinning against them. They are things that you think only you know about, but they are each and every one accounted for and written up against you. There is no sin secret from the eyes of the Lord. It is an ironic thing to think of the fear we have of people knowing our secrets or bad deeds, and yet we commit these things openly in front of God every day. You may have done something and gotten away with it, maybe stealing, maybe adultery, or even murder, and time goes by and relief sets in because no one found out and they may never find out at all, but God knows, and it is written down in heaven. You too will sit in this chair one day.

I don't know if it is naivety or a defense mechanism that allows us to continue on through our days in apparent disbelief to the fact that we will be judged for our actions one day. Still others believe if a crime is committed and the criminal is caught and goes to jail or pays a fine or something, that is the end of it. Perhaps we wouldn't be able to look ourselves in the mirror every day if we thought over the wrong things we have done against ourselves, others, and God himself. Though as Christians, our sins are covered by the blood of Christ, and we will not be condemned to hell because of our sins; there is still had to be a judgment. There is a hierarchy in heaven; it is not an even playing field. People think they can do what they want without having to own up to their wrongdoing. They think if no one on earth finds out of the wrongs they have done, then it is as if it never happened, but the Bible repeatedly speaks on how God has given Jesus power to judge us.

> Moreover, the father judges no one, but has entrusted all judgment to the Son. (John 5:22)

> And he has given him authority to judge because he is the Son of Man. Do not be amazed at this, for a time is coming when all who are in their graves will hear his voice and come out-those who have done good will rise to live, and those who have done evil will rise to be condemned. By myself I can do nothing; I judge only as I hear, and my judgment is just, for I seek not to please myself, but him who sent me. (John 5:27-30)

> He commanded us to preach to the people and testify that he is the one whom God appointed as judge of the living and the dead. (Acts 10:42)

> For we know him who said, "It is mine to avenge; I will repay," and again, "The Lord will judge his people." (Heb. 10:30)

> But they will have to give an account to him who is ready to judge the living and the dead. (1 Pet. 4:5)

But I tell you that men will have to give an account on the Day of Judgment for every careless word they have spoken. For by your words you will be acquitted, and by your words you will be condemned. (Matt.12:36-37)

For if God did not spare angels when they sinned, but sent them to hell, putting them into gloomy dungeons to be held for judgment; if he didn't spare the ancient world when he brought the flood on its ungodly people, but protected Noah, a preacher of righteousness, and seven others, if he condemned the cities of Sodom and Gomorrah by burning them to ashes, and made them an example of what is going to happen to the ungodly, and if he rescued Lot, a righteous man, who was distressed by the filthy lives of lawless men (for that righteous man, living among them day after day, was tormented in his righteous soul by the lawless deeds he saw and heard)—if this is so, then the Lord knows how to rescue the godly men from trials and to hold the unrighteous for the day of judgment, while continuing their punishment. (2 Pet. 2:4-9)

I had been through a lot of things in my life before this event, and many were trying or scary and even horrible, but this by far was the scariest thing I had ever experienced. I was just sitting there listening while sin after sin was spoken out in front of me. My accuser was by my side, brimming with hatred for me, constantly accusing me of this and that. If I chose to look, I could see the pit of hell full of people in agony, waiting for me to join them. Still, I tried to keep my eyes fixed on Jesus the whole time, who, despite what was being said of me, was still defending me. When the list was finished, I did not get flung into hell as I surely should have been because

he himself bore our sins in his body on the tree, so that we might die to sins and live for righteousness; by his wounds you are healed. (1 Pet. 2:24)

He was oppressed and afflicted, yet he did not open his mouth; he was led like a lamb to slaughter, and as a sheep before her shearers is silent, so he did not open his mouth. By oppression and judgment he was taken away. And who can speak of his descendants? For he was cut off from the land of the living; for the transgression of my people he was stricken. He was assigned a grave with the wicked, and with the rich in his death, though he had done no violence, nor was there any deceit in his mouth. Yet it was the Lord's will to crush him and cause him to suffer, and though the Lord makes his life a guilt offering, he will see his offspring and prolong his days, and the will of the Lord will prosper in his hand. (Isa. 53:7-10)

Before I formed you in the womb, I knew you; before you were born I set you apart. (Jer. 1:5)

But we ought to always thank God for you, brothers loved by the Lord, because from the beginning God chose you to be saved through the sanctifying work of the Spirit and through belief in the truth. He called you to this through our gospel that you might share in the glory of our Lord Jesus Christ. (2 Thess. 2:13-14)

So you can see that it was nothing that I had done that saved me. It was through God's mercy and Jesus's sacrifice on the cross. God knew me, and he knew Rosie even before we were born. God knew what plans Rosie had for me and knew what choices I was going to make that would hinder me also, but he made provisions for me. He sent people to warn me about Rosie, but even knowing that I would not listen, he sent people to minister to me. My acceptance of Jesus into my heart as my personal savior did actually save me! All those things that would have condemned me to hell were null and void because of Jesus's death on the cross.

For the wages of sin is death, but the gift of God is eternal life in Christ Jesus our Lord. (Rom. 6:23)

Truly it is a gift to us, undeserving as we may be. God doesn't force himself on us. He makes a way to him available to us through people we know, or strangers, circumstances, Christian radio, Christian TV, and books. Sometimes he will even send angels to us, but it is up to us to receive them. When the opportunity makes itself available to you, don't pass it up. That time when I met that stranger on the street, it was only two months later that I found myself in that situation with Rosie, and thusly into the judgment seat. I had made many decisions before this incident, both good and bad, but that was the best decision I ever made with immediate results. Don't let anyone fool you into thinking that you can get into heaven without knowing Christ. It doesn't matter if the list of your good deeds rivals that of your past sins. Certainly, that list doesn't outweigh your own list of sins. Those good deeds do not exempt you.

In reply Jesus declared, "I tell you the truth, no one can see the kingdom of God unless he is born again." (John 3:3)

Whoever believes in the Son has eternal life, but whoever rejects the Son will not see life, for God's wrath remains on him.(John 3:36)

For God so loved the world that he gave his one and only Son, that whoever believes in him shall not perish but have eternal life. For God did not send his Son into the world to condemn the world, but to save the world through him. Whoever believes in him is not condemned, but whoever does not believe stands condemned already because he has not believed in the name of God's one and only Son. (John 3:16-18)

Who are you believing in today—Mary, Peter, Allah, Buddha? Only God can save you, and if he sends someone into your life with his message, don't turn away; you don't know how many more opportunities you might have to find the truth before you die. God's blessings are on those who go out and minister in places where the Bible isn't readily available and those who do ministry in hospitals and in jails, for they are servants of God. There are those who walk the streets at night, preaching to prostitutes and drug addicts. It is to all our benefits to listen to these people who go out of their way to spread the Gospel. Thank God for all the people on this earth who are not afraid, even in the face of adversity, to preach God's Word. Be thankful to them, but more than that, be thankful for God working through them, for that is the only thing standing between you and the pit of fiery hell.

I Entered Heaven

After my judgment was over, the Lord disappeared, and another angel came and took my hand and led me away from the seat and asked that I follow him. We didn't run, and yet we travelled so fast and ended up in front of another door. The door opened on its own accord, and I heard the Lord's voice say to me, "Welcome to heaven." The moment I stepped through there into heaven, there was such a joy that I had never felt before on earth. There was nothing that I have ever done that brought me a pleasure such as this. I don't even think that this type of joy, not one drop of it, is on earth at all. After he had welcomed me, Abraham appeared, and the Lord said to him, "This is your descendant." At the time, I didn't know what the Lord meant by me being a descendant of Abraham. When I saw Abraham, I commented to him that he looked just like I had imagined he would, and then we hugged. Next, twelve men came to me, and Abraham said, "These are the twelve disciples." I hugged them each also, and I noticed that one of them was shorter than all the others. We then all spent some time together.

> I say to you that many will come from the east and the west, and
> will take their places at the feast with Abraham, Isaac, and Jacob
> in the kingdom of heaven. (Matt. 8:11)

As I spent some time there, I was able to observe many things. I saw different people of all shapes, sizes, and colors there. There were lots of babies there too. Never fear for a baby you or a loved one have lost for they are there in heaven, as well as many, many children. I also saw a lot of angels. There were some angels there whose job seemed to be only to sing nonstop. There were angels playing various instruments, as well as angels who were constantly just praising the Lord. I have never heard voices lifted in song before that sounded so beautiful or any song that could compare to what I was hearing there. As I listened, my soul was filled with such a joy that I had never experienced before.

> Praise the Lord. Praise the Lord from the heavens; praise him in the heights above. Praise him, all his angels; praise him, all his heavenly hosts. (Ps. 148: 1-2)

I can't describe to the fullest how beautiful heaven was. Again, there is nothing on earth to compare with its splendor. I did see streets of gold, and the edges of them were inlaid with precious jewels. I saw what can only be described as a city. There were buildings of varying sizes and design, some that looked to be mansions. Some buildings there were covered with jewels like diamonds and rubies, as well as others with gold on them. I was so overwhelmed with everything I saw. To myself, I said, "This where I want to spend the rest of my life."

I wandered around through the streets for a while when I then came upon a place that was filled with a lot of angels. They were taking turns worshipping God. Some would just call God Holy, Holy. It really is indescribable to recount how they were worshipping; my words cannot do it justice for the reality is beyond words. In this place, I could see beams of light shining down in a particular spot. These beams were crystal clear, like glass surrounding the place, and yet I could not see the center. I tried, but no matter how I turned myself, I could not see the center. I believe that God was there; I could not see him, but I think that is where he was.

Heaven is a place that is full of love, the greatest love. I believe that there is where I really felt love for the first time. The love I thought I had for my mother or other family members or husband paled in comparison to the love I experienced there. Love is something that God created, and what we experience on earth is a mere interpretation or a reflection of the love in heaven. After a while, I was brought to a place in heaven where God expressed his love for me. He said that he was sorry for the things I had gone through on earth. He said that he knew me before I was born and called me his child. As I stood there, I could feel no other emotion, no pain, no nothing except for love. The love of God is a must-have! This is the greatest thing there is; that is why it pleases God when we love one another.

> "Teacher, which is the greatest commandment in the Law?" Jesus replied, "Love the Lord your God with all your heart and with all your soul and with all your mind." This is the first and greatest commandment. And the second is like it: "Love your neighbor as yourself." (Matt. 22:36-39)

After God finished expressing his love for me, he rewarded me for all the good things I had done on earth. A list of all the good deeds I did came out, and they were read to me one by one. They were written down and included the date and the time they had occurred. As they were spoken, I remembered each and every one. As my deeds were being read out, we came upon one where God thanked me, and Jesus said that I had done it for him. They were speaking of when I would go out in the streets and give my money to those who were less fortunate than me. I didn't have much money to spare, but the little I did give pleased God. They were also thankful for the times where I encouraged others. One of these times happened when I came upon a woman in the bathroom of a club who was sitting on the floor, crying. I asked her what was wrong, and she told me that she was homeless, that she had a good life but that it was no more; she had lost everything. She related to me the bad things that had happened to her, and after hearing it, I felt bad for her and offered that she could spend the night at my house. She said that she would stay for a few days and then get transportation to her village. Well, she stayed for a month. I took care of her and gave her money for the bus fare to her village. She acted very gratefully.

The next day, I left her at my place for a few hours, and when I came back, I saw that she had packed her things. She didn't have a lot of things, and when I asked her if she wanted me to go with her to the bus station, she said that she would be fine and she left. A few days later, I realized that she had packed all *my* best outfits and had taken them with her! I couldn't believe it; I was so hurt. Still, that wasn't the end of it. I went to the club one day and I saw a girl carrying a bag that looked like mine, and when I asked her about it, she said that a girl had sold it to her the other day. I asked for a description of the girl, and it turned out that it was the girl that had stayed with me. As if that wasn't enough, one day I was in the market, and a few girls approached me like angry bees ready to sting. One lady pushed me and asked me where my "friend" was. They claimed that she had stolen from them and said that I was a thief too. Some bystanders rescued me before things got out of hand, and I was able to tell them that the girl had stolen from me also.

I am telling you this story because God still remembered the good deed I did by letting that girl stay at my house. You too will be rewarded for helping others, regardless of how things turn out. It doesn't matter if those people are grateful or if they repay you with kindness or not. God will reward you in heaven. If people have taken advantage of your good nature, don't take this to mean that you should stop helping others, forgive them, and continue on doing the good that is in your heart. God will remember both your good deed and their bad one, for it is all written in heaven.

If you love those who love you, what credit is it to you? Even "sinners" love those who love them. And if you do good to those who are good to you, what credit is that to you? Even "sinners" do that. And if you lend to those from whom you expect repayment, what credit is that to you? Even "sinners" lend to "sinners," expecting to be repaid in full. But love your enemies, do good to them, and lend to them without expecting to get anything back. Then your reward will be great, and you will be sons of the Most High, because he is kind to the ungrateful and the wicked. Be merciful, just as your Father is merciful. (Luke 6:32-36)

As he was going into a village, ten men who had leprosy met him. They stood at a distance and called out to him in a loud voice, "Jesus, Master, have pity on us!" When he saw them, he said, "Go, show yourselves to the priests." And as they went, they were cleansed. One of them, when he saw that he was healed, came back praising God in a loud voice. He threw himself at Jesus' feet and thanked him—and he was a Samaritan. Jesus asked, "Were not all ten cleansed? Where are the other nine? Was no one found to return and give praise to God except this foreigner?" Then he said to him, "Rise and go; your faith has made you well." (Luke 17:12-19)

Can you imagine how Jesus must have felt? He healed ten lepers who, without his help, would have remained as they were for the rest of theirs lives, and only one came back to thank him. Did this stop Jesus from healing others in the future? No. So too should we act in the same manner. Keep giving to the poor and helping those in need when you can. Even if you are tithing at church and find that your money is not being used in the manner that you believed it should be or would be, don't stop giving, for you are acting faithfully even if others are not. Find another church that you can trust that the money you give is going where it should, don't just stop giving altogether, but staying at that church for if they are doing something like that wrong, there are probably other things as well.

Then the King will say to those on his right, "Come you who are blessed by my Father . . . For I was hungry and you gave me something to eat, I was thirsty and you gave me something to drink, I was a stranger and you invited me in, I needed clothes and you clothed me, I was sick and you looked after me, I was in prison and you came to visit me . . ." The King will reply, "I tell you the truth, whatever you did for the least of these brothers of mine, you did for me." Then he will say to those on his left, "Depart from me, you who are cursed . . . For I was hungry and you gave me nothing to eat, I was thirsty and you gave me nothing to eat, I was thirsty and you gave me nothing to drink, I was a stranger and you did not invite me in, I needed clothes and you did not clothe me, I was sick and in prison and you did not look after me . . ." "I tell you the truth, whatever you did not do for one of the least of these, you did not do for me." Then they will go away to eternal punishment, but the righteous to eternal life. (Matt. 25:34-46)

The eyes of the Lord are everywhere, keeping watch on the wicked and on the good. (Prov.15:3)

The lamp of the Lord searches the spirit of a man; it searches his inmost being. (Prov. 20:27)

For God will bring every deed into judgment, including every hidden thing whether is good or evil. (Eccles. 12:14)

For me it felt really good to be rewarded for the good things on earth, but more than that, to be thanked for the things that God felt I did for him. So know that as you live here on earth that God is watching and is ready and willing to reward the good deeds that you do here. Just remember that of those rewards, salvation is not one of them, for that can only be gotten through belief in Jesus Christ.

My Experience with God in Heaven and the Love He Has for Us All

After I was rewarded for my good deeds on earth, I was taken to another area, and the Lord spoke with me about what had happened to me on earth. He confirmed that indeed Rosie had killed me, and he told me that Rosie's hatred for me started back to the first month she had met me. Again he expressed his love for me and his sorrow for the things I had suffered on earth. I realized that God's love is what I had been looking for on earth. I used to hear people on the streets say that God loves me, and I used to think to myself that if God loved me, why doesn't he do this or that for me. Truly God did love me, and I remembered all the things that God had blessed me with when I was on earth and the people he sent in my life to tell me about him so that I might be saved.

God explained to me that Rosie had in her heart an envy for me and that the devil saw that and used that to feed her desire to see me not succeed in life. For that reason and many others, we must purify our hearts of any evil so that the devil cannot use us to sin against others. I have heard people say that the devil made them do things, but as we discussed before, this just isn't true.

> But each one is tempted when, by his own evil desires, he is dragged away and enticed. Then, after desire has conceived, it gives birth to sin; and sin, when it is full grown, gives birth to death. (James 1:14-15)

An example of such, again, is Judas of the twelve disciples, who we know had a love of money.

> Then Mary took about a pint of pure nard, an expensive perfume, and she poured it on Jesus' feet and wiped his feet with her hair. And

> the house was filled with the fragrance of the perfume. But one of
> his disciples, Judas Iscariot, who was later to betray him, objected,
> "Why wasn't this perfume sold and the money given to the poor?
> It was worth a year's wages." He did not say this because he cared
> about the poor but because he was a thief; as keeper of the money
> bag, he used to help himself to what was put in it. (John 12:3-6)

It doesn't say here that the devil made him do anything. He did it himself.

> Then dipping the piece of bread, he gave it to Judas Iscariot, son
> of Simon. As soon as Judas took the bread, Satan entered into him.
> (John 13:26-27)

> Then Satan entered Judas, called Iscariot, one of the twelve. And
> Judas went to the chief priests and the officers of the temple guard
> and discussed with them how he might betray Jesus. They were
> delighted and agreed to give him money. (Luke 22:3-5)

You can see that Judas already had an open door of greed in his life, which made it possible for Satan to come in and guide his actions. It was the same with Rosie, and it's the same for anyone else. I was so surprised as I was listening to the Lord explain this to me. I used to have a bad habit of gossiping. I would be the one going around asking if anyone had heard this or that about so-and-so. Mind you, this wasn't even me relating firsthand experience to those that needed to know something; it was hearsay. I felt pressured to gossip, and sometimes my gossip hurt others, but it wasn't until it happened to me that I stopped. The first thing I did was stop going to the places where I was hearing the gossip. I did not engage in gossip if I heard it, and even now, I don't like to talk about people. Now I will just talk about whatever just to talk, not to gossip. You should know that when I was in the judgment seat, my gossiping was brought up as a sin.

As I said, I stopped going to the places where I could even hear gossip in the first place. That is important. It is important to be aware of where the seed of sin is even being planted. For example, if you are a married man and one of your coworkers tells you that they are going to have a bachelor party for someone and it is being held at a strip club, don't go. Why? This is what can happen (and I've heard of this happening before): You go to the club, and you and everyone else is having a good time. You watch these women stripping, and you like what you see, and you get all these ideas in your head—this can open the door to the spirit of perversion. You get home to your wife, and you are dissatisfied that she doesn't look or act like the strippers you saw at the club. The desire for that kind of stimulation grows and grows until the next thing you know, you are looking for girls like that on the Internet. Once these spirits enter, you get caught up in all this, and you begin behaving in ways that you wouldn't normally do. Maybe you begin by watching porn all the time or can't get interested in sex with your wife unless you watch porn first. Perhaps you begin to frequent strip clubs or even pick up prostitutes.

Soon after this, dissatisfaction spills over into other things, and your marriage falls apart. It all began in a way that you might think is innocent enough, but the devil only needs a crack to get in. He just needs a small thread before he unravels the whole sweater. Though it may seem that the spirits are the ones causing the trouble, we are all responsible for letting these spirits in our lives in the first place and, still further, for not being aware of them and subsequently not getting rid of them before significant damage is done. Every decision we make, even the seemingly innocent ones, can have serious ramifications. Again I say, we really should ask ourselves, what would Jesus do? Stop things before you get started. Is it too late? Are you already involved in something? Don't be naive and think only certain people can be afflicted with sexual demons, because it really can happen to anyone who opens a door. It is hard to break free from this type of thing for sexual interaction is a natural urge, but you can ask for deliverance from the perversions that are out there that entrap us. You must repent and ask God for deliverance, and he will deliver you.

We see people all the time who are addicted to drugs, who we know just started by getting high one time with their friends and it turned into something else. So we tell ourselves, "Just say no to drugs," but there are other things besides drugs, sexual matters, or greed of money that the devil can use against us. They all begin with the condition of our hearts, things we may not think mean anything in the day-to-day life. Perhaps it is jealousy or prejudice against others. These might be things that don't necessarily cause you to act against someone personally, as in maybe you don't go around slapping everyone who is richer than you or beating up everyone that has a different color skin, but it matters, and they are open doors in your life. Perhaps you take bribes, or you have an anger inside that causes you to treat others like trash. Maybe you just don't like anybody for no reason, or maybe you are very persuasive, and your boss uses you to deceive others with a smile. Whatever it is, you must get rid of it. You must purify your heart, or the devil will find a way to use you like he did Judas and my friend Rosie.

> Submit yourselves, then, to God. Resist the devil and he will flee from you. Come near to God and he will come near to you. Wash your hands, you sinners, and purify your hearts, you double-minded. (James 4:7-8)

Your hands are full of blood; wash and make yourself clean. Take
your evil deeds out of my sight! Stop doing wrong, learn to do right.
(Isa. 1:15-17)

O Jerusalem, wash the evil from your heart and be saved. How long
will you harbor wicked thoughts? (Jer. 4:14)

Next, God spoke with me about the love he has for all his children on
earth. He was saddened and told me that some don't know him or don't love
him or even think to ask him for help. He talked about those who are lost and
are serving his enemy. Even them, he has intervened in their lives and yet has
gotten no response. He says that when we hurt, he hurts and that he hates to
see any in poverty or those that are sick or serving his enemy, the devil. He
said still, they are all his children, for he has created us all and that he knows
us, each and every one, and loves us equally. I asked God why he didn't just go
there and help them. He said that they don't ask him for help, and moreover,
they blame him for every bad thing that happens (I was among one of those
people). He says this type of behavior leads people away from him. He talks
about people who pray to nonexistent gods or other beings they think are gods,
or they think they are praying to them, but they don't know these gods, so they
are praying in vain. I told God that I had prayed to him my whole life, and he
said no, I hadn't. He then said he will take me to the place where the gods
that I and others prayed to in vain.

We left and travelled to the second heaven. Remember, the third heaven
is paradise. In this second heaven that I had passed through before with the
angels, God showed me the first god, which was a sun with a human face on it.
He said that it was the sun god that lots of people on earth worship. He showed
me the god Buddha, the god the Catholics and the Protestants worship that they
think is him. I saw so many gods. Every religion in the world has a god that
they think is the true god. God said that it hurts to hear the prayers of people
who are praying to the wrong thing, and then they become disappointed when
there is no response, where none can be given. God sounded like he was in
pain when he shared this with me. No more was said, and then we travelled
back to paradise. God told me that in the church I had been attending before
I was killed, they worshipped the sun god, but that in my heart, I had been
worshipping him; so therefore, he received my worship, and he was very
pleased to do so.

I was very happy to hear that, but at the same time, I was saddened to
think of people who put a lot of time and dedication into worship only to not be
worshipping the Most High God. God told me that religion not only separated
us from each other, but that it can separate us from him because of misbelief
or misdirection. I used to think, "Why fight each other about religion? We are

all worshipping the same God, but that is not so." Fundamentally, religion is about doing all these various things in order that God might accept us. I know I had been looking for God for a while, first through Protestantism, but that felt too empty to me; Catholicism was too much work, and you can recall my time spent as a Muslim before I gave up. In my time looking for a religion, I was moving farther and farther away from God without knowing it culminating in me, declaring that there was no God at all.

As you know, I gave my life to Jesus in the marketplace. After I had done so, that gentleman that had led me to Christ told me to go and find a church, which I did, but it was the wrong one. I have a friend who, along with his wife, was Muslim, and they gave their lives to Christ, after which they sought a church and ended up becoming Mormons. If you come from a religious background in the first place before you find Christ, it is likely that you are going to find a "religion" that is familiar to you and your past experiences. Beware though; not every church that talks about God is of God, and not every church that talks about Jesus is of Jesus. If you lead someone to Christ, don't just let them flounder off on their own. Take the time to help them find the right church.

I may have shocked you by saying there is more than one god, but why? The first commandment says in Exodus 20:2-4, "You shall have no other gods before me." Why would he say that if there weren't other gods out there somewhere? Some people take that to mean we shouldn't worship anything or anyone else or have idols, but the next commandment after that says that already. "You shall not make for yourself and idol in the form of anything in heaven or above or on the earth beneath or in the waters below. You shall not bow down to them or worship them; for I the Lord your God, am a jealous God."

A funny thing happened to me. When I first arrived in Ohio that day, I saw a statue of Buddha for the first time in a Chinese restaurant that I went to. I saw it immediately as I entered, and it shocked me so bad that I jumped and immediately went outside. I was amazed because it looked exactly like what I had seen in the second heaven. Another time I saw one was when I went to get my nails done, and when I asked someone what it was, an American lady told me that it was art. In Africa, there are different tribes that worship different gods, and they make carved images of them. Lots of tourists like to buy these images. They call them masks or use them as art, but that is not what they are. Be wary of what you are taking into your home. That same mask that they would sell to white tourists is not something they would sell to me in Uganda. Africa is not the only place with carved images or idols. Even those of Christian faith have images of Christ on a cross or Mary that they will hang in their house, and some people even make altars and light candles to pray to these images; however, they don't consider them idols. Why not? Is it because they know Jesus is real, therefore the image has a power or something? Perhaps they think it isn't an idol because Christ is real, so the image is just a representation. Either way, Exodus 20:2-4 says we are not to make these images or bow down to them. We should not even stare or stand in awe of or have reverence for them.

He specifies in that verse that he is the Lord our God; he is the one who created the world and us, and therefore, he is superior to anything else. Why else do you think he is called the Most High God? There would be nothing to be the "Most High" of if there were no other gods below, right? Exodus 34:14 says again, "Do not worship any other god, for the Lord, whose name is Jealous, is a jealous God." Moses says in Deuteronomy 3:24, "O sovereign Lord, you have begun to show to your servant your greatness and your strong hand. For what god is there in heaven or on earth who can do the deeds and mighty works you do?" Does Moses know something we don't know? If not, then why would he say that if he didn't know that there were other gods? Deuteronomy 31:18 says, "And I will certainly hide my face on that day because of all their wickedness in turning to other gods." We are told again in Deuteronomy 6:13—15, "Fear the Lord your God, and serve him only and take your oaths in his name. Do not follow other gods, the gods of the people around you; for the Lord your God, who is among you, is a jealous God and his anger will burn against you, and he will destroy you from the face of the land."

Again, I would say, why would there be a need to specify things by saying "the Lord your God" or to even command us not to worship any other if there was no other? (For fun, I would suggest you look in the Bible and see how many times it says the specific term the Lord your God.) Moreover, we are to make sure that others around us aren't worshipping other gods. Deuteronomy 29:18 says, "Make sure there is no man or woman, clan or tribe, among you today whose heart turns away from the Lord our God to go and worship the gods of those nations; make sure there is no root among you that produces such bitter poison." That is a great job indeed, and one that has been put to the test in "holy wars" for centuries. It doesn't say here that we must kill each other to achieve that, but as humans, that is often what we have done. In John 17:2—3, Jesus says, "For you granted him authority over all people that he might give eternal life to all those you have given him. Now this is eternal life: that they may know you, the only true God, and Jesus Christ, who you have sent." There is only one God of creation. There is only one God that forgives sin and can give eternal life to those who believe. Perhaps that is the criteria for being the "true God" or "the Most High God." There are lots of verses both in the Old and New Testament that urge us to turn away from the worship of other gods and to instead worship the only one true God that is to be the Lord and God of our lives. It would take much time to note them all. You could do a search online or in some study bibles; there are keywords in the back where you could look up the Word God and find every reference where it tells us to not put any gods before him, so there must be others.

As I said before, God showed me these other gods. Every god has a connection to the people who worship it. Just like when you are saved, you give your life to Jesus and you connect to him through the Holy Spirit, so as the people who connect with the god they are worshipping. Of course, not everything that people worship are gods; some are demons that masquerade as something else, and some things are just that—things and nothing else. When I was attending that one church where they were worshipping the sun god, there were strange things happening there, and I assumed that because I was saved and attending church that it must have been the power of God working there, but it wasn't. These other gods have false power; they are counterfeits, trivial in the face of God's true power. They can't do everything that God can do. Think back to Moses and the pharaoh's priests.

Another thing these false gods do is block you from God. Worshipping them, praying to them or whatever, is a sin; and as such, it acts like a barrier, like what we talked about before. The Lord gave me a vision. In it, I saw the three gods I had been worshipping—the Protestant, Catholic, and Muslim gods—and visually, I could see them hindering my prayers to God. Because of this, I also couldn't receive the joy of my salvation to its fullest. When I woke up, I knew I had to denounce those false gods and pray that God would destroy the power they had in my life from me, having been connected to them. After that, I had another vision of God doing just that; and afterward, I was able to pray and get answers and the guidance I needed. It is important that we do this, for not to do so is to enter upon confusion. There is an empty slot in our lives where God fits. If we fill it with other gods, God himself cannot fit; there is only room for one or the other. If you are saved and you want God to be in your life, you must remove these obstructions first. Otherwise, you can get disheartened when you pray and get no response. You put the blame on God without realizing that you failed to get rid of the old when you got the new. It's like moving and not changing your address, you're not going to get your mail if you don't notify the post office of your new address. So in the same way, we must notify these gods of the change. Say this prayer:

> You foul spirits, you false gods [call them by name or description],
> I break you off my life in the name of Jesus. No longer do you have
> place or power in my life. Jesus, please come into my life and take
> full control of it. Amen.

Take the time to pray this prayer with family or friends in your life whom you have led to Christ so that they too can be free to experience the full joy of salvation that God wants us to experience. These religious spirits are strong, in that they are heavily entrenched in people's lives from generation to generation, but they can be broken in the name of Jesus.

You may wonder how people who are in churches that are teaching about God can, in fact, be worshipping something other than the *true* God. Well, some things are obvious. You must look to those in charge and listen to what they are saying and what they are teaching. What are they doing themselves or trying to get you to do? If it is in any way contrary to what is in the Bible, that is an indication that something is wrong. For example, I saw a priest on TV in England who said that God told him to marry another man. I believe a voice told him that, but you can believe it wasn't the Most High God, for homosexuality is a sin. God is not going to tell you that a sin that wasn't okay before is now suddenly okay. God never changes.

A lot of people in different religions say that God has spoken to them, and I believe that is true because he can speak to anyone. However, it is more likely they heard one of the false gods and believed them to be the Most High God. Still, that won't save you. Let's talk about the Pharisees for a moment. In biblical times, they were respected by everyone, and of course, they thought highly of themselves. They were known to be representatives of God and supposed keepers of the Word. They had all that information for generations and still, they got it wrong. God had spoken to their ancestors, gave them the law, and prophesized Jesus's coming; and yet they were the main ones making it the hardest for Jesus to do what he came on earth to do. They knew of God, but they didn't *know* God. They were not truly serving him, for if they were and were in fellowship with the true God, they would have known who Jesus was. Listen to what Jesus said to them in Matthew 23:13.

> Woe to you, teachers of the law and Pharisees, you hypocrites! You shut the kingdom of heaven in men's faces. You yourselves do not enter, nor will you let those enter who are trying to.

What of these people who strap bombs to their chests and kill innocent people? They say that they are doing it for God. They are not doing it for the true God, for he said, "Thou shall not murder." Yet they say God told them to do that. Do you recall that woman who killed her children in the bathtub? She said voices were telling her to do it; I believe her. Remember what I said about testing spirits who tell you things? This applies here, for if something is telling you to do something that the Bible says not to do, don't do it, for it is not from God. God is not going to tell you in the Bible not to do something, and then turn around and say, "But in this circumstance, you can do this or that." The devil and his minions have a hatred for human beings, and anything they can convince you to do that is going to be harmful to others is priority to them, for they know how much God loves us.

When God was telling me about these other religious spirits, I asked him why he didn't stop them; he said that he has told his children to stop worshipping these other gods, but that they are rebellious. We have free will, so God isn't going to shake us like a bully until we decide to worship him. Every time we hear the Gospel of Jesus but refuse to listen, there are angels keeping track of that. Every opportunity that we pass up is written in heaven. Remember Sodom and Gomorrah? They had opportunity to change their ways; they didn't, and eventually their cup of iniquity was filled. Every time a relative or a coworker talks to you about giving your life to Jesus, every stranger that gives you a flyer or book about receiving Christ, every instance that you flip past a channel on TV that have a pastor preaching about giving your life to Jesus is accounted for in heaven, and when you refuse to listen, that is recorded as well. You will never be able to say that God didn't try to communicate with you, for he speaks to us all in different ways all throughout the world. People get caught up sometimes, wondering about these tribes and other people that aren't civilized and wondering what happens to them because no one told them about Jesus. Well, God can make himself known to anyone, but in conjunction with that is the fact that we are told to go out and minister to people of all cultures and races; that means sometimes, others' salvation is dependent on us getting the Word out. Scary, huh? Still, you can't underestimate the power of God; he can and will use us where he can, and if he can't, he will find other ways of reaching people.

On the other side of this, there is no person on this earth that the devil can't speak to. He uses the same means of communication that God uses. The difference is that the devil knows he is bad and that what he wants for us is bad, so most times he disguises himself and his purpose. He arranges things to distract us, like leading us to a potential boyfriend or girlfriend of bad character but obvious wealth. Your friends or family don't like them, but the devil whispers to you that they don't really know them, and besides, that person has money to buy you stuff or take care of you. Money is a powerful motivator. It is not uncommon to be offered money to do things that people know they shouldn't do, like theft or murder, but the devil wraps it up in these packages that tell us that we need the money or we'd be better off with more money or who-is-going-to-know-anyway-type scenarios. Regardless of the vessel of reasoning from him to you through your friends or other associates, religion, or TV and radio, the bottom line is that he is communicating with us all. There are so many things, both good and bad, that bombard us every day, forcing us to make decisions of one kind or another. We need to have a filter for it all to keep the good and remove the bad. God wants to be our guide, but we have to make a step in his direction. We have to get out of religious ruts and away from the worship of other gods, even if that is all you have known your whole life. My mother told me that she was born a Protestant and that she would die a Protestant, but it wasn't as simple as her just being a "Protestant"; it was about the hell that I saw when I was in heaven. I didn't want that for her, so I didn't give up on her. For that matter, I don't want Rosie in hell; it is not even a place you want your enemies to be in.

The next subject brought up was that of abortion. I wish I could describe to you properly how much it grieves God's heart when people do this. God said that women all over the world are shedding innocent blood, and the devil has convinced people that it is okay. Lots of people believe that the fact that fetuses' hearts aren't beating until a certain time, they aren't really alive. How is that though? There are live bacteria and other things that don't have heartbeats, but they are still considered *alive*. Some people are okay with abortion because they think fetuses don't have souls until they are in a certain stage of development. Who decided that? The devil came up with that idea—believe it. There are other things that don't have souls or spirits that we know of, like plants, but they are *alive* and shouldn't be arbitrarily discarded. People even try to save the rain forests and everything; why not save the unborn child? They are both *alive*. God says that he blesses people with children. This is regardless of the circumstances. Having a child out of wedlock isn't a sin; it is the *fornication* that led to the conception of the child that is the sin. God chooses to bless people even in the midst of their sin. If someone conceives after a one-night stand, it isn't a consequence but a blessing, for God is telling you that he hasn't given up on you yet, and he is blessing you with this child through whom he is going to teach you new things. What better method is there to show you a reflection of the love he has for you than to have a child of your own to love unconditionally, for whom you want the best for, for whom you teach right and wrong to so that they can go out into the world and be a great person—a representative of you. When people look at the good your child does, they think, "Wow, they must have had some great parents." When your child shows compassion and understanding to others, people around them know that they learned it at home. So too then are Christians, children of God through whom God shows his love and purpose for in our lives.

God took me and showed me the spirits of aborted babies right there in paradise. God said that abortion is a sin and that it is in fact murder. I was surprised. I was one of those uninformed people who did not really know anything about abortion. The only thing I knew was from my experience in Uganda, and there it is considered an abomination to do that. I didn't know what abomination meant though. I had heard also that you could die from it, but other than that, it wasn't something I heard much about until I moved to the United States. I didn't have any technical knowledge about fetuses and babies and whatnot; I didn't even know where babies came from until I was thirteen! Those kinds of subjects were very private and not spoken of around children back in Uganda. So astonishing it was to me to be speaking of such a thing to God and seeing how grieved he was by it.

If you are a woman who has aborted a child or someone who has encouraged a mother to abort a child for whatever reason, repent of it and ask for forgiveness. You will be forgiven of this, for it is as simple or as complicated as any other sin in God's eyes. Make it a point to dissuade others you might hear contemplating on aborting a child. Remember, children are a gift from God, and any gift God chooses to give you should be treated with gratitude and reverence for it is a gift, not a right, a privilege, not an entitlement. Do not let the circumstance of the conception or the circumstances surrounding the impending birth cause you to sin against that child and God. Don't give up on God, for he has not given up on you. Again I say, if you have committed this sin, repent and receive forgiveness. God is not there just waiting to punish us; he wants to forgive us and receive us back into the fold, back into his arms. There is no sin too big for God to forgive.

> Then I acknowledged my sin to you and did not cover up my iniquity. I said, "I will confess my transgressions to the Lord" and you forgave the guilt of my sin. (Ps. 32:5)

> He who conceals his sins does not prosper, but whoever confesses and renounces them finds mercy. (Prov. 28:13)

> If we confess our sins, he is faithful and just and will forgive us our sins and purify us from all unrighteousness. (1 John 1:9)

My Mansion Was not Finished

When we had finished that conversation, the Lord Jesus asked me to follow him, and we walked down a street that was full of beautiful mansions. In that neighborhood, it was so peaceful, like no place on earth. When we got to a particular mansion, we stopped and the Lord told me that it was my mansion. I was so ecstatic! He continued on by saying that this is where I would stay and that he had been building that mansion for me.

> Do not let your hearts be troubled. Trust in God, trust also in me. In my Father's house are many rooms: if it were not so, I would have told you. I am going there to prepare a place for you. And if I go and prepare a place for you, I will come back and take you with me that you may be where I am. You know the way to the place where I am going. (John 14:1-4)

We walked around it, and I could see it was like no house I had ever lived in. He took out the keys and opened the door and allowed me to enter first. The Lord then told me that although the outside was finished, the inside was yet to be completed. I saw around me that the floors were not yet finished, and some of the walls were not complete. Still, what else I saw looked fine; it wasn't in total disrepair, but the Lord said it was not fixed well enough for me to stay there. That was laughable to me for when I was on earth, I was staying in a slum with Rosie, and here I was in heaven, and the Lord is telling me that this mansion wasn't good enough for me yet! Really, I didn't care that it wasn't finished yet; I was in heaven. Heaven! There was no evil there, no lack of anything, no crying, no pain, no working or looking for a job. It was all good, and I was ready to stay in that incomplete mansion for the rest of my life. Isn't that typical though of human behavior and Christian behavior in particular? God always has so much for us, and yet we are always ready to settle. God begins a work in us, and we are ready to settle even if his work is not yet complete in us, but oh, how much more he want to give us. How much more beautiful would the completed mansion be? Curious, I asked Jesus where I would stay while my mansion was being finished. Again, the Lord asked me to follow him, and we ended up back where God was. Jesus looked at me and again said that my mansion was not yet finished and that it was not yet time for me to live in it; therefore, they were sending me back to earth!

I immediately said, "No no no no. I am not going back to earth, please!" I was on my knees before God and Jesus, begging them not to send me back. I told them how I felt that earth was a terrible place for me. I talked about all the evil spirits down there that I didn't want to deal with and my fear that I couldn't stop sinning since there was so much sin there on earth. They listened quietly to me as I went on and on explaining about the earth as if I had been the one to create it. Jesus interjected and reminded me that I had a life down there that I hadn't lived yet on earth. I asked the Lord what life there was for me on earth that is better for me than in heaven. I told him that I didn't like living on earth and how I had barely survived down there. I told him that I didn't want to have to go back and then have to come back to heaven and sit in the judgment seat again, for I saw no way that I could get by on earth without sinning. Jesus then said that I needed to go back so that I could preach and minister to others and that God would lead me. Again I said no and added that the people down there were so unloving, and I didn't want to go back there. I began begging again for them to not send me back.

As I was there, I just kept thinking about hell and all the sins that were written against me that I had committed on earth. I was so panicked and I felt that I didn't have any assurance that I wouldn't go back to earth and mess things up so badly that next time, I would end up in hell. More than that, the difference between heaven and earth is so stark, so different, like night and day; there really is no comparison, and now that I knew, how could I go back? When I finally stopped babbling and trying to rationalize to them all the reasons why shouldn't and didn't want to go back, they spoke to each other, though I couldn't hear them. Afterward, God turned to me and he said that his children were still down there and that I needed to go back and tell them what he had told and shown me. He said hell waits for many who do not know and that I needed to tell people about how much he loves them and is waiting for them to come back to him. He wanted me to remind people as to how forgiving and merciful he is and how he has no wish that any should perish. He told me that he had chosen me for this purpose since before I came into my mother's womb.

God went on to say how daring the enemy and his angels are becoming against his children and how they are enslaving us. He even said that these demons marry each other using human bodies. I couldn't fathom this statement at all, so I just ignored it, saying to myself that I must have misunderstood, that it just couldn't be so, no way. God did not even explain himself to me. I know I have said a lot of things that may seem alarming or unbelievable to some people, but for me, of all the things God had shown me or told me, this was one issue that I just couldn't believe. To myself, I said that of course God would not lie, but the idea of it was so shocking, so abhorrent that I couldn't take it in. Yet he did say it and he left it at that, and there must be a reason that he said that to me, although I don't know it now. As he spoke, again I could hear his pain, his hurt and grief for us, his children here on earth. I felt the pain as well, for it is overwhelming to think of all that goes on down on earth, but still I could not say yes. I pleaded with God to please find someone else who is already there on earth who could serve him in this way. I still felt like I had gone through too much on earth to go back down again. I couldn't let go of the memories of the suffering I had gone through, the worshipping of wrong gods, the torment of those demons, and of course, Rosie. Was I being selfish? At that time, I guess I was. I could only think of myself and all I would have to go back to. The images of those people in hell with that fire burning them without relief were still fresh in my mind. For someone like myself who did not believe in hell and, for a time, heaven, to see both, I think someone else would feel the same as I did.

Before arriving in heaven, I had regiven my life to Jesus and then died about two months later. Before that, I hadn't had much experience really reading the Bible for myself, and the only thing that some people might term as *spiritual* that happened to me was that for two days, I spoke in tongues. Just one day out of the blue, I came home, and the words started pouring out of my mouth, and I couldn't stop. Before that time, I had no prior knowledge of speaking in tongues, had never heard of such a thing. I never knew that it was a God-given gift. Everything before that point that I knew about God was secondhand; what I had learned mostly about the Bible was the Ten Commandments that my mother had read to me. I remember as child once, when I had broken one of the Ten Commandments, I hid myself in a bush, thinking that God was going to consume me or whip me. I remember waiting in that bush for God's punishment and how fearful I was, for my mother had told me that no matter where I was, God was watching me.

> The eyes of the Lord are everywhere, keeping watch on the wicked
> and the good. (Prov. 15:3)

I felt incapable of knowing what was true from what were lies; I didn't want to mess up.

I don't think I have ever begged for anything in my life like the way I begged them not to send me back. This time I even said to the Lord that there was no one on earth who cared about or loved me. My best friend turned out to be my enemy. I ran away from my parents because I felt that they obviously wanted to get rid of me by marrying me to that man. As I said that, it seemed as if a door in heaven opened up for me to see down to earth, and I could see my brother in Uganda doing his business, and then I saw my mother washing dishes. They were both minding their own business, and Jesus asked me where I thought they would end up. The Lord said to me that if my mother died right now that I would never see her because she would end up in hell and I would be in heaven, and that the same fate awaited my brother. He looked at me and said that he knew that I didn't want them to die the second death. I then remembered my mother telling me that she was born a Protestant and that she would die a Protestant. After that thought, I hung my head and I gave up on me and my desires. I could not relegate my family to hell if there was a chance that I could save them from that by telling them the truth about Jesus and how to truly get to heaven. So I said yes, I would go back; then just as quickly, I said no again before again finally saying yes. Jesus then reminded me again that I had a life waiting for me on earth, that God had ordained and will bless me with that I hadn't lived yet.

In my mind, I wondered what that could be, for nothing could be better than heaven itself. Still, Jesus said that God had a husband for me and that I was destined to serve God on earth and that this husband would help me. I told God that I didn't believe in marriage and that all men cheat on their wives, for I had seen it. I asked who was this man that will not do that. The Lord said that this man will love me and that God would show his love for me also through this man. Jesus said that he would be with me on earth. I was happy to hear that God had a man for me who was going to love me. I had always had a picture in my mind of this dear man who would be mine, but I had given up on this man, thinking that it was just a dream. For some women that must seem silly, but you must understand where I come from. Where I am from, women are not valued. Ninety percent of them have no say in their marriage. The man is like a king, and only what he says goes. Things are not like they are here in the United States or Europe.

For God to promise a husband for me and say those things, it was so wonderful. I couldn't believe it, but at the same time, I could. I mean, here I was—dead but living, in heaven, and talking to God. Indeed, it must be possible. I was excited at the prospect of experiencing a form of human love, the likes of which I had never experienced. The thought of Jesus being with me as well was such a wonderful feeling. Still, I had to ask, will I ever get back to paradise? I asked God to assure me that I would come back to heaven. He said, "All will be well with you." Honestly, I just wanted a straight yes or no answer, you know? He also told me some things that I needed to do back on earth.

Why Didn't God Force Me to Go Back to Earth?

Many may wonder why God didn't just send me back to earth. Why didn't he just wave his hand and send me plummeting back to earth? He is all powerful, isn't he? Yes, he is. However, we, little unworthy humans that we are, have something very powerful inside us called free will. God created us in his image and gave us dominion over the earth and ultimate control over our lives. We are not robots programmed to do anything but are individual personalities and characters put here on this earth, and essentially, we can do whatever we choose to within reason. God has a will and a purpose for our lives, but many of us never accomplish it because we are not aware of it or we flat out refuse to do what God has called us to do. At the end of the day, we have to accept God's will in our lives; he doesn't force us to it. God could have sent me to earth and ordered my body to say and do certain things (certainly if demons can possess people, God has a power that is as great or better to do the same), but that is not how God operates. You could say that it's against the rules.

Let's talk about Moses. God talked to Moses and told him to go and free the Israelites from under the pharaoh's rule.

> And now the cry of the Israelites has reached me, and I have seen the way the Egyptians are oppressing them. So now, go. I am sending you to Pharaoh to bring my people the Israelites out of Egypt. (Exod. 3:9-10)

In later verses (Exodus 3:11-4:17), you can read that Moses was doubtful of his abilities and even asked God to send someone else in his place because he didn't want to do it, even after God had said that he would be with him and showed him some of the miracles he would perform through Moses. Eventually, Moses decided to do as God had instructed, but it was his decision. The Bible

146

even said the Lord's anger burned against Moses when he had asked to be replaced by someone else. Even though the Lord was mad, he still did not use his great power to force Moses to do anything. Early on in the Bible, God told Abram (later called Abraham) to leave and move somewhere else.

> The Lord had said to Abram, "Leave your country, your people, and your father's household and go to the land I will show you." (Gen. 12:1)

Abram didn't question God; he just did exactly what God said. He could have protested though, and think what would have happened if he had done that. God didn't have to ask or tell Abram to do anything. He has great power; he had previously flooded the earth, right? Even then though, he told Noah to build an ark. He allowed Noah to be an active participant in his own salvation.

> So God said to Noah, "I am going to put an end to all people, for the earth is filled with violence because of them. I am surely going to destroy both them and the earth. So make for yourself an ark of cypress wood." (Gen. 6:13)

Noah could have refused, and he would have suffered the fate of all the other people and animals left behind. So too could Lot have suffered. God had his angels warn Lot to leave Sodom and Gomorrah, and when Lot asked for a modification of where they should escape to, he was granted it and time to get there. They were told not to look back as the cities were destroyed. Lot and his daughters did as they were told, but his wife chose not to, and she ended up suffering the consequences. (See Genesis 19:1-29.)

God could have supernaturally put Noah and the animals in a bubble so that they wouldn't drown in that flood. He could have snapped his fingers and transported Abram to where he needed to go. God's angels could have destroyed everything and everybody except Lot and his family if they felt like it, but no, they were each given a choice in their own destiny. We too have a say in the things God asks us to do, and also, we may ask for mercy in a situation where God may have previously decided not to have any. If not for Abraham asking that God not sweep away the righteous along with the unrighteous, Lot and his daughters would have been destroyed. (See Genesis 18:23-33.) My situation was just the same. God didn't just toss me back. I chose to do as he called me to do.

Why God Wanted Me to Go Back to Earth

It was not yet time for me to leave the earth. God didn't strike me down and raise me up to be with him because he couldn't wait to see me any longer. God had so much for me here on earth that I was to accomplish before I went to heaven. I wouldn't call myself special, only that God had chosen me to do something on earth, just as each of us has a purpose here. Remember I told you about that dream I had, the one I told Rosie, wherein a messenger of God had come to tell me that God was going to take me to America to serve him? He also said that I was going to sing in a choir, and then he allowed me to hear a song that I would hear there and that hearing it would be a sign that that was the church I was to sing in. He told me that I was going to be persecuted but that I would live and that God would be with me. He also told me that I would have a salon of my own and that I would do hair for women who have come from all over the world and that God would allow me to minister to them. He urged me to treat everyone who was sent to me in that salon with love and respect. He said that I would be a vessel to share the Gospel to God's children and that the devil would try to take my life, but that I would get it back and come out victorious. After that dream, I woke up, and I was so happy, and I was bursting to tell everyone I knew. I told all my friends from A to Z and, of course, that included Rosie. By the way, the year I had that dream was in 1998.

God did not bring me to the USA until 2003. In the meantime, a lot of things happened. In fact, during this time, I forgot about this dream and started coming up with my own plans instead. I woke up one day and decided I would try to come to the USA and study to be a nurse or a midwife because that was what my mother did for a living. That did not happen though. I didn't have the money to go to school here. I had so many demands on my money that was split between sending money to my brother, my cousin, and my sister's children. It was either send the money to my family who was in desperate need of it or go to school for nursing and midwifery. Doing hair was just a hobby. I had always loved to do hair, but I never knew that I could make a living from it. It seemed by chance that I started doing it seriously at all. One day I braided a lady's hair, and I got a call from another lady who had seen that hairstyle and liked it. She asked if I could do hers, and it all started from there, ending up with me now having my own salon.

While I was in Africa planning to come to the United States, I didn't even know where to go. I was sitting in a small nail shop and I overheard a man talking about how he used to live in America. After I finished getting my nails done, I went over and asked if I could speak to him. Well, we talked for a little while, and he told me that I should go to Columbus, Ohio. He said that it was nice there and that the cost of living was cheap. This might sound funny, but before speaking with this man, I thought that I might go and live in Texas. I had heard about Texas rangers and thought they were all cattle keepers and horse raisers. I figured that I would like it there because that was close to the type of life that I was used to. To me, they represented what real Americans were. He told me that Texas was nice too, but that things were big and expensive there. So I ended up in Ohio in October, and it became so cold there, and I didn't like it. The main thing that set me against being there was the snow! Still, I was there, and I made an effort to ignore the cold and the snow and just make the best of things. There was one thing that I like there though, and it was a church. In fact, I had seen this church on television when I was in Africa. I wanted to go there so much, so one Sunday, I went to this church, and it was the biggest church I had ever been in. I became a member there, and one day, they announced that they were going to be having a choir rehearsal and invited anyone who wanted to sing in the choir to attend.

One evening after that, a man approached me as I was walking out of church and said, out of nowhere, that I should sing in the choir. I told him no because honestly, I don't sing that well. Then another time, a woman that I had met who attended that church and who was also from Africa told me that I should join the choir. When she said it, this time I knew that it was from God. So I joined the choir. It was very nice, and I made some friends, and the choir became my everything. Some months after I had joined the choir, a Wednesday rolled around and we were rehearsing, and the choir director said that we were going to learn a new song. I swear to you that this woman opened her mouth, and out of it came that song the angel had sung to me in my dream! As she was singing, the memory of that dream came to me, and tears started streaming down my face. The joy was so powerful, I just couldn't believe it. I knew that the time had come for me to serve God in that church, and I served in that choir with everything that I had, with all my heart. I knew for that time it was my calling. Slowly, though, the persecution started. It went on and on in that church until I couldn't take it anymore. It was heartbreaking what was happening to me in that church.

This was a great church. The pastor was a God-fearing man who cared about his people. His heart was consumed with a desire to serve the Lord and his people. It was a great honor for me to have served God there under that pastor's anointing. This church was huge, and I don't believe that the pastor was aware of everything that was happening there though. I served there for a year and I never shook that man's hand or spoke to him personally. I don't know why I was surprised at what happened, for the angel had warned me that I would be persecuted at that church. Eventually, I left there. I should mention that while I was there in Columbus, I had a dream one night that I was in a bar and I was preaching to a man about Jesus. I remember waking up and rebuking the devil, thinking that he had sent this dream to me, but I don't know why I felt that way at the time.

After the reality of that dream I had about serving in that church was over, I was emotionally distraught. I didn't know what I was supposed to do, had no idea where I was going. I trusted God though, and I just kept on braiding people's hair in my apartment. One day it was about 4:00 p.m., and I decided to go out and get something to eat, and I saw a sign that said Smokin's Food and Drinks. I thought that it was a place where they smoked ribs. When I went inside, I saw that all the seats were taken and that people were watching football. I ended up sitting at the bar. I ordered some ribs and the waiter told me that they didn't sell ribs there. He said that they had hot dogs and pizza. So I ordered some pizza and while I waited for it, something happened. A white man came up to me, and he said that he was the manager and welcomed me. I said thanks, and he noted my accent and asked me where I was from. I told him that I was from Uganda, and he went and told a bunch of other guys, and they came up to me and asked me about Uganda. They were all nice to me. Well, I ate my pizza and left, but decided to come back there again. When I came back the next time, the place was pretty empty, but I decided to stay. There was one guy there and he asked me to sit next to him, and I did. He started talking to me and told me what he was going through at the time. He mentioned that he was going to have an operation on his abdomen, and I started talking to him about Jesus.

I told him about how Jesus went around healing the sick and doing other things. We talked for a while and afterward, he gave his life to Christ. I prayed for him and for healing for him. He told me that I was his angel and that God had sent me to him in that place. Tears were streaming down his face, and I was very happy that he had received Jesus. Suddenly, I remembered that dream I had about preaching about Jesus in a bar. I knew then that the dream had come from God, and I repented of not having received it as such when it had happened. After that, I started preaching to guys at that bar and praying for them as they received Christ in their lives. There came a day when that guy I had preached to the first time came back, and he asked me if I remembered him and I said no. He reminded me and said that after that day he had spoken with me, he had begun to feel better and that he had changed his mind about the operation because of that. He said that he thought that my prayer had worked. Imagine that, from singing in the choir to preaching in bars! I was also ministering to the women who came to me to get their hair done as well. Doing hair really is a great opportunity to minister to people, especially when you do what I do, which is braid hair. Just think about it, hour upon hour of hair braiding. People get bored and they start talking, and of course, so do I. Really, if you think about it, I am essentially holding these women captive, for they are not going to get up and leave in the middle of me doing their hair. After I am done, since I do a good job, they are compelled to come back and get their hair redone, which is just another opportunity for me to talk to them again!

Time passed, and soon, it was time for me to leave Ohio. I still didn't know what state to move to, so I thought maybe I should just go to Texas since that had been my original plan before talking to that man. I moved to Texas, and I liked it. I went to some farms and stuff, but at the end of the day, Texas was just too big for me. So to make a long story short, I ended up moving to Orlando, Florida. When I arrived, I had one thousand dollars, no home, no job, no friends or family, nothing with me but joy. It was so hot—so, so, so hot in Florida—that I fell in love with it. It felt like I had reached home. There was so much to do; I went somewhere different every weekend. I didn't have any family yet in the United States, and sometimes I felt lonely, but I knew in my heart that God had brought me to America for a reason; that is what kept me going.

Eventually, I got a job braiding hair in a shop, and I worked there for nine months, and from there, I decided to move out on my own. One day, two ladies came in, and one of them asked if I could do her hair the next day, and I said yes. The two ladies were sisters, and one of them was a pastor's wife (I didn't know that when I first met them) whose church was in Louisville. The other lady was originally from another state too. I told them to come in the next morning, and I took them to the beauty-supply store to buy hair extensions. I must tell you that when they got in my car, I could feel such an anointing on them that it seemed to fill every nook and cranny of my car. I started ministering to them about Jesus, and then I came to find out who they were and that they hadn't come to me really to get their hair done. The Lord had sent them to me, and they invited me to come to their church and speak there. Let me tell that the power of God was so infective in that church; God's people came there and were set free. It was such a blessing for me to be there, such a great joy to see God working in people's lives.

Every day, I could see the dream that the angel of God had told me coming true. God is never one to lie. He gave me that dream to tell me what was going to happen, what he was going to bless me with, and even Rosie's evil machinations could not stop it from happening. He sent me back to earth so that I may fulfill the purpose he had for me. Yeah, it was five years in the making, but that doesn't change the fact that it came to pass. I must say that I am not the only one who God speaks to or tells one's purpose to. I must encourage anyone who has received a word from God to hold on to it, keep it close to your chest, and don't give up on it due to circumstances or the passage of time, for God is not a liar. What he says will come to pass. When I was given that message, I was poor, uneducated, and without a job. I was a new Christian without the means or the training some might think I needed to minister to others. I didn't think I was valuable to God, and my lack of confidence in myself and God made me susceptible to people like that roommate who discouraged me and, of course, Rosie, who mocked my dreams as well. I started to believe what people said about dreams just being dreams, but the devil knew that what had happened was more than just a dream but rather a reality yet to happen. He saw me as a threat and took steps to make sure that dream did not turn into a reality. He was worried, and rightfully so. I was destined to sing the Word, to preach the Word, to bring others to Christ, and he wasn't having it. The angel told me that the devil would interfere but that I would come out of it victorious. I didn't know what that meant at the time, but of course, he was talking about my death and being sent back. The devil did everything he could to the point of my death, where his power ended.

To anyone who is reading this, I say to you if God gives you a vision about his kingdom, be ready for the devil to do what he can to stop it. He will attack you however he can. In my case, I made the mistake of telling my enemy what God had planned for me. That saying "Keep your friends close and keep your enemies closer" is dead wrong. You need to know who your enemies are and stay away from them because they are your enemies, and they want to bring you down, and the devil will use them to do it if you are a child of God. Be careful what you say and who you share certain things with. Ask God to whom you can reveal certain things to. Still, if you stay strong in the Lord and he in you, you will overcome whatever the devil has planned for you. No matter how God's plan came to pass, it came to pass. Yes, I live in America. Yes, I own my own salon. Yes, I have customers from all over the world. Yes, I sang in the choir that the angel told me about. Yes, I preach the Word to whomever the Lord leads me to. My dream was more than just a dream; it was my destiny.

Don't be scared if God gives you a vision or speaks to you about something he has for you; just be wary. The devil doesn't know everything that goes on in your life, and just because you open your mouth and say that the Lord has great plans for you doesn't mean you will be immediately inundated with trials and tribulations. However, if he does get wind of it, he isn't just going to sit around and do nothing about it; he will start to fight. This happens with things that are not even concerning a special plan God has for you. It could be something as simple as telling your spouse that you want to save up some money to put down on a house. Suddenly, it seems that everything starts happening to prevent that from happening. It could be that the devil is attacking you, and more than that, it could be that the Lord is allowing it because what you are trying to do is not the right thing. The Lord will allow stuff like that to happen to you in order that you turn to him and ask him for guidance. Instead, why don't you pray in advance for things? Ask for guidance and further protection over the plans you have.

Another I must say is don't put God in a box. If God has asked you to do something for him, don't make excuses for why you can't do it. If he says that it is something you are going to do, he is going to make a way for it to happen. If God has called you to preach, don't get stuck thinking that you need to preach in a big church or tell yourself that you won't do it unless there is a big group of people to preach to. No, start wherever you are. When God gave me the dream and said I was going to be preaching the Gospel, you better believe that I didn't think I would be preaching at some sports bar. Yet there were people giving their lives over to Christ despite the noisiness of that bar. God used me where he needed me at that time, and he will use you wherever he needs you, so yield to him. Don't think that if you aren't preaching, you aren't working for God because you can. As a Christian, giving words of encouragement, showing mercy to others, giving godly advice, listening to people's problems, and praying with others is all part of ministering, all part of being representatives of Christ on this earth. I have prayed with people who have not immediately given their lives to Christ, but the Lord still used me to touch them in that place, at that time. It is not my job to choose people to save; God leads me to them or leads them to me. This doesn't mean you just stand still and wait for people to come to you, although God can still use you if you stand in the same spot every day. Jesus set a great example for us by going to the places that the so-called religious people wouldn't even go. He talked to the people that the "religious" people wouldn't even associate with. He mingled with criminals, prostitutes, tax collectors, and foreigners. He did his Father's business no matter where or who it lead him to. We can only aspire to do the same.

Why Doesn't God Do Everything Himself Here on Earth?

When I was a child trying to survive like others during and after the war, I can remember milling about through the streets full of dead bodies and hearing others wondering aloud to themselves or others why God didn't stop the senseless slaughter of innocent people. Then when I was a little bit older in Rwanda, during the war between the Hutu and Tutsi tribes, I asked the same question. During my own life, as terrible things happened to me, I would question God repeatedly as to why he was letting these things happen to me. I remember talking to a young man here in the United States one day about God, and he stopped me and said that he didn't believe in God. I asked him why that was so, and he said, "If God is real, why didn't he stop my parents from divorcing when I was seven years old?" Like this man, myself, and many others worldwide, every day we all wonder why doesn't God stop bad things from happening, especially things that happen to children who can't stop things from happening to them in instances like molestation or excessive beatings.

Let's start from the beginning.

> Then God said, "Let us make man in our image, in our likeness, and let them rule over the fish of the sea and the birds of the air, over the livestock, over all the earth, and over all the creatures that move along the ground." . . . . God blessed them and said, "Be fruitful and increase in number; fill the earth and subdue it. Rule over the fish of the sea and the birds of the air and over every living creature that moves over the ground." (Gen. 1:26, 28)

We also know from Genesis 1:1-24 that God was pleased with everything he had created before he created man; it says for all those things, "And God saw that it was good." When God created man, the Bible did not say that he saw it was good. Why? I guess that was yet to be determined. We were created in his image, but we weren't clones. We, unlike the animals and such, are given free will and the knowledge to decide whether or not to do what God intended us to do, i.e., rule over the earth. Problems start to emerge when we don't do as God commands us.

Furthermore, Genesis 2:16-17 says, "And the Lord God commanded the man, 'You are free to eat from any tree in the garden; but you must not eat from the tree of the knowledge of good and evil for when you eat of it, you will surely die.'" So now we can see that there was clear understanding between God and man that (a) he could eat from the tree, as in there was nothing stopping them like a ring of fire nor would God himself stop him from eating from it; and (b) he is being told, however, not to eat of it and given the consequences of what would happen if he did. Nowhere else before this was man told not to do anything in particular. He was only put in the garden to work in it and take care of it. Everything that Adam and Eve needed was provided for them in that garden, and later in the earth as a whole; there was no lack of anything, no sickness, no dying, no evil—they had it made. Everything was all well and good until

> now the serpent was more crafty than any of the wild animals the Lord God had made. He said to the woman, "Did God really say, 'You must not eat from any tree in the garden?'" The woman said to the serpent, "We may eat any fruit from the trees in the garden, but God did say, 'You must not eat fruit from the tree that is in the middle of the garden, and you must not touch it, or you will surely die.'" "You will not surely die," the serpent said to the woman. "For God knows that when you eat of it your eyes will be opened, and you will be like God knowing good and evil." (Gen. 3:1-5)

The devil is very crafty in that he sets us up for failure from the first breath, from the first taste, from the first touch, of something that's bad for us. What is interesting to note in these verses is that the serpent first spoke to Eve to make sure she understood what the rule was, for how can you be held responsible for breaking a rule if you don't know what it is? He asked specifically what the parameters were before moving on. The next thing was the fact that he wove in the truth while at the same time making it seem as if Eve was missing out on something great. He didn't lie to her on this point. She would become like God in the sense that she would know the difference between good and evil, up until that point she didn't have that knowledge. Second, the serpent knew that eating the fruit wasn't going to cause Eve to instantly drop dead on the floor, so saying that she wouldn't die wasn't exactly a lie. However, it did cause her to sin, which caused her to be separated from God, which equated to death.

Every day, the devil uses these kinds of tactics to get us to question God and his motives. He also takes great pains to make bad things look good.

Still, what the devil meant for bad, God turned for good. Even though man no longer has access to the Garden of Eden and direct access to God because of the barrier of sin, we have salvation through Christ our Lord.

> For God so loved the world that he gave his one and only Son, that whoever believes in him shall not perish but have eternal life. (John 3:16)

> But the scripture declares the whole world is a prisoner of sin, so that what was promised, being given through faith in Jesus Christ, might be given to those who believe. (Gal. 3:22)

> But now in Christ Jesus you who once were far away have been brought near through the blood of Christ. For he himself is our peace, who has made the two one and has destroyed the barrier, the dividing wall of hostility, by abolishing in his flesh the law with its commandments and regulations. His purpose was to create in himself one new man out of the two, thus making peace, and in this one body to reconcile both of them to God through the cross, by which he put to death their hostility. (Eph. 2:13-16)

> Therefore, just as sin entered the world through one man, and death through sin, and in this way death came to all men because all sinned-for before the law was given, sin was in the world. But sin is not taken into account when there is no law. Nevertheless, death reigned from the time of Adam to the time of Moses, even over those who did not sin by breaking a command, as did Adam, who was a pattern of the one to come. (Rom. 5:12-14)

This last verse is very important, for it shows how the problem was caused by one person and solved by one person, Jesus Christ. It shows that people sinned even when they didn't know that they were sinning and therefore suffered the consequence of it—death—but even that is overcome by Christ, for we can live eternally with him if we believe. We are reconciled to God through the death of Jesus Christ. God threw us a lifesaver, literally. We don't have to drown in our sin. Still, we have the choice to drown. We can see the life preserver (Jesus) and still not grab on to it. It is our choice since we have free will, but if you refuse to grab on, you can't go to judging and say that you never saw a life preserver. But if you believe and you let Christ come into your life and let the Holy Spirit come to live inside of you, well you will have salvation, but you will acquire another problem as well—the devil.

The devil is a liar and a thief, and he wants to take control of what God had given us: dominion over the earth. Every day, we allow him another piece of the pie, and God is not going to say to the devil, "Give back what you have stolen," for we allow the devil to steal stuff in the first place. We give him permission. By sinning, we give the devil authority in our lives. So too do we give God authority in our lives by coming to him and asking for protection for our loved ones, for our homes, for our nation. We have to acknowledge God; we can't just expect him to just pick us up over puddles, to block the path of every bullet, to redirect the path of every out-of-control car if we don't do our part as well. So too, we can't expect the devil to stop waving temptation in our faces, to stop whispering lies, to stop destroying if we keep inviting him closer by the sins we do and the immoral lives we live. That is why bad things happen to good people or, rather, why bad things happen at all, because there are none of us good.

Yeah, we do good things from time to time, and some of those times might not even benefit us in some way by making us feel good or look good to others, but at the end of the day, we are all sinners and fall short of the glory of God. God is not going to work in our lives like a robot and fix everything that is wrong; would we really appreciate it if he did? How long before we demand it of him or take it as our due even when the majority of bad things that happen are the result of someone somewhere involved in bad behavior? This goes for weather too. People want God to change the weather, stop storms from destroying towns or tsunamis from ravaging coastlines, when we are the ones messing up the environment in the first place. We are the direct cause of environmental changes that affect the weather all around the world! So first and foremost, we need to stop causing problems. When we can do that, then we can ask God why he doesn't do this or stop that.

So where to start? God sent his Word to us via the Bible. God wants us to know his principles, his character, his love, his capacity for wrath. He teaches us what to do in our everyday life. The Bible should be titled *How to Live Life for Dummies* because it is all in there, everything we need to know, as well as directions and prayers. There are parables for those of us who need a little imagery or story to help us cement things in our minds. When I really started reading the Bible, my life was never the same. Believe it. The devil can't deceive me anymore. Yeah, he can do other things, but at least he can't do that, and that is significant because that is part of the devil's main arsenal. The Bible makes it possible for me to discern the voice of God from the voice of the devil because I can take what I am feeling or hearing or having someone else tell me, and I can put it to the test of the Bible and see what it says about a particular issue, and if it is contrary, I can speak and rebuke the devil on the spot, and you can too! The Word of God is a sword; it is what gets the job done. And the spoken Word of God is what created the world; how powerful is that!

Remember also, in the Bible, it constantly says "if you" this and "if you" that because everything is a choice. If we do what we are supposed to do, then God can do his part. It is a push-pull relationship. God wants us to take control of our lives by letting him in and pushing the devil out. He wants us to be aware of the devil and stop saying that God did this or that bad thing, because God is incapable of doing bad; he can only do good. Even in the Bible, where God is letting loose his wrath, it is a good thing, for he is just. Just because there is a consequence and you don't like it or it doesn't feel good doesn't mean it isn't good or isn't for your own good. You will be surprised how many good things will happen to you when you spend your time doing good things. Think of what the world would be like if we were all doing what was good, right, and just. Would we be complaining that God doesn't intervene and do more good, more right, and be more just? The saying "Shoot first, ask questions later" applies here. We need to do as Isaiah 1:16-19 says:

> Wash and make yourselves clean. Take your evil deeds out of my sight! Stop doing wrong, learn to do right! Seek justice, encourage the oppressed. Defend the cause of the fatherless, plead the case of the widow. Come now, let us reason together, says the Lord. Though your sins are like scarlet, they shall be white as snow; though they are red as crimson, they shall be like wool. If you are willing and obedient, you will eat the best from the land; but if you resist and rebel you will be destroyed by the sword. For the mouth of the Lord has spoken.

We have been given pretty clear commands here with pretty clear results and/or consequences. We have to stop doing wrong, put away our evil ways and lifestyles. We need to help those in need. The world in general is hypocritical in that it says one thing and does another. We say we want to get drugs off the streets, yet we let drugs fly into the country every day. On top of that, we shun those who have become addicted to these drugs, who then turn around and hurt others to get more of them. Then we cry at the funerals of those shot by drug related drive-bys. It is a cycle. People say porn is wrong, stripping is wrong, yet the majority of people dress provocatively, and we all know the saying "Sex sells." We use sexual content to sell merchandise. We make it seem like sex is the way to be cool, to fit in, to be loved. So little girls dress like women and get picked up by men or start having sex earlier with boys who use sex as a weapon, and we wonder why there are all these babies born out of wedlock or why abortion is on the rise. How can we expect God to be putting out a fire that we keep adding tinder to?

God commands us to seek justice and encourage the oppressed. There are people all over the world, in Africa specifically, that are being oppressed. You know there is always battle over oil. There are people still being sold into slavery today in Sudan. God has allowed us dominion over ourselves and the world; there are those in power who don't do anything about these kinds of things happening, but people have the nerve to ask why. Why does God do this or not stop that? He has given us the power to do it, he has commanded us to do it, so we need to do it ourselves. If you are at work and your boss tells you to do something, tells you everything you need to know, and tells you where to find what you need to get the job done, do you then turn around and ask him why he doesn't do it himself? Do you dare? He has his job and you have yours.

I recall recently that there was a war between Russia and Georgia, and people sent aid to the people of Georgia. There was talk about helping them rebuild, and that is not only the right thing to do but the *biblical* thing to do. We need to pray for those people, and in addition to that, we need to pray that God will send a man that will help destroy the people that are currently oppressing others in Rwanda, Sudan, the north of Uganda, and elsewhere. We have also specifically been told to help those who are fatherless and women who have lost their husbands. I admire people who do outreach programs in their neighborhood that help children who are living without a father or male role models in their lives, and also those who help widows and single mothers. Again, it is not only the right thing to do, but also a God-given command that we do so.

Who else should we be helping?

> Is it not to share your food with the hungry and to provide the poor wanderer with shelter—when you see the naked, to clothe him, and not to turn away from your own flesh and blood? (Isa. 58:7)

There are always going to be poor people among us, no matter what. Several places in the Bible urge us to take care of those less fortunate than ourselves. If God has blessed you with money, then it is your obligation to help those in need. It is not just a right thing to do but a biblical principle as well. Do not say to yourself that if God wanted them to have money, they wouldn't be poor; instead say, "God blessed me abundantly with money that I may provide for myself and family as well as help those in need." There is no specific way that you need to do this, for there are so many options available to us when it comes to helping the needy. Perhaps you prefer to do as I did and walk the streets and help those you see begging. Maybe you would feel more comfortable doing a food drive with your church or children's school. Some people like to donate to certain charities, and still others like to do stuff like participate in building homes, like Habitat for Humanity does. If you have your own business, you can give discounts to those in need as well. For example, if you have an auto repair shop, maybe you would charge for parts and not for labor. In another business, perhaps you charge for your products and not for the delivery. Again, I say there are so many things we could all be doing to help those in need. It is not enough to just tithe in church on Sunday, for that is a separate matter altogether.

This verse also commands that we don't turn away from our own flesh. Some people would say, "Of course, I would never do that. I will at least take care of my family." Yet there are people every day who don't support their children via child support or other means. Men in particular, from coast to coast, abandon their children after a relationship fails. We all know statistically, this leads to so many problems. Yes, a woman can raise her children without the financial support or input of the father, but at what cost to herself or their children? Giving up the financial and relational obligation for a child is a big problem, for what are we then teaching our children? There are still other people who don't take proper care of their children, who then end up in foster care or put up for adoption. How many people amass wealth and yet don't share any with their family because they feel like they are entitled to it all? Yet those same people will donate to a charity at a company function to make themselves look good.

Honor the Lord with your wealth. (Prov. 3:9)

Certainly, if God has blessed you with money, you shouldn't be squandering that money on strip clubs or gambling or excessive shopping and other like things. That is like a slap to God's face, and it grieves him when we misuse what he has blessed us with. God has asked that we honor him with our possessions. For example, if God has blessed you with money and you want to buy something for yourself with it, that is okay, for God wants us to be content and happy. However, we must consider this thing that we are going to be purchasing. Is it going to take you farther from God or your family, as in will you then be spending more time with this thing than with God or your family? I think that people as a whole pray to God and ask that he increase their money or their status or other things, then when they get it, they become so focused on that thing they forget that God blessed them with it. Before they got this thing, they were in constant prayer, they were seeking the Lord and so on, and then afterward, there might be a quick "thank you" or a "praise be to God" and then that is it. Certainly, that is not honoring God with your possessions.

Let's move on to another topic.

A righteous man is cautious in his friendships, but the way of the wicked leads them astray. (Prov. 12:26)

Who would know this better than I? God warns us to choose our friends wisely lest they lead us astray. This is a solid principle that was important in the past and is even more important today than it ever was with the invention of the Internet. Parents, we must acknowledge the fact that there can be a real danger to our children if they make the wrong friends. Children consistently mimic the bad behavior of their friends; we see it every day. Children are ever ready to follow the lead of their peers. We can't be there every second of every day that our children interact with potential friends, but we can give them the foundation for recognizing a person who has good friend potential versus one who is lacking. I never knew how to choose a good friend until I read the Bible. It is a fact that when you hang out with people, they will influence you or you will influence them, period. That is just the way it goes. People either build each other up, or they tear each other down. We are constantly shaped by those around us, and this is even more significant in the life of a child who is yet unaware of how the world works or what the wisest course of action in a certain situation might be.

So what are signs we should look for? Well, for one, when your child is hanging out with the wrong children, you will see the results almost immediately in school or at home. Kids will become disruptive or disobedient or downright rebellious. Parents, we must pray for our children. Pray that they make good friends and that also, your child can be a positive person in other children's lives. If your child has already fallen in with the wrong crowd, you have to pray for God to intervene in their lives and the lives of those other children as well, that they might get back on track. It also helps if you place your children in environments that are more likely to produce positive results. For example, if you have a godly friend that has children, there is a good chance that they are raising their children in a godly way. Try and arrange outings where these children can mingle. Youth groups at church are a good place for children to make friends. A big thing is, you should invite your children's friends to your house or to a place where you can observe them, because you need to know who these children are that your child is hanging out with.

For adults, the same basic rules apply. Be wary of the people you interact with. Feel them out. Pay attention to how they conduct themselves. Find out what they believe. Are you in a relationship? Get to know your significant other's friends, for they have an impact in your relationship whether you believe it or not. People always talk to their friends about problems they might be having in their relationship, and if they have friends of low morality or character, you better believe they will give out bad advice that could lead to more problems in your relationship. So pray also that your significant other will find and keep friends of godly character. Pray this for yourself so that you too will have positive people in your life. Pay attention to the signs when you are in relationship with someone else; this includes friendships. Keep away from prideful, lazy, racist, lying, slandering, immoral people. That may sound easy enough, but it isn't also always right in your face. That is why prayer is important, and it is also important to pay attention to what your heart or your instincts might tell you about a person. Don't be afraid to discontinue an association when you realize stuff about a person. There is a difference between you being a good influence on them and them being a bad influence on you. Perhaps your moral character will make an impression on this bad person, but if you find that they are leading you into sin or are consistently acting negatively against you, then it might be time to walk away. Again, in this, prayer is important. Maybe God has you in that person's life for a reason; you need to find out if that is so. Either way, be careful of who you associate with lest they bring you down.

A friend loves at all times. (Prov. 17:17)

So again, I say that God has given us dominion over the earth and ourselves. He has given us all the tools necessary to function and, on top of that, made a new covenant through Jesus Christ that we may have salvation and eternal life with him. Think of God in a managerial light. He delegates stuff out to each of us. We all have certain qualifications that we bring to the table. Thusly, God gives us each a purpose and a direction so that together, we might all function as a whole for the betterment of the whole. God is always there to appeal to when we need help. He will also sometimes step in when we court disaster and to rebuke us when we mess up. He gives us rules to live by and expects us to follow through or reap the natural consequences of wrong actions. He is there to pick us up when we fall, comfort us when we grieve, and strengthen us when we are weary. In our efforts to be godly people, we must endeavor to be the same way in our lives, in our interactions with others.

Let us talk about discipline. Proverbs 3:11-12 says, "My son, do not despise the Lord's discipline and do not resent his rebuke, because the Lord disciplines those he loves, as a father the son he delights in." So parents, let us not shy away from disciplining our children. Our children are accountable to us for their behavior, as we are accountable to God for ours. Confused about how to bring up godly children? The Bible gives us instructions on how to accomplish this so that they will grow up to be good God-fearing adults who make good members of society and good husbands and wives. God has given us, as parents, the responsibility to discipline our children, so we need to do so and not sit idly by, expecting God to do it for us. He has given us the tools and stands at the ready should we ask for his help, but he is not going to do it for us. Proverbs is full of verses regarding discipline. Let's look there.

These verses are telling us not to ignore bad behavior—take action.

> He who spares the rod hates his son, but he who loves him is careful to discipline him. (Prov. 13:24)

> The rod of correction imparts wisdom, but a child left to himself disgraces his mother. (Prov. 29:15)

These verses serve as a reminder that sin leads to death—separation from God.

> Discipline your son, for in that there is hope; do not be a willing party to his death. (Prov. 19:18)

> Apply your heart to instruction and your ears to words of knowledge. Do not withhold discipline from a child; if you punish him with the rod, he will not die. Punish him with the rod and save his soul from death. (Prov. 23: 12-14)

> Discipline your son, and he will give you peace; he will bring delight to your soul. [So too does God delight in our good behavior.] (Prov. 29:17)

Remind your children that it is not just you as their parents that call them to obey, but more than that, they are commanded by the Bible to heed your instruction.

> Honor your father and your mother, as the Lord your God has commanded you, so that you may live long and that it may go well with you in the land the Lord your God is giving you. (Deut. 5:16)

> Listen, my son, to your father's instruction and do not forsake your mother's teaching. (Prov. 1:8)

Don't be afraid to explain things to children. Some parents believe blind obedience by their children is the only acceptable way to rear children. Let me say that explaining things to children is worthwhile, for they are more likely to listen if you do. Explain to your children the sacrifices you make on their behalf. Relate to them similar situations that you went through when you were younger so that they understand that you are speaking from experience and are not just trying to make their lives miserable. There are times when blind obedience is necessary. Tell them when this is so, and in addition to that, allow for opportunities to explain things to them. Show them passages in the Bible that back up your decisions so that they can see that you too are accountable to God for your disciplinary actions. This will take some weight off your shoulders while also getting children familiar with the concept of searching the Bible for advice and instruction. They need to know that we are given specific instructions to follow in the Bible. Lest we or they forget, check out another verse that speaks clearly about this.

> So that you, your children and their children after them may fear
> the Lord your God as long as you live by keeping all his decrees
> and commands that I give you, and so that you may enjoy long life.
> (Deut. 6:2)

Remember also that some things in the Bible are very specific about how we should conduct our lives, and other things are concepts that are applicable to our current circumstances and environment. For example, there are places in the Bible that tell us to eat healthy or to be good stewards. How do you know exactly what that means? If you are unsure about something like that, pray to God for clarity and discernment. I know that God sent people to me when I first moved to America that helped me wade through the adjustments I needed to make, now that I was in a place that had so many options available to me that I had never been exposed to before. Let's take food for instance. When I first came to the United States, I was told by some people that I should stay away from fast food. They informed me about the hormones and preservatives in lots of those foods that lead to certain types of diseases and can cause weight gain. God also placed in my life someone that explained to me the pitfalls of using credit cards. A man explained to me how he had acquired unnecessary debt that he was trying to dig himself out of. So with this information, I have managed to stay away from fast food, and I have only one credit card for emergencies. I have been here for a while, and I have noticed that, hey, I am not the only one with this information, and yet many people choose to ignore this advice. So why then become mad at God or blame God for the troubles that plague us? God is not going to destroy fast-food restaurants or cause your hand to cease functioning before you apply for yet another credit card.

> Do not forsake wisdom, and she will protect you; love her, and she
> will watch over you. Wisdom is supreme, therefore get wisdom.
> Though it cost all you have, get understanding. (Prov. 4:6-7)

My son, pay attention to what I say; listen closely to my words. Do not let them out of your sight, keep them within your heart; for they are life to those who find them and health to a man's whole body. (Prov. 4:20-22)

I, like others, had to learn the hard way sometimes to listen to instructions. It cost me a lot in dealing with Rosie, had I listened to God and others, I would have spared myself a lot of hardship. God didn't stop me from being Rosie's friend, but he gave me the knowledge to make better decisions, and yet I had the free will to ignore it. Take it from me, listening to godly advice and wisdom from the experienced and immersing ourselves in the Word for God's instruction will spare us a lot of problems in life.

When God Does Intervene in Our Lives

Now some people would take that previous chapter to mean that God can't or won't intervene in our lives, but that isn't so. God can intervene in our lives whether we are saved or not. I remember in my own personal life that even when I gave up on religion and God, he was still there in my life. He made himself known to me, even if I chose to ignore it or was ignorantly unaware at the time. For example, there were times when I was so poor that I didn't know where my next meal would be coming from. I would be hungry and unsure about what or how to get something to eat, and someone would come up and offer to buy me or give me something to eat. Things like that would happen to me often. There were times that I would desire a particular dress. There would be a picture of it in my mind, and eventually, I would come across the design of that dress and acquire the money to buy it. Mind you, I had not seen the dress before in actuality nor had I told anyone my desire for it. God put the desire for it in my mind and heart and then provided it to me. At the time, I didn't recognize this, but God was faithful even when I was not.

God uses symbolism in our lives every day to get our attention, but we have to be aware of when it is happening. For me, God has used snakes often to warn me of danger and, alternately, to show me that he can protect me from this danger. I have already told you my dreams about snakes in reference to Rosie, but another thing I didn't mention was about one time Rosie and I were playing together and hiding in the grass and I lay down on a poisonous snake, but it did not bite me. Do you recall the other snake that should have bitten me as a child? There was another time when a snake fell from a tree immediately in my path, I could have stepped on it, but I didn't. I have come across people who say they don't believe in God, yet they tell me of things that have happened to them or for them, and I can clearly see that God is helping them or talking/warning them about something. Remember, God is love. Imagine that you have six children, but two of them are evil. As a parent, do you abandon those two because they are bad? No. God is the same way. No matter how lost you may be, God will make the effort to reach you. He can intervene on your behalf, but you have to be aware of when it is happening so that you can yield to God.

Does God use different methods to reach, warn, or guide the lost than he does to those who are already saved? No. There are people who aren't walking with God who have been given dreams from God. I came across a certain lady one day who was going through a divorce. She was very unhappy in her life. She started talking to me about what was going on in her life, and she mentioned to me how she had lived a crazy lifestyle when she lived in New York. She said that she had no care for the future, only what was happening at the present time. However, she said that one day she had a dream, and in this dream, she saw two trains. One train was full of evil people, and it was heading for and ending up in a dark road. The other train had a few good people on it, and it was heading for and ending up in a road full of light. She said that in the dream, she was drawn to the train that had the evil people in it, but someone in the dream spoke to her and told her to stop and to get on the other train that was headed for the light. After relaying this to me, she looked at me curiously and said that she had never told anyone this dream before. I asked her if she believed in God, and she told me no. I asked her if she knew that God cared about her, and she said that no he didn't, and she knew that to be so.

Well, I ignored that statement and translated that dream for her. I explained to her that the trains represented both life and death, heaven and hell. The train full of evil people was going to end up in death, with the final stop being hell, while the other train with the few good people was headed for salvation and heaven. I told her that the reason she was attracted in her dream to the evil train was because that was how she was currently leading her life and that the voice that told her to stop was from God. She laughed and skeptically asked me if God would actually speak to her. I assured her that God had spoken to her, but she was disbelieving and said that she was too evil for God to have spoken to her. I told her again that God did give her the dream, and I asked her if she changed anything after she had the dream all that time ago, and she said no. She said she had continued in that lifestyle and eventually got married. She said that things didn't get better, and then she asked me if God would actually forgive her for her adulterous behavior in her marriage. I told her that he would forgive her, and the fact that she recalled this dream while speaking to me shows that God has not forgotten the dream he gave her and that he allowed me to be there to interpret it for her. Long story short, she accepted that God has been with her and she gave her life to him.

When we pray to God through Jesus Christ, we give God permission to intervene in specific situations where he might otherwise not have. The Bible tells us to turn to God in our times of trouble or suffering.

> Is anyone of you in trouble? He should pray. Is anyone happy? Let him sing songs of praise. Is any one of you sick? He should call the elders of the church to pray over him and anoint him with oil in the name of the Lord. And the prayer offered in faith will make the sick person well; the Lord will raise him up. If he has sinned, he will be forgiven. Therefore confess your sins to each other so that you may be healed. The prayer of a righteous man is powerful and effective. (James 5:13-16)

People don't seem to understand how powerful or how important prayer is. Prayer is how we communicate with God. This is how you let him know you are thankful and how you can ask for his help in your life. God doesn't respond to crying, complaining, having attitudes or specific religious habits or behaviors. It is amazing how much people will do to try and substitute prayer. They wear charms that they think will protect them from harm. They hang crosses to ward off evil spirits. They wear special items of clothing that supposedly bring luck for upcoming situations. It is all nonsense. I for one was a crier. When something went wrong, I would cry and cry and bemoan my fate. God didn't hear my crying and then zap my problems away. Self-pity doesn't make your problems go away either. Life is full of problems; one goes away and is replaced by another. Turn to God first. Before you pick up that phone to call that friend that always listens to you go on and on, call on God. Let's look at some familiar verses pertaining to prayer.

> And I will do whatever you ask for in my name, so that the Son may bring glory to the Father. You may ask me for anything in my name and I will do it. (John 14:13-14)

> If you remain in me and my words remain in you, ask whatever you wish, and it will be given to you. (John 15:7)

> Therefore I tell you, whatever you ask for in prayer, believe that you have received it, and it will be yours. (Mark 11:24)

> Ask and it will be given to you; seek and you will find; knock and the door will be opened to you. For everyone who asks receives; he who seeks finds; and to him who knock, the door will be opened. (Matt. 7:7-8)

We should not take these verses to mean that we should pray whatever, whenever, and expect to receive whatever it is that we ask for so long as we tag "In Jesus's name, amen" at the end of the prayer. We are to pray in accordance to God's will and purpose. God is not a genie who grants wishes. You can pray all day for something that God feels isn't good for you, and he will answer that prayer by not granting you what you are asking for. Trust that he knows that some things are not good, that they will harm you in some way. The thing that people forget is that sometimes, the answer is no. God will not give you everything and anything you ask for. When you pray, you should be applying God's words to your prayers. The Bible says that God can grant healing, so you should feel free to pray for that. The Bible says that God can grant comfort during times of grief, so you should feel free to ask for that. Do you understand what I am saying? Also, there are things we shouldn't do while praying. For instance, Matthew 6:7 says, "And when you pray, do not keep on babbling like pagans, for they think they will be heard because of their many words." I am sure a lot of us have come across people who think a long-winded prayer assures the wanted response, but that is not true. Also, there are no key phrases that you should use to get a desired response. Remember also that things like unforgiveness or sins in our lives will hinder our prayers from being answered.

> And when you stand praying, if you hold anything against anyone,
> forgive him, so that your Father in heaven may forgive your sins.
> (Mark 11:25)

As born-again Christians, we have the benefit of having the Holy Spirit residing in us. The Holy Spirit is here to guide us through life. The Holy Spirit will help you to even know what to pray to Jesus for. It can give you the words to speak or the passages in the Bible to look up for guidance. I could not go on if I didn't have the power of the Holy Spirit working with and in me every day. He is my helper; he shows me the hidden things of God that I would not otherwise know. The Holy Spirit is the only thing besides water that I believe people can't truly live without, for without it, you really aren't living. The Holy Spirit will give you peace when there is nothing around you to be peaceful about. He will lead you to what to pray for and will bolster you up when things are pressing you down. The Holy Spirit will give you discernment for when people are lying to you. God will guide you through the Holy Spirit as to what decisions to make. The Holy Spirit also gives us power to do battle against the enemy. Some people believe in God but don't believe that the Holy Spirit exists or that it resides in them.

> And I will ask the Father, and he will give you another Counselor
> to be with you forever—the Spirit of truth. The world cannot accept

him, because it neither sees him nor knows him. But you know him, for he lives with you and will be in you. (John 14:16-18)

When the Counselor comes, whom I will send to you from the Father, the Spirit of truth who goes out from the Father, he will testify about me. (John 15:26)

But you will receive power when the Holy Spirit comes on you; and you will be my witnesses in Jerusalem, and in all Judea and Samaria, and to the ends of the earth. (Acts 1:8)

But I tell you the truth: It is for your good that I am going away. Unless I go away, the Counselor will not come to you; but if I go, I will send him to you. When he comes, he will convict the world of guilt in regard to sin and righteousness and judgment. (John 16:7-8)

In the last days, God says, I will pour down my Spirit on all people. Your sons and daughters will prophesy, your young men will see visions, your old men will dream dreams. (Acts 2:17)

Do not worry about what to say or how to say it. At that time you will be given what to say, for it will not be you speaking, but the Spirit of the Father speaking through you. (Matt. 10:19-20)

But when he, the Spirit of truth, comes, he will guide you into all truth. He will not speak on his own; he will speak only what he hears, and he will tell you what is yet to come. (John 16:13)

If you then, though you are evil, know how to give good gifts to your children, how much more will your Father in heaven give the Holy Spirit to those who ask him! (Luke 11:13)

So you can see that even though you may not think God is intervening in your life, recall that he has left us the Holy Spirit, which is a part of him, that is here with us always to guide us and help us in all things. You don't need to go to a psychic or a palm reader to find out things. The Holy Spirit will guide your words when you are reaching out to others in Christ. I can't tell you how many times the Holy Spirit has led me about what to say to certain people. People become shocked and wonder how I knew what they were coming to or how to tailor advice specifically to them. These things that I tell them come straight from God to the Holy Spirit, to me, to them.

Another way the Holy Spirit is a help to you is it gives you power over unclean spirits and demons. You have the power and authority to cast them out of your life and the lives of others. You can also lay healing hands on people so that they might become well. God is not going to come down and cast demons out, for he has given us the power to do so. God has already intervened by giving us the Holy Spirit, through which we can do these things. As we read earlier, Jesus told the disciples that it was to their advantage that he leave them so that they might receive the Holy Spirit in his place. Instead of Jesus, one lone man preaching to the masses, praying for the sick, and working miracles by himself, there would now be several people infused with his power, doing God's work all over the world, conceivably at the same time. Upon Jesus's ascension back to the heavens, the Holy Spirit came down and was received by each of the disciples. Their fear of what to say or what to do was nonexistent, for when the Holy Spirit is upon you, you need not be afraid to speak of God to whomever, wherever. The Holy Spirit can guide your words, your steps, and will also let you see in the spirit what God wants you to see. With this advantage, you can help to also guide others who are in need of spiritual guidance. Many times the Holy Spirit has guided my prayers about friends or relatives that were in need of something. The Holy Spirit imparted the knowledge to me, not them. How comforting for me to know that even though I have family members and friends across the ocean who are sometimes unable to contact me to ask for prayer or guidance, I can still be of help to them without them having to ask.

The Holy Spirit is also known by another name, and that is the Spirit of Truth. This is because the Holy Spirit can unerringly guide you in every decision you must make. The Holy Spirit can hear directly from the Father and guide you. The verse we read earlier, John 16:13, tells us that the Holy Spirit repeats what he hears, as in he doesn't change what God says in any way, doesn't sway either left or right, depending on how we may feel about something. He strictly tells us like it is. The Holy Spirit can give you insight and wisdom from God when you are reading the Bible. When I tried to read the Bible before I was saved, it was very difficult. I would have trouble understanding lots of things, and to be honest, I was oftentimes bored. Now with the help of the Holy Spirit, the Bible has come alive. I am no theologian; the Holy Spirit has guided me as I have written this book and pointed out the verses I needed to emphasize the truths that God has shown and told me. As a Spirit of Truth, the Holy Spirit will help you to discern good people from bad people; he will expose them to you. He will guide you to the right people. Also, this might sound weird, but the Holy Spirit will also remember stuff for you. Did God give you a Word five years ago? The Holy Spirit will remember it, and when the time has come for fulfillment, the Holy Spirit will remind you so that you will know that God is faithful in what he tells us.

God said that he would pour out his spirit on all people, and people will prophesy and see visions and dream dreams. This is the Holy Spirit that enables these things. It is through him that God will give information to us. Let the Holy Spirit be your guide if you are single, for he will point out the right people to you and expose the wrong ones. I am sure there are many people out there that wish they had some warning about a person they dated or married that was the absolute wrong person for them. If you are filled with the Holy Spirit, you will have that advantage. I remember when I first moved to the United States and was single; there were a lot of guys that were interested in me. I remember one man in particular who was interested in me who seemed like a nice guy. To myself, I thought he seemed interesting and that maybe I would give him a try. That night, however, the Holy Spirit told me that no, this man was not my future husband and that in fact he was an abuser of women. He told me that the spirit of abuse was attached to his family and that he was not the only man so inclined. I was also told that this man's father and other members worshipped another god. Well, I was so thankful for the information and praised God for revealing it to me through the Holy Spirit. Still, I had told the young man that I would meet him the next day, and I felt bad about not showing up, so I did.

When I arrived where we said we would meet, he was there waiting. We started talking, and he said to me that there was something he hadn't told me the day before about his family. I inquired as to what it was, and he told me that he had left his father's house because his father was abusive to him and his mother. He then went on to reveal that his father believed in some crazy gods. I was stunned to hear him tell me exactly what the Holy Spirit had revealed to me the night before. I know I must have had a very shocked expression on my face as he was speaking. Let me tell you something, you don't have to date someone for a year to get to know them and decide whether to marry them. This man had a history of violence that he said he escaped from, but the Holy Spirit knew that it was only temporary, for the spirit of abuse was upon him and his family. It was only a matter of time before he began to engage in the same activities. If you are filled with the Holy Spirit, he can tell you right off that this person you have in mind is or isn't the person for you. When I first met my husband, the Holy Spirit told me that this man was my husband. The Holy Spirit also reminded me that I had dreamed about this man a year before I met him. Why did it take a year before I met this man? Let me tell you something. It is very important to God that you meet and marry the right person. God does not like divorce. He doesn't want us to hurt each other by being involved with the wrong people. To this endeavor, God is going to try and work on you first before he sends the person he has for you into your life, if you let him. If you are praying for a mate, make sure you are also striving to be the right person for that mate. Let God work on you first. If you don't, you will be waiting in vain and more likely choose the wrong person in the midst of your impatience, for God is not going to send a good person for you to then bring down.

It all seems so complicated sometimes, which was one of the reasons I was afraid to come back to earth. I couldn't figure out how I would navigate my way through life without help. I felt like I had to do everything myself and do everything in my own power. That train of thinking led me to the conclusion that I was going to fail and perhaps be worse off than I had previously been. I couldn't bear the thought of it. However, I didn't count on the impact the Holy Spirit would have in my life. The Holy Spirit can convict you of sin, thereby inducing a confession and repentance, for which God can then forgive you. What a weight off my shoulders. I don't have to walk around with guilt weighing heavily on me or doubt riding on my shoulders, because I have the Holy Spirit to ferret out stuff for me. This is why I say I could not live without the Holy Spirit. I know how my life used to be and how it is now. How wonderful it is to have the Holy Spirit residing in me, for he gives me joy, shows me love and enduring kindness, and is patient with me when I stumble or halt in confusion.

> But the fruit of the Spirit is love, joy, peace, patience, kindness, goodness, faithfulness, gentleness, and self-control. Against which such things there is no law. (Gal. 5:22-23)

> Now the Lord is the Spirit, and where the Spirit of the Lord is, there is freedom. (2 Cor. 3:17)

Knowing this, if someone claims to have the Holy Spirit, look at them and see if they are bearing the fruit of the Holy Spirit. The Holy Spirit is the Spirit of Truth, and when he is inside you, he will speak and show you the truth. So then, how can people that say they have the Holy Spirit be prejudiced? How can such people then be kind to some people, but not to all? How can they be in a relationship with someone they are not married to but live with, and then come to church and act as if they are living right? You see these types of people all the time—they play drums in the church band, they lead worship in the choir, and are the ringleaders in church committees. Don't be a hypocrite. Remember that the world is watching and judging us as Christians. They hold us to a higher standard, and they should, but we have to live up to it, and with the help of the Holy Spirit, we can. Don't be one of the people that the world looks at and say that they don't want to believe what we believe because they don't see the difference between us and themselves. All they see is rules and regulations with the same results they are having, without being involved. This pains me to see and hear, and you know it grieves God's heart as well. You don't have to be a negative influence on society, but rather a positive draw when you allow yourself to be filled with the Holy Spirit. I guarantee that if you let him fill you, you will never be the same.

Let's look again at all the things the Holy Spirit does in our lives: He is a teacher (shows us in the Bible the things we need to know), a wisdom giver (helps us make wise decisions), a translator (lets us know what God is trying to tell us), an advocate (helps our prayers to reach God by telling us what to pray for), a whistle-blower (convicts us of sin in our lives), an x-ray technician (he sees through the lies and barriers of others), and a comforter (comforts us in our times of strife or grief). As if that wasn't enough, the Holy Spirit is so much more! The Holy Spirit gives us gifts as well. These gifts include the ability to heal, to teach others, to evangelize, to prophesy, to discern things in the spiritual realm, and also to work miracles. Note the following verses:

> There are different kinds of gifts, but the same Spirit. There are different kinds of service, but the same Lord. There are different kinds of working, but the same God works all of them in all men. Now to each one the manifestation of the Spirit is given for the common good. To one there is given through the Spirit the message of wisdom, to another the message of knowledge by the means of the same Spirit, to another faith by the same Spirit, to another the gifts of healing by that one Spirit, to another miraculous powers, to another prophecy, to another distinguishing between spirits, to another speaking in different kinds of tongues, and still to another the interpretation of tongues. All these are the work of one and the same Spirit, and he gives them to each one, just as he determines. (1 Cor. 12:4-11)

I find it to be a great shame that there are churches around that claim they are followers of Christ, and yet they deny these spiritual gifts. They like to say that those were gifts given only to the disciples, that the powers they possessed were for that time only and not for today. However, if you read the Bible for yourself, you will find that it is not so. The early church would not have grown if Jesus hadn't have left and the Holy Spirit hadn't come down. Jesus himself had these gifts that I mentioned, but the disciples did not until the Holy Spirit came and filled them. It was the Holy Spirit that enabled Jesus to do the things he did while he was otherwise limited in his human body. The Holy Spirit gave him the words to speak to the Pharisees, the insight into what they were thinking/planning; he relied on the power of the Holy Spirit for healing and miracle working. This is not just me saying this.

> How God anointed Jesus of Nazareth with the Holy Spirit and power, and how he went around doing good and healing all who were under the power of the devil, because God was with him. (Acts 10:38)

So I say then, how can there be a pastor of a church who doesn't believe in the Holy Spirit or the power and necessity of the Holy Spirit in their own life? It is impossible to truly be a person after God's own heart if you are not in constant partnership with the Holy Spirit. I myself cannot effectively pray for someone without the leading of the Holy Spirit, for how will I know what the real problem is? People lie to each other and even to themselves, which is why it is important to have the leading of the Holy Spirit in prayer so we know what to pray for. For example, you might have someone ask you to pray because they are having financial problems. What they haven't told you, however, is that they are bad stewards of money or that perhaps they have a gambling problem. The Holy Spirit can let you in on what the real truth of the matter is so that the actual problem can be solved, not just the symptoms or the consequences of that problem.

So again I say, these gifts are available to Christians, and further, it doesn't matter who we are, for we are all the same in God's eyes.

> For we were all baptized by one Spirit into one body—whether Jews or Greeks, slave or free—and we were all given the one Spirit to drink. (1 Cor. 12:13)

There is no distinction among Jews, Greeks (Gentiles), slaves, and so on. We are all one in the body of Christ. We all receive different spiritual gifts from God through his Spirit.

Sometimes people get discouraged by thinking that because they have or know someone who has the Holy Spirit, then certain things should be happening, like miracles or increase in church membership. If there is someone around with the gift of evangelizing or the power of miracle working, then it will happen in God's time; if not, then there needs to be specific prayer requests that some people be infused with those gifts. Remember that not everyone who is filled with the Holy Spirit will have the ability to lay hands on someone and have them be healed; that might not be their spiritual gift no matter how much they may want it to be. Still, these spiritual gifts can be given to anyone. Let it also be known that every Christian can be filled with the Holy Spirit, and when they are, unbelievers will notice that something is different about you, even though they might not know what it is. Demons that are dwelling around your home or workplace will know also and try to fight your presence. Being filled with the Holy Spirit myself, I can also sense when I meet someone if they are filled with the Spirit also. There is a feeling of familiarity, like meeting a brother or sister—which is essentially true because we are one with the Spirit.

Let's talk more in depth about another gift that the Holy Spirit can bestow upon us—speaking in tongues. When a person is speaking in tongues, it's as if God is speaking himself. This is a gift that we find rarely among people and one also that can be falsified or misused by people trying to make a spectacle by babbling and claiming that they are speaking in tongues. Still, when someone has been gifted with this ability and also sometimes when we can't find the words to pray, the Holy Spirit will lend us the words of God to use. Speaking in tongues is the same as speaking in a foreign language. It is the language of God, understood only by him, Jesus, his angels. The devil and his demons do not understand it, but they know what it is and will flee from it. It is not something that we can write down or translate for ourselves. This is not a language that your pastor or deacon can teach you. You can't learn it at a seminary school or any such place. This can only be given to you by God through the Holy Spirit. If you recall, sometime after I received Jesus Christ as my personal savior, one day out of the blue, I started speaking in tongues. What I didn't mention to you was that I was thrown out of my church because of it.

Yes, this church, which I mentioned earlier that turned out to be not worshipping God after all, told me that speaking in tongues was from the devil and that I was not welcome there. In reality, the devil himself was offended and scared that I was doing it there. In any event, that church is not the only church that frowns upon speaking in tongues or doesn't actually believe that it is possible or an ability given to people other than pastors. After I was kicked out of that church, I was hurt and embarrassed, and not knowing that it was a blessing at the time, I didn't want to speak in tongues anymore. One day, though, I received a vision from God asking me to speak in tongues, but I didn't. Again, I received that same vision, and then I did. After that, my spiritual life seemed to reach a new level. When a person speaks in tongues, they are speaking the ministry and words of God, and the power infused in those words, although secret in meaning, are effective weapons against the devil and, at that same time, aids to the children of God.

The devil will do whatever he can to keep Christians and the world as a whole from speaking in tongues or recognizing the power that they wield. He will use doubt and disbelief to make people hesitate. He will use fear of mockery to make people hesitate. He will also use outright rejection to make people hesitate to use this gift. I use the word hesitate because just being given a spiritual gift means nothing if you don't use it. Remember the story in Matthew 25:14-28 about three servants who were entrusted with talents while their master was away? Only two used what they were given and amassed more than what they had started with, while the third took his and buried it in the ground. The master was upset at that third servant because he hadn't used what he was given. The same concept applies to the spiritual gifts that God gives us. We must use them to further his kingdom; otherwise, they are useless. The devil knows that speaking in tongues and other spiritual gifts further the purpose of God here on earth. Let's look at an example of someone using their gifts of evangelizing and speaking in tongues in the Bible.

> "He commanded us to preach to the people and to testify that he is the one whom God appointed as judge of the living and the dead. All the prophets testify about him that everyone who believes in him receives forgiveness of sins through his name." While Peter was still speaking these words, the Holy Spirit came on all who heard the message. The circumcised believers who had come with Peter were astonished that the gift of the Holy Spirit had been poured out even on the Gentiles. For they heard them speaking in tongues and praising God. Then Peter said, "Can anyone keep these people from being baptized with water? They have received the Holy Spirit just as we have." So he ordered that they be baptized in the name of Jesus Christ. (Acts 10:42-48)

The people that came with Peter were astonished that these Gentiles had received the Spirit and were speaking in tongues. They didn't realize that those that were uncircumcised could receive these gifts. Peter, however, rolled with the punches, having recognized that God doesn't play favorites.

> They saw what seemed to be tongues of fire that separated and came to rest on each of them. All of them were filled with the Holy Spirit and began to speak in tongues as the spirit enabled them. (Acts 2:3-4)

> And these signs will accompany those who believe: in my name they will drive out demons; they will speak in new tongues. (Mark 16:17)

Jesus himself said that last verse. He didn't say that these gifts were for a period of time only. They are for those who believe. Still again, you find churches that are proclaimed followers of Christ who deny the spiritual gift of speaking in tongues. My question is, how can you believe part of what Jesus said or that which the Bible teaches and not the rest? Something is wrong there. Right now, this very second, someone is receiving the ability to speak in tongues even if they don't know it, like I didn't at first when I was living with Rosie all those years ago. I am not writing to bash churches or misguided believers, but instead to make people aware of the truth that the Bible speaks about on this and others issues. Don't be one of those people that Jesus mentioned in the Bible who will call "Lord, Lord" but don't actually know him or the truth for what it is. I don't want anyone sitting in the judgment seat and finding out that what they thought they knew was wrong, and therefore, they must be cast into hell.

If you are a born-again Christian who is filled with the Holy Spirit, know that you *can* cast out demons, and you *can* be given the ability to speak in tongues, and you *can* also be given other spiritual gifts that I've mentioned earlier. You have to believe that it is so and not let the devil sway you otherwise. Jesus went to the cross first to die for our sins, then to give us peace of mind that we may believe and be sure in our salvation, to free us from demon oppression, to free us from diseases so that we may have joy and fellowship with him so that he may also bless us in our lives. Furthermore, he left us as a lone man that we, as the body of Christ, might receive in his place the Holy Spirit in our lives. Jesus went through so much for us so that we could be free of those things that I mentioned, but that doesn't mean that we *will* be free of them as if we live in a protective bubble, but rather, he has given us the means to do battle against those things and prevail. Not only will you prevail, but also you can have joy and peace in adversity, in a declining economy, in a war-torn world.

> A righteous man may have many troubles, but the Lord delivers him from them all; he protects all his bones, not one of them will be broken. (Ps. 34:19-20)

A church that doesn't believe this is way offtrack and is not some place that you need to be. God made a new covenant with us through the death of Jesus Christ, and he will operate and intervene in the lives of those who give him permission by receiving the filling of the Holy Spirit.

The Power of Your Mouth

Most of us know that it was with words that God created the universe. (See Genesis 1:3-24: "And God said, 'Let there be light,' and there was light.") We know from our previous discussion that angels and demons alike respond to our words as well. With our mouths, we can also give praise to God and ask for God's intervention in our lives. I think we all know on some level that words have power, and although we may not like to admit it, we know that it is very difficult to tame our mouths sometimes. I didn't used to know how powerful the words that came out of my mouth were. Let's face it though; people can speak words in your life that can forever alter your future. Most parents know that the words they speak to their children can either make them or break them. Teachers find themselves with that same power over children every day. Friends and acquaintances either build each other up or tear each other down in seconds. There are people among us that are living defeated lives because of words that were spoken to them early in their lives at school or by close relatives and such. People abuse others verbally more than many of us care to admit. Words we say can be infective, think of mob mentality. On the other hand, we can bless others with our words as well.

As you know, I had a message spoken to me from an angel about my future before I came to the United States. That was all it was—words. No money, no plane ticket, no nothing else but words. Still, later on, those words became reality in my life. We have that same kind of power when we speak to others. When you tell your child over and over that they will never achieve anything in their lives, chances are that they won't because words can be defeating. When husbands and wives fight and they throw mean words around and name-call or say they want a divorce, that kind of stuff stays with them and causes further problems because people don't forget stuff like that. The Bible mentions the power of words in several different places; let's look at a few:

The tongue has the power of life and death, and those who love it will eat its fruit. (Prov. 18:21)

Whoever of you loves life and desires to see many good days, keep your tongue from evil and your lips from speaking lies. (Ps. 34:12-13)

Jesus called the crowd to him and said, "Listen and understand. What goes into a man's mouth does not make him 'unclean' but what comes out of his mouth, that is what makes him 'unclean.'" (Matt. 15:10-11)

As you can see, one of the things it says in the Bible is that if we love life and we want to see good things happen, we need to watch our mouths. How many of us know someone who constantly lets their mouth get them in trouble? How many of us *are* that person? Certainly, we all know someone or have known someone who can't get through more than one sentence without cursing. Some people have lots of money and think they can do and say whatever they want because they have that money, but the Bible tells us that if we expect to have a good life, we need to watch what we are saying. I think we have all lived enough life to this point to know that money isn't everything. It may bring you status and material things, but it doesn't ensure joy or happiness, and if you are constantly unmindful of what you say, it definitely won't. What do you think it means when it says, "The power of the tongue has the power of life and death"? Do you think that is too extreme? It's not. It is important to stay away from negative people who are always speaking negative things. Have you noticed how a person like that can bring you down? Their words can bring an oppressing atmosphere around you that can, in actuality, make you feel bad. Why? Because words have power. We can, and often do, speak negativity into physical existence. It works in reverse too; that's why motivational speakers are wanted to promote products or ideas. Their positive words and energy create a positive atmosphere that makes people feel like they are on top of the world and can accomplish whatever is being asked of them.

Do you know that lots of people's unhappiness is due to their *own* negative thinking and negative words? Some people have a negative dialogue that constantly revolves around in their heads that says stuff like "I never do anything right" or "Nothing ever good happens to me" or "No one likes me or will ever love me because I am _____." Repeating these things in your mind actually brings things to pass. You don't try as hard when you think that things are gonna turn out wrong anyway. You think there is no sense in hoping for something good or praying for that job promotion because you have convinced yourself that you won't get it. You keep yourself closed off to people so they don't get close enough to maybe hurt you when, in actuality, you are setting yourself up for failure every time. Perhaps this doesn't describe you; perhaps you are unhappy because of some negative words that someone spoke to you that you decided to believe. Yes, I said *decided*. If a small part of you didn't believe that negative thing they said to you, it couldn't hurt you or make you unhappy. So what to do? You have to speak positivity into your life, and you will be amazed at what things come to pass. Sounds silly or too easy, right? Surely we have all heard what I am saying in one form or another. No? Talk to any successful athlete, and I bet they have a mantra of positivity that they speak to themselves before a game or a fight or a tournament. What are you speaking in your life or your children's life or your friend's or spouse's life?

> The good man brings good things out of the good stored up in him, and the evil man brings evil things out of the evil stored in him. But I tell you that men will have to give account on the day of judgment for every careless word they have spoken. For by your words you will be acquitted, and by your words you will be condemned. (Matt. 12:35-37)

Well, if you didn't know it before, you know now that it doesn't stop here on earth. What you have said and done will follow you after death and all the way to the judgment seat. There will be no mercy for those who say stuff like, "Everybody else was doing it." Nope, there will be you and only you in that judgment seat without a defense lawyer in sight. So I suggest that you pray and repent and start watching what you say to yourself and to and around others.

I guess the next thing to talk about is awareness. We need to be aware of where negativity is flowing from in our lives, for like I mentioned before, when a person is positive, then other people want to be around that positive person. Contrarily, we need to be aware of when we are being exposed to negative things and take pains to avoid these things or these people. I myself had to take such steps. Take for instance the radio or TV news. I was always reading or hearing about something bad going on, and I would ask myself how could someone do this or that, and of course, the answer to that is that there is evil alive and present in this world. However, when I was twenty years old, I made a decision. I decided that I was going to stop reading newspapers, stop listening to negative news, and stop watching violent movies.

I can honestly tell you that I saw a big change in my mental life. You don't realize how long these negative types of things stay with you long after you ingested the negativity to begin with. Another thing I have done is that I don't hang around negative people anymore. Sounds easy enough, right? But is it? How many people do you know that you hang around with or tolerate and make excuses for their negative behavior, saying stuff like, "Oh, that's just how so-and-so is" or "So-and-sos are that way because they just got out of a bad relationship, or they just lost their job, or they are just having a bad day" when you know they are like that all the time? You have to take action and remove as many negative things from your life as you can. Not only that, but you also need to then infuse some positivity in its place. I, for one, started watching comedies. No hardship, right? I would watch these comedies on TV and laugh and laugh. I also found some of those judge shows amusing. By the time I came to the United States, my mind was already trained not to watch negative news or expose myself to other such things. You too can train yourself both mind and mouth; you'll be happy that you did.

The Word of God Is Powerful

So if our words are powerful, how much more so is the Word of God? God's Word is anointed with power, not just his spoken Word as in the creation of the universe, but the written Word in the Bible. God gave us his Word in order that we could study in and have it with us always. God responds to his Words in prayer as well, as we previously discussed. The devil knows, of course, that there is power in the words of the Bible, which is why he will go out of his way to keep us from reading it. How many people have bibles in their houses that they don't read? Lots. I remember the first time I got my hands on a Bible and started reading it, I fell asleep. The next time after that, I felt as if I couldn't understand it. Still after that, I thought to myself that the Bible was boring. I wondered why it was possible for me to read a newspaper and not fall asleep or read a novel and not have trouble understanding it or be consumed with boredom. Has this happened to you? How about this? How many of you get up and get ready for church, having had the same hours of sleep you usually get during the week or even more because it's the weekend, however, as soon as you sit down in church after the worship session, you start to fall asleep? Ha! Yeah, you know what I believe? I believe that the devil was attacking me and attacks others as well in an effort to keep us from reading and hearing the Word. Such a simple strategy, but oh, so effective. I tell you what though, when I gave my life to Jesus and accepted the Holy Spirit into my life and body, after that, I could read the Bible without falling asleep. If you are suffering from the same problems, pray to God and ask for deliverance. Truly, it is a serious enough problem to warrant prayer.

Why do you think that here in America, Bible study or even Bible reading is not allowed in schools? All different types of philosophy can be taught—Darwinism, Buddhism, mythology, the big bang theory, and so on—but not creationism as per the Bible. There are all kinds of books that children read that aren't uplifting or edifying to others, but they must read and converse on them; however, not the Bible, unless they are in a private school. Why is that? It's because the devil has a serious toehold, no, foothold here in America. People don't want to hear that or don't want to say it out loud, but it is true. Like I said, the devil knows how powerful the Word is, and he will do what he can to hinder people from reading or hearing it. What reasons do they really have for not studying the Bible in school? None that make any real sense. All that is ever taught in public schools about the Bible or Christianity is not the good it is or does, but rather how many wars were started and fought in the name of Christianity.

We are leaving our kids defenseless against the bombardment of other ideas and ways of behaving. We are currently at a historical low when it comes to our youth today in the world and in America especially. I have never seen such discontent, such rebelliousness, such callous disregard for morality. It is madness . . . no, it is *evil* insinuating itself overwhelmingly at an alarming rate with noticeable results. Children today in general have no real respect for authority or themselves for that matter. These girls are certainly not respecting themselves by dressing in such scandalous manners. The boys are no better with the way they speak and the trouble they get into with no thought for the future. Drug use is available even in elementary schools now at a level that is astonishing to me, and we all know that children are sexually active earlier in life than they ever were before. With the ready access to sites like Facebook and MySpace, kids have been introduced to and are involved in stuff that would never have happened ten or even five years ago. By the time your child has gotten to high school and beyond, the devil has had so much time to get a hold of them in so many ways that it is unfathomable.

Satan knows the same thing about kids that we know. He knows, whatever it is, you got to get it in and get it in early. We know kids are like sponges when they are little, so it is up to us to make sure that they suck up the right things, and that starts with the Bible. It continues with us showing kids how to handle adversity in a Christian manner by modeling it to them and then backing it up with the Bible. Are you upset about something? Are the finances in trouble? Don't get all depressed about it or argue in whispering tones with your spouse. Talk to your kids; you don't have to give them too much of the specifics, for they won't have true understanding and you don't want to worry them, but show them where they and you can find comfort in the Bible in reference to that problem. Show them, let them hear you praying and crying out to the Lord about certain problems or illnesses so they too can see that God listens and is faithful. We have already talked about how God operates and how he intervenes and the power of prayer; let your kids in on this too. How many of us have ever said, "If I only knew then what I know now"? Give your kids a jump start in the right direction. Put into them what you want to get out and stop letting the world and the devil babysit and raise your kids while you are out doing what, trying to get what? We all know that you can't take it with you. What you *do* take is your actions on this earth; that's what you take to the judgment seat, and your kids will too. Don't you think they should know that? Just as you would equip yourself or your child to jump out of a plane into the unknown, here are a few verses that you and they should know.

> Praise be to the Lord my Rock, who trains my hands for war, my fingers for battle. He is my loving God and my fortress, my stronghold and my deliverer, my shield, in whom I take refuge, who subdues peoples under me. (Ps. 144:1)

> For the word of God is living and active. Sharper than any double-edged sword, it penetrates even to dividing soul and spirit, joints and marrow; it judges the thoughts and attitudes of the heart. Nothing in all creation is hidden from God's sight. Everything is laid bare before the eyes of him to whom we must give account. (Heb. 4:12-13)

> Then they cried to the Lord in their trouble, and he saved them from their distress. He sent forth his word and healed them; he rescued them from the grave. Let them give thanks to the Lord for his unfailing love and his wonderful deeds for men. (Ps. 107:19-21)

> Let them praise the name of the Lord, for his name alone is exalted; his splendor is above the earth and the heavens. (Ps. 148:13)

> He sends his command to the earth; his word runs swiftly. (Ps. 147:15)

We see here that God sent his command to the earth, and his Word runs swiftly. We see also how powerful his Word is, like a sword that can pierce both spirit and soul. Whatever the problem might be, the Word is there for us to use. It is the best weapon there is, and it is here to work for us. There are angels around, and they are at your disposal, waiting for us to speak the Word so that they can see some action. I know for a long time the angels that were around me must have been bored out of their minds, for I never spoke any of God's Word or had them do any battles for me! God was patiently waiting for me, and so were they. I tell you the truth, my brothers and sisters, this is the way it works. I can't stress enough that healing of sicknesses or diseases is for today, not just the past. Use the Word of God before you call your doctor or your friend that is always online, reading up on illnesses. Remember this verse?

> But he was pierced for our transgressions, he was crushed for our
> iniquities; the punishment that brought us peace was upon him, and
> by his wounds, we are healed. (Isa. 53:5)

Memorize that. Believe it. Speak it over yourself and your loved ones before you go to the doctor. Not suffering from a disease? Are you experiencing depression, overwhelmed by sadness and negative thoughts? Stand on this familiar verse:

> I tell you the truth, whatever you bind on earth will be bound in
> heaven, and whatever you loose on earth will be loosed in heaven.
> (Matt. 18:18)

Memorize it. Believe it. Speak it over your loved ones. Add this: "And now, you spirit of depression, I bind you in the name of Jesus, and I loosen peace and joy in my life right now!" That spirit of depression has to obey and leave. You might say there is no spirit of depression, doesn't matter; if you say that, the spirit will have to leave. Of course, if you leave the door open, it can come back. You can get and stay on medication that will give you a false sense of freedom from depression, but is that what you want? You need to get rid of that spirit and replace it with something else, and then there will be no room for it in your life.

> Take the helmet of salvation and the sword of the Spirit, which is
> the word of God. (Eph. 6:17)

The helmet is your protection, your assurance, your covering that you can rely on to keep you from the pit of hell. The Word, or the sword of the Spirit, is your weapon that you do battle with. Why do you think it is called the sword of the Spirit if you are not supposed to use it against spirits? They do exist. Remember also:

> For our struggle is not against flesh and blood, but against the
> rulers, against the authorities, against the powers of this dark
> world and against the spiritual forces of evil in the heavenly
> realms. (Eph. 6:12)

You are fighting against that person you have problems with that is possessed by dark principalities or practices. You are battling the rulers of darkness, the demonic spirits of diseases and conflict. All this stuff is real, whether you want/choose to believe it or not, but regardless, God wanted us to know what we were dealing with so we could be prepared, and he gave us the resources to do so. I'm telling you, reading the Bible will open your eyes and answer so many questions you have and even the ones you didn't know you had; it certainly did for me. When Jesus was on this earth, he dealt with the same things, the same kind of people we deal with every day.

> Then Jesus said, "Am I leading a rebellion, that you have come with swords and clubs? Every day I was with you in the temple courts, and you did not lay a hand on me. But this is your hour—when darkness reigns." (Luke 22:52-53)

Jesus was talking to those who had come to arrest him. These people were stirred to action by Satan. Jesus did not want his disciples to fight those who had come for him, for he knew it wouldn't change anything. They would have just come another day, with another group. The hour of darkness is still upon us and will continue until the Second Coming of Jesus.

I know there are still some naysayers out there who don't want to believe there are demons out in the world or that we have to deal with them. If you think that after all I have written, I suggest you pick up your Bible and read for a while. Are you one of those people who think that the Bible is just a book or a fairy tale? If so, please explain to me why a man will molest or rape his own daughter or another family member or friend. Tell me what will make a young man get a gun and go to school and kill random students and then himself. If it is not the influence of the devil or his minions, then tell me what will make someone repeatedly kill other people that they don't even know, or blow up buildings containing innocent people. There are so many wicked things going on in the world, so many wicked spirits in high places. They insinuate themselves in every aspect of people's lives, from their jobs to their home lives. Still, none of this is unknown to God, and he has given us his Word to do battle against these powers. I know what I am talking about. I have had to do battle with the demons in my life using God's Word.

Speaking about the power of the Word of God makes me remember something important. Recall we spoke earlier on about how sometimes people don't even realize their need for deliverance in a specific area. For example, hunger. There are people, and maybe you are one of them, who think they are always hungry. Every time you turn around, this person is eating. Perhaps this person comes to terms with it and admits they have a problem, so they seek out some kind of group or start some hunger management counseling or program. They learn these skills and get better by applying them while they are in the program. However, once that is over and they are left to their own devices, they fall back into bad habits. Why? Because they are battling the spirit of hunger/gluttony, and you can't fight a spirit with counseling; you are only fooling yourself. Yeah, it worked for a while, and the devil will let you alone for a little bit because he knows it won't last, and then afterward, he can then have the spirit of guilt and depression attach themselves to you also. In this situation and similar ones, you have to stand on God's Word and speak to the spirit that is hindering you. You say to it, "You foul spirit of _____. I have authority over you in the name of Jesus. I break your power over me, and I command you to go in the name of Jesus!" I tell you, that spirit will go. You have to analyze how it came into your life in the first place so that you can prevent it from showing up again. It's like getting an alarm system; you have to secure all the points of entry, or it's pointless.

You might say, "Well, what about people who have committed crimes, should they be excused because they were beset by or possessed by spirits?" To this, I say no. This person has allowed these spirits to have a hold in their life, and by not being in the Lord, they didn't allow for the awareness to come so that they might fight these spirits. If a man is convicted of child molestation, he should be put in jail to serve his time. However, if this man comes out of jail without having been delivered of his tendencies or gotten rid of those demons that were influencing him, then when he gets out, he is going to hurt another child. If no one tells that demon to leave that man, it won't. Another scary thing to mention, and this is something that people forget about, is there is such a thing as generational curse or inherited sin. So should this man have children of his own before he has cast these demons out of his life, they can attach themselves to his offspring. Thusly, as God abhors sin, he will chastise the children of this man and their children and so on until the cycle is broken.

> The Lord is slow to anger, abounding in love and forgiving sin and rebellion. Yet he does not leave the guilty unpunished; he punishes the children for the sin of the fathers to the third and fourth generation. (Num. 14:18)

If the child molester casts out these demons, confesses, and repents, then it will stop there with that man.

We really must take this seriously, really take it to heart. People don't want to admit to this kind of stuff; everyone wants to think they are their own person, separate from their parents or other family, but there are some things you just can't get away from without help from God. Certainly, we have all heard of a family wherein most of them drink heavily, or they have a history of violence, a history or gambling, or a history of adultery, and/or divorce. That is what I am talking about when I say generation curse or inherited sin. For this reason, my friends, you must take care in the decisions you make, for when you commit sin, you are inviting bad spirits into your life, and your children and family will pay for it. Before I got married, the Lord revealed to me that

I had a spirit of adultery in my life and that I needed to pray and break it. When I woke up, I wondered how I could have a spirit of adultery in my life when I wasn't even married yet. I wasn't sleeping around either, so I didn't pray. A few days later, I was reading my Bible, and I came across that verse in Numbers, and then I understood. That spirit was attached to my family. Realizing that, I started to pray and ask God to deliver me from it. You would be surprised to know how many people are walking around who are suffering from the sins of their forefathers, and if they don't have a relationship with God or they aren't in his Word, they will probably never find out and will then pass it on to their children as well.

I knew a young man, back when I lived in Uganda, who suffered from a generational curse. I used to pay this young man to clean my yard. Once, I went to pay him, but then I realized he had not completed the job. I decided to go to the house where he lived and find out what happened. When I didn't find him there, I asked the neighbors if they knew where he was. They told me that he was in police custody because he had been caught having sex with a cow! I told her that it was impossible; it couldn't be true. Well, she called the neighbors, and they also told me it was true. Well, I left there in a state of shock. I couldn't believe that of the young man for he was so nice and so able; I just couldn't settle the thought of him doing that in my mind. Sometime later, I saw this young man, and I didn't know what to say to him. He came to me and immediately apologized to me for not finishing the work I had assigned him. He told me that he had been in police custody for a crime he had committed. He then rushed on to say that he had a problem and then explained that it had been the second time he had been caught mating with a cow.

Since he was being so open with me, I couldn't help asking him how this kind of thing could happen. He told me that it happens when he is asleep. He said he would be dreaming and a beautiful naked woman would appear to him. She would call to him and tell him to come outside. He told me that she was so seductive, and he couldn't resist her. He would then be sleepwalking as he followed her so that he could have sex with her. He says that he never sees a cow at all until someone finds him, and he wakes up to find himself on the cow. He continued by saying that his father had been caught many times mating with cows, and they sent him away from village to village. It turned out that his father had just died six months before this started happening to him! Tears came to my eyes as he told me this, and I told him how sorry I was. He asked me if I would permit him to finish what he had started so that he could make some money so that he could leave the area per the police's request. I just gave him the money so he could go. People get shocked and disgusted when bestiality is mentioned, and many don't believe that it really happens; or if it does, it is rare. Still, there is no sin that is new under the sun, and even the Bible mentions it.

Cursed is the man who has sexual relations with any animal. (Deut. 27:21)

Do not have sexual relations with an animal and defile yourself with it. A woman must not present herself to an animal to have sexual relations with it; that is a perversion. (Lev. 18:23)

In this young man, we can see that the father was guilty of the sin of bestiality first. I don't know if he was the first family member or if his father or other relative had been afflicted with this predilection as well. However, we do know that the son was not so afflicted until the death of his father. Subsequently, this eighteen-year-old boy is now suffering from the same problem. If you are a father and you are involving yourself with prostitutes or habitually watch porn or practice any other kind of sexual immorality, you need to ask yourself, "Is this what I want for my children? Do I want my children acting in this same manner?" Your answer should be no. You need to turn to God, confess, repent, and ask for deliverance from these sexually immoral sins. You can stop these habits in your lifetime and keep them from transferring to that of your children. Don't have children yet? Think you are only behaving a certain way because you are single? Nope, it doesn't work that way. You have opened doors with the sin in your life, and it will follow you until you get rid of it. You may think you are in control, but you are not. Still, don't despair; this is why Jesus went to the cross for us, for all our transgressions—present, past, and future. Through him, you can be delivered. The chains can be broken.

When evening came, many who were demon-possessed were brought to him, and he drove out the spirits with a word and healed all the sick. This was to fulfill what was spoken through the prophet Isaiah: "He took up our infirmities and carried our diseases." (Matt. 8:16-17)

The same Jesus stands ready to cast out any demons in your life at any time, just like he did in biblical times; nothing has changed. Some people back then were influenced or possessed by demons, and so are people nowadays. Don't hesitate; remove these demons from your life. Say this prayer:

Dear Jesus, I come to you as a sinner. I ask for forgiveness. Lord Jesus, forgive me and cleanse me from sin. Deliver me from _____ and _____ and change my life. Fill me with your Holy Spirit. Satan, I remove you! I will serve you no longer! I break your power in my life! Dear Jesus, thank you for forgiving me of my sins.

Remember, words are powerful! Pray this prayer and be forever changed. Welcome the kingdom of God into your life. Get a Bible. If you have one, read it for yourself. Pray to God and ask him to show you the verses he has for you. You'll be surprised at what you come across and how the Bible can speak to you right where you're at in your life. Tell God that you want to have a personal relationship with him and ask that he help you find a good church or to open your eyes to the good in your current church. Ask God to show you the demons that have a hold in your life. After you have confessed your sins, these demons will no longer have authority or legal right to be in your life any longer. Remember to stand on these verses:

No weapon forged against you will prevail. (Isa. 54:17)

I tell you the truth, whatever you bind on earth will be bound in heaven. (Matt. 18:18)

I have given you authority to trample on snakes and scorpions. (Luke 10:19)

So I say to you: Ask and it will be given to you. (Luke 11:9)

And I will do whatever you ask in my name. (John 14:13)

If you remain in me and my words remain in you. (John 15:7)

I am not special. Jesus delivered me from the demons that were in my life because of the sins I had opened the door to. Jesus delivered me from a generational curse. In fact, he delivered me from seven generational curses that were upon my life. After the first one of adultery, I was anxious to know if there were more generational curses in my life that I was unaware of. I prayed and fasted and beseeched God to deliver me from them. God then showed them to me one by one. There was one for adultery, another for poverty, one for murder, and still another for idol worship, as well as others. I don't think there is a family alive that isn't beset with some form of generational curse. Jesus delivered me from them, and he can deliver you too. You just have to ask.

Yes, We Can Live Happily on Earth, but How?

We want to feel good. We want to laugh and be merry. When we laugh, our souls and spirits fill with such joy and our bodies feel good all over. People who learn to relax, laugh, and enjoy life tend to live longer and are healthier over all. Happiness is what every human being on earth is looking for. Oftentimes, although we don't mean to, we look for happiness in the wrong places. Some people have a misconception that money will bring them happiness. Others think they are clever enough to know that money doesn't bring happiness, and yet they strive to get money so they can then buy the things they think will make them happy or buy them the lifestyle they think will make them happy. Still, there are lots of people who have more money than they need, and they are not happy. Beauty doesn't guarantee happiness either, despite what the populace may think. There are others who believe that religion itself will bring happiness and joy, but that just isn't how it works.

I can admit that I used to believe that having enough money to buy anything at any given time, combined with a good marriage, equaled happiness. In Uganda, most people don't have the money they need, let alone the money to spend on things that are unnecessary. Many don't have the money they need to send their children to school. Health insurance? Forget about it. The government certainly doesn't help people like they do here in America. In America, people are ashamed to ask for certain things, but back where I grew up, it is not shameful to knock on someone's door and ask for a spoon of salt. It's not an embarrassing thing to walk across the street to ask a neighbor for some cooking oil. I have done those things myself, and life was hard when I was growing up. There wasn't a TV, so we spent a lot of time talking and sharing. If a neighbor of ours gave birth, we would go over there and help clean her house and cook for her. We would go to someone's house and mourn with them if they lost a loved one. It was not unusual for someone who had a job to share their paycheck with their mother or other family members. Still, at the time, I did not think there was happiness in these things.

When I came to the United States and saw these big houses, people driving fancy cars, people going to ATMs and getting money immediately to spend in retail shops, I thought to myself, "These are big people." In Uganda, a rich person is thought to be big. In Uganda, if you are fat, you are automatically considered rich, for the average person can't afford to eat enough to be fat. So when I came to America, I looked around me, and I thought, "Wow, there are a lot of rich people here, and I just knew that these people were happy." Really, I had never seen so many people with so much money and stuff. I figured, "Well, this is it. I will be happy if I can also get a job and work really hard so I could have the same things that all these other people have." I remember one time when I visited a couple in California, and I went to their house and was quite astonished. Their house was very large, and they had big cars. The kind of cars they had were abnormally big to me because in Africa, they use cars of that size to go on safaris. Their house was filled with expensive furnishings and accessories, but I didn't feel any happiness around them.

As I was in America longer and started interacting with people more, I started to realize how much people around here complain. Where I am from, people had nothing, but they didn't complain. I remember meeting people who were unhappy and who would say that they were stressed. I had never heard the word *stressed* or its equivalent in Uganda. It took me about three years of living here to realize that money doesn't give happiness, although it can make you comfortable. I also found out that material things don't make you happy, although they can make things more convenient or aesthetically pleasing. Marrying a rich person isn't going to make you happy by association either. So if everything the world has to offer doesn't give happiness, what does? Where does true happiness come from? Is there anyone here on this earth who is filled with happiness? How can we change our lives and live in true happiness?

For me, happiness came from reading, understanding, and acting in accordance to the Word of God. It really works. It really is the things we choose to do that can bring happiness and health or unhappiness and unhealthiness. Let's look at some things we can do.

> Give generously to him and do so without a grudging heart; then because of this the Lord your God will bless you in all your work and in everything you put your hand to. There will always be poor people in the land. Therefore I command you to be openhanded toward your brothers and toward the poor and the needy in your land. (Deut. 15:10-11)

That is just one of the many verses in the Bible about helping those in need. Giving to the poor is something we all know that we should do. When we do so, it touches the very center of God. It really is a win-win situation, for God is blessing that person through you, and in turn, he will bless you as well for following his commands. God will bless the work of your hands. That means God will help you with what you are trying to accomplish in your life. He can intervene by bringing to your notice people who can help you achieve what you are trying to do, or bring *you* to the notice of people that can open the right doors for you. He can help you conceive ideas and follow them through to completion. God can bless you with money and help you to enjoy it the right way. Still, first, we need to be giving to the poor. Let me ask you, what do you do with your paycheck? Do you use it to help others, or do you spend it all on yourself?

So you can give to the poor and receive blessings, but what's the reverse?

> He who gives to the poor will lack nothing, but he who closes his
> eyes to them receives many curses. (Prov. 28:27)

Let's talk again for a second about how clever and crafty the devil is. I think two of the devil's most used weapons are that of blindness, in the form of unawareness, and disbelief/doubt. In America, people don't really believe in curses or bad luck for the most part. People believe that things just happen and that it is just life. Believing in curses is considered an antiquated notion, and people who do believe in that stuff are looked down on or not taken seriously. Why do you think that is? The devil has engineered it to be that way, tailored that way of thinking to suit his own purposes. He knows that if people really believed that they were cursed, they would then try to figure out why that was so and take steps to correct the behavior that brought it on, which would eventually lead to Christ.

Let's think about some of the things that may happen to us (maybe something similar has happened to you) that we just brush off as unfortunate or bad timing or some such thing. For example, you get paid, and then all of a sudden, your car breaks down. There didn't seem to previously have been anything wrong with it, but there you are, calling AAA and shelling out money to a mechanic. You can't pay the bills you needed to pay because of the car incident. Meanwhile, you missed some days at work because of that as well, so you are gonna have less money on top of that. Maybe you should've sent a check to that homeless center you pass every day going to work or donated to that charity food drive at your kid's school. It really is a simple concept—give to the poor, reap the benefits. Sounds callous, maybe, but it is right there in the Bible. Money, or lack thereof, is one of the ways God will use to get your attention. Why? Because if your focus is only on the money or things you are trying to accumulate, then it isn't on him, and we know he is a jealous God. The problem is that a lot of times when God is trying to get our attention, we aren't aware of it, or we chalk it up to be just some unfortunate thing that happened; we have to remedy that.

So giving to the poor can net us some blessings, which, I don't know about you, can certainly make us happy. What other things can make us happy here on earth?

> A good man obtains favor from the Lord, but the Lord condemns a
> crafty man. (Prov. 12:2)

Favor from God is a wonderful thing. When you have the Lord's favor in your life, things seem to be a little simpler. There are less hiccups, and things seem to work out just as they should. Have you ever faced a situation where there was no way you could dig yourself out of it? Has there ever been a time when you had done all that you could do in your power, and it was now up to some strangers to decide something or do something that impacts your life and not theirs, as in they won't lose any sleep over it but you will? How about a situation like this: You want to rent a space for your business. You look through some rental advertisements, and you find the perfect location, the perfect square footage, the perfect rental obligation. The problem is, they have all these requirements that they want from you, and on top of that, they want six months rental payment in advance. Well, you don't have that kind of money, but you know you're good for it. You don't meet those requirements, but you're passionate about your business and know what you need to know to be a success. It comes to you that you should just go meet this person, and when you do, suddenly you hear them say that they don't need that stuff the ad said and that they are willing to accept two months in advance instead! Sounds to me like someone has God's favor.

Ever get a job you don't qualify for without even having an interview? Did the IRS send you a check in the mail saying that they messed up your taxes? This is God showing you his favor, and that comes from following God's commands and being a good person. You know how they say the mob takes care of its own? Well, God takes care of his own too. There are earthly rewards for following God's precepts and living righteously. God stores stuff up in heaven for us based on our earthly behavior; of course, you won't get any of it if you don't get to stay in heaven in the first place. Conversely, if you are not a good person and you regularly have a disregard for God's precepts, you are gonna live a condemned life. That is not a happy way of life. Have no peace? Things constantly going wrong? Being mistreated regularly? Maybe you are living a condemned life.

God is also looking at our intentions or the conditions of our hearts and will reward us accordingly and vice versa. For example, maybe you purposely bumped as if by accident into a white person at your job, and they fell down and injured themselves and were then unable to perform their job properly and got fired. You could have helped them somehow, but you didn't because you don't like white people. Maybe you didn't hire a black person for a job that they were qualified for and instead hired a less-qualified white person because you don't like black people. These are some things that happen that a person from the outside looking in wouldn't notice. It might seem like nothing was amiss, and yet God knows the conditions of our hearts. He knows our intentions. You wonder why your homelife isn't going so well or you aren't getting enough sleep or money seems to be going out faster than it is coming in. Perhaps you are living a condemned life.

Let's look at another verse.

> A kind man benefits himself, but a cruel man brings trouble on himself. (Prov. 11:17)

Do you consider yourself a kind or merciful person? Do you usually have a kind word to say to people? Do you always reach out to others and oftentimes give more than you get? I know it sounds corny, but being kind to others is a reward in itself. It makes you feel good to help others when it comes from your heart and not begrudgingly given. When you give to someone in need, it sparks joy in your soul. Coincidence? I don't think so. I believe God designed it that way. However, being a cruel person has its own consequences. Being a bitter, hateful person hurts you as much as it does others. Ever notice that a lot of the most ruthless people also have lots of stress? They get ulcers and other like problems. They suffer from heart attacks and strokes. It takes a lot of energy to be mean regularly. It's not worth it.

I love the book of Proverbs in the Bible because it is full of verses that are easy to understand and yet hard to dispute. Here is another verse I'd like us to look at.

> A heart at peace gives life to the body, but envy rots the bones. (Prov. 14:30)

It is no secret that some people live a long time and others die young. Regardless of what the case may be, envy is one of those things that can torment you once you let it get a hold of your life, and no amount of healthy eating or exercise can rid you of the effects. Can you recognize an envious person? Are you one? An envious person will give dirty looks to a beautiful woman they don't know because they feel unattractive. An envious person hates for anyone else to have something good happen to them because they feel they are lacking in their own life. An envious person will constantly analyze their own life and find it wanting, and instead of finding out why that is so, they will plot ways to bring others down, for spite is a product of envy. The Bible gives a good description of what an envious or jealous person goes through.

> The wicked man will see and be vexed, he will gnash his teeth and waste away; the longing of the wicked will come to nothing. (Ps. 112:10)

That is some powerful imagery, but it is accurate. An envious person can't stand to see someone who seems to be better off than they are in some way. It doesn't even have to be true, but they think it is. A person who has no place in their heart for envy has no contempt for anyone who is better-looking than them. Such a person is genuinely happy when a coworker is promoted. This person can compliment a friend with a car that is of a higher quality than theirs.

The Word of God says in **Proverbs 17:22,** "A cheerful heart is good medicine, but a spirit dries up the bones." How true that is. There have been studies that say that people who laugh a lot are likely to live longer and get sick less often than their sour counterparts. Doesn't it feel good to laugh? Coincidence? I don't think so. I am a laugher; I love to laugh. I remember laughing so hard once that my husband said that he wasn't going to take me to the movies again. Sometimes I really can't control myself when I watch comedy. I don't know why, but I do know that I love to laugh! How many of you out there are like me? I appreciate listening to comedians who don't feel the need to curse, and I like to hang out with people who can make me laugh. I remember when I first met my husband's family, I felt as if I had known them for a long time already. That day, we laughed so much. They were happy people, and it showed both in spirit and in body, for they are healthy people, but not everyone is like them.

On the flip side of this, a person with a broken spirit is easy to spot. They say things like, "I will never love again, I don't like people because they are bad, and I don't like people getting close to me." Somebody hurt them. Some situation crushed them. They feel like they need to be alone so that they can wallow in that hurt as a testimony or punishment for letting it happen in the first place. Whatever their reasoning, they are only hurting themselves more. They have got to get out of that brokenness, away from those defeating thoughts. How? The first thing they need to do is forgive the person who hurt them in the past, even if it is their own self. Sometimes we bring problems on ourselves, and instead of learning from the mistake and moving on, they lie there among the devastation. If you don't forgive, you can't move on, and those bad feelings will stay. We've got to forgive, for when we do, eventually the hurt will go away, and equilibrium will be restored. It doesn't happen overnight, but it will happen.

Rejection, divorce, betrayal, family disputes—some people think that their situation is too big or too bad. To them I say, have you ever been forced to marry someone you don't know and never seen before? Has anyone ever had witchcraft worked on you to the point that you went mad? Have you ever been killed by someone who you thought was your best friend? The pain of that was so great, so overwhelming. I don't know what I would have done had God not taken that pain from me. I am not saying this to say that my problems are greater than anyone else's, but rather to say that I too have been broken by people, but I didn't stay broken. Why? Because I chose to forgive. Nobody asked me for forgiveness; I did it on my own. There is true power in forgiveness. When I forgave my parents, I felt a relief in my spirit. When I forgave my best friend, it felt like a vacuum cleaner had sucked all the pain out of my heart. There is no need for anyone to continue walking around with a broken spirit. No need to suffer from the symptoms of a broken spirit. I remember feeling so down, like my heart was shaking on the inside, ready for a heart attack or something. Sometimes you feel so down as if you are headed for a breakdown. I know how that feels. I had to ask God to help me, and he did. Still, my part was the forgiveness.

I am encouraging anyone out there who is carrying around unforgiveness to let it go. Feel too hurt, too betrayed, too angry? Ask God to help you put those feeling aside so that you can forgive others who have wronged you. Do you think I felt like forgiving Rosie? I remember telling God one day that I couldn't forgive her, that it just wasn't in me to do. I was honest with God, and I asked him to help me. Maybe you are in a similar place. It wasn't as hard for me to forgive my parents because although what they did was hurtful, they were doing what was culturally accepted. They weren't trying to hurt me. It was acceptable where I came from to choose a spouse for your child and to exchange money or goods for them. It took me about a year to forgive them. During that year, I would cry every time I thought about what they did to me. Maybe you are not a crier. Typically, women cry, and men shut down and turn to things like drugs and alcohol to mute their pain. Of course, there are women that also behave in such a manner, but it is more common that they choose instead to cry or try to be so extra busy that they don't have time to think about who or what hurt them. Regardless of your method of coping, God can take away the pain if you reach out to him.

He heals the brokenhearted and binds up their wounds. (Ps. 147:3)

An anxious heart weighs a man down, but a kind word cheers it up. (Prov. 12:25)

Let's talk for a moment about depression. There are a lot of people suffering from depression. People are overworried about how they are going to pay their bills, what is going on in their lives, or whether this or that is going to happen. Some people are constantly thinking about money and how they can take care of their families in the way that they think they should. I say overworry and constantly thinking because therein lies the problem. There is nothing wrong with a natural concern for you and your family's personal welfare. It is when these types of thoughts begin to take over your mind, begin to color everything that you do or every decision you make. It is when you decide that you are so depressed that you need medication for it. We have talked before about such medication being a false relief and the spirit of depression hanging on to people. I want to talk now also about how a lot of times people suffering from this not only avoid looking at what the real issue is, but also how such people can make things worse by hanging out with negative people. I can't stress enough how important it is to hang around positive people.

For example, what if you lose your job? You come home and you tell your spouse and they in turn start fussing at you and blaming you for what happened; that makes you feel worse. It doesn't matter if it was truly your fault; you know if it is or not. How much better would it be if that spouse instead turns to you and says positive and uplifting words of encouragement? Perhaps you are in a situation where your spouse is oblivious as to how they could have avoided a situation like being fired. Even if it is their fault this time or every time, there is a positive way to go about helping them to correct their behavior. Yelling and screaming or placing blame in a negative way versus in a corrective manner just adds to the problem and doesn't help fix it. Be positive and helpful without being an enabler, and that person will be motivated to go out and look for another job and do better in the future. Being depressed or feeling sorry for oneself is a powerful thing. There are people every day who, having felt rejected or put down by their loved ones on top of the problematic situation, commit suicide or even murder the ones who they feel caused the problem. Being a positive person in someone's life when they face a difficult situation could turn out to be a matter of life and death. Keep that in mind when dealing with a loved one, a coworker, or a friend.

You know what else can help you live happily on earth? Finding a good spouse to share your life with. Sounds cliché, but it is true. Who we marry plays a big part in our lives. We can be happy or troubled depending on who we marry. Let's look at some verses regarding wives:

> He who finds a wife finds what is good and receives favor from the Lord. (Prov. 18:22)

> A wife of noble character is her husband's crown, but a disgraced wife is like decay in his bones. (Prov. 12:4)

> And a quarrelsome wife is like a constant dripping. Houses and
> wealth are inherited from parents, but a prudent wife is from the
> Lord. (Prov. 19:13-14)

It says here that a good wife comes from God, and a man who finds her has received favor from God. Well, we already know how great it is to have God's favor. There are so many people whose lives are destroyed because they married the wrong person, and certainly a large part of that is because just as God can give you a good spouse, the devil also is a supplier of spouses, although he specializes in the bad ones. Don't think for a moment that the people you meet are coincidentally in your life. They are either sent by God or the devil. At some point, they made a decision that caused them to enter your life, and it can be for good or bad. Imagine for a second two roads that run parallel to each other, never intended to meet or merge. People are traveling down their own road. Each one comes to stop signs, traffic lights, construction, and such. Perhaps this person who came into your life was waiting at some train tracks, and it is taking forever for the train to come and pass by. Perhaps God allowed that train to be there because that person needed to slow down or wait before continuing on, or perhaps that train came because God wanted them to stop and take a side road now that would lead them straight to you. On the other hand, perhaps that train is put there by the devil to keep that person from continuing on to what God has for them. Instead of waiting for it to pass, the devil has them take that side street that causes them to be lead straight to you, thereby distracting you both from your true purpose. Either or could be the case, however, but only one is for both your mutual good.

There are people that are good for you and others that are not. How can you tell the difference? I am going to mention some things that may seem obvious to some and not to others. I say that first because a lot of people have a high tolerance for misbehavior demonstrated by their girlfriend or boyfriend or spouse. Sometimes, this tolerance comes from what they observed in their own family while growing up. Some of it comes from having low self-esteem, thereby making people feel like they don't deserve better. Still others feel like they deserve it because of their own past behavior that wasn't the best it could've been. I want to say today that you shouldn't have tolerance for some types of behavior. For example, if you are with someone who lies, cheats, watches porn, wastes money on things unnecessarily, is jealous, or would rather spend their time hanging out with friends and family rather than with you, this person is not sent from God and will end up damaging or destroying you. If you are with someone who always puts you down, is physically or verbally abusive, tries to keep you secluded from others, or only wants you for what you can give them—money, sex, food, lifestyle—that person is not for you and has not been sent to you from God no matter what it may have seemed like in the beginning.

Don't be discouraged. There are good people out there. I have met my share of good people with good hearts that are naturally good, even if they aren't Christians. A good spouse will make your life happier, more comfortable, and will help bring favor to your marriage. A good wife is not going to be quarrelsome to the point where you can't solve any problems. A good wife is not going to spend money like it's water. A good wife knows how to plan for her family. A good wife is a God-fearing wife. A good wife respects her husband and is understanding. Even having all these things doesn't mean there won't be problems, but a good wife will be part of the solution and not part of the problem. A man who finds such a woman will be a happy man indeed. He will be happy to go to work and provide for his family. He will take the time to speak with and confer with his wife on things. He will love her, and their being together won't be beset with strife due to dysfunction. It will truly be a union blessed by God.

If you are a man who wants to be happy with his wife, you have to monitor your behavior as well. It is really hard for a woman to support and respect a man who is verbally abusive. It is hard to communicate with a man who doesn't listen. It's hard to submit to a man who is irresponsible. It's hard to make love to a man who watches porn or reads porn magazines because it makes a woman feel self-conscious and inept. It's hard to trust a man who has cheated because then she will always think the husband is cheating. It's hard for a woman to nurture and care for a man who only pays attention to them when they want something. All these things bring your wife pain and doesn't glorify God.

> Husbands, love your wives, just as Christ loved the church and gave himself up for her . . . Husbands ought to love their wives as their own bodies. He who loves his wife loves himself. After all, no one has ever hated his own body, but feeds and cares for it, just as Christ does the church. (Eph. 5:25-29)

A good man loves his wife as he loves himself. A good man puts his wife first and respects his wife both indoors and out. A good man listens to his wife and will pray with and for her. A good man doesn't waste money on unimportant things at the expense of needed ones; he will provide for her. A good man doesn't participate in sexually immoral behavior. A good man will say good things about his wife. A good man will make a great father. If you have a man with most of these qualities, consider him a blessing from God. It should also be noted that a good husband or a good wife will confess their wrongful behavior and ask for forgiveness, for if they love you and love God, they will be remorseful for their misbehavior.

If you are not married or in a relationship, ask God to bless you with a spouse that you can spend the rest of your life with. Pray earnestly for this person, but beware of the devil, for he too knows your desire and will seek to send a substitute in the place of who God has for you. This person may look, sound, and smell like Mr. or Mrs. Right, but they are not. You must pay attention, for many earnest and innocent people have been led astray. People will pray and ask for a person that is like this or like that, and when they meet someone who seems to have those qualities they have been looking for, they jump right in. Next thing you know, vows and rings have been exchanged, and that person turns out to not be who the person thought they were. In fact, the devil has orchestrated this whole thing from the start. Certainly, we have all heard of cases or have been involved in a situation where someone will say that so-and-so was like this, and the moment they said, "I do," they changed. The thing is that they didn't change. Who you thought they were was an illusion perpetrated by the devil to mess things up. The devil or his minions can hear you just as well as God can. With that information, they can set up a detour to get you offtrack. When stuff like that happens, people get distraught and blame God, thinking that he sent them the wrong person. This, of course, is just what the devil wants. He has, in fact, killed two birds with one stone. He messed up your life and drove you farther away from God.

The logical question then becomes, how do you know if a potential spouse was sent by God or is in fact a substitute sent by the devil? Well, the first thing you should know is that it doesn't matter how good the person might appear to be. It is not all about outward appearances or certain actions, although those are important. The most important thing for you to do is pay attention. God will intervene and show you things to alert you to whether or not this person is for you at that time. It will be almost like a voice inside you telling you yes or no. God can tell you whether or not these outward showings of affection are genuinely or falsely contrived just to get you interested. Make it a point to ask God to show you if he led that person into your life. As I mentioned before, God has different ways of communicating with us. You need to figure out how he does that so that when you ask something of him, you will be able to hear the answer when he gives it to you. You have to be careful also about having sex with a person because you then become spiritually tied to them, for good or for bad. If you try to ask God about this person after that, you are going to have trouble hearing the truth, if at all. Of course, God can make himself clear in any situation, but you have to get the sin out of the way first, remember?

Back to the signs—just because you met someone at church doesn't mean they are meant to be your spouse. Remember there are men who only go to church to find a woman, and there are women that only dress up at church to attract a man. I have had men hit on me at church, and they try to say stuff like, "The Holy Spirit told me we should be together." I also had a man hand me a note with some verses on it; he didn't say anything to me. The note read as follows:

> Two are better than one, because they have a good return for their work: If one falls down, his friend can help him up. But pity the man who falls and has no one to help him up! Also, if two lie down together, they will keep warm. But how can one keep warm alone? (Eccles. 4:9-11)

I read that note and wondered to myself how many other women he had given this note to. He had the nerve to ask me if I read it and requested that I reply to it. So be careful. I am not saying that you can't find a good spouse at church; I am just saying that the fact that they go to church and are polite while there or are dressed nicely isn't enough. Two are better than one—that is true. But that guy used those words for his own benefit. Remember that if you think you want to use God's Word in such a manner. Question yourself and your motives, for you don't want to be mocking God. God's Word is beautiful and can often explain things or express things that perhaps we could not, but your heart has to be earnest in reference to what you are using it for. Try to catch a mate by using God's Word like it is; poetry may not be the best course of action.

> Remember him—before the silver cord is severed, or the golden bowl is broken; before the pitcher is shattered at the spring, or the wheel broken at the well, and the dust returns to the ground it came from, and the spirit return to God who gave it. (Eccles. 12:6-7)

As we live on this earth, we have to remember that we are not going to live here forever. Life on earth is short, but where you spend eternity is forever. So as we live here on earth each day, we need to ask ourselves, "What will happen to me if I die right now?" Some people think that all they have or will have is what their life is like on earth right now, so they say stuff like, "Please let me enjoy life before I die," but the Word of God says that our spirits will return to God, who gave it to us in the first place. As you know, I had this experience wherein when I died, my body remained on earth, but my spirit went back to God so that I could be judged for the good and evil I had done. I sometimes feel bad for people who die while still under the command of their sins, for example, being shot while caught stealing or some such thing. I always wonder to myself what is going on up there in heaven where that person's spirit has gone to be judged. I don't think God's first question will be whether or not that person enjoyed themselves on earth. Keep that in mind and remember your creator before it is too late.

The Instructions God Gave Me on My Way Back to Earth

I was told to leave my best friend's house immediately when I got back to earth. The Lord also told me to look under the bed that I was lying on because that was where Rosie had put some of the voodoo stuff. I was instructed to throw it in front of her and leave and not to worry about where I would go, for the Lord would tell me where to go. He also told me not to be fearful, for he would be with me. When I got back to earth, I did as I was told, but I must say that I was so shocked at the things I discovered under my bed. There were very short sticks, about four things tied up with paper; there was also a long sheet of paper that was hanging under there with words that were written in Arabic. I didn't know specifically what the words meant, but I knew in my heart that they were very powerful and had contributed to my downfall. I guess I am getting ahead of myself. I am sure you all want to know what happened when I entered my body back on earth.

After God had finished giving me the instructions, two angels appeared, and I recognized them as being the two angels that had brought me up from earth. They said that they were ready to take me back, and the next second, we moved out of heaven and passed through the other heavens on our way back to earth. As we approached, I could see my body lying down and people around it. The angel then warned me that I was about to reenter my body. I can't really describe the transition. I just know that I felt myself enter my body, and when I did, I felt cold, too cold. I sneezed and opened my eyes, and the people who were around me started running, calling out that I was a ghost. One woman was so shocked that she fell down.

I pulled those things from under the bed and brought them outside to where Rosie was and threw them in front of her. She was the only one standing there, for everyone else had run away from me except her. I looked her in the eye, and I could see the shock in her face; she couldn't believe what she was seeing. As I was about to leave, a man came and asked her where the dead body was; he had a vehicle that carried the dead bodies to the *mochele*. Seeing that car really brought the whole situation home to me. I knew that I had been dead and had come back, but seeing that car confirmed it, and I knew that I had been dead long enough to have been pronounced dead. Back in Africa, when a person dies, all the neighbors come to mourn with the family member or friend that has been left behind. The family stays with the body for two days before it is then buried. Even if a person dies in the hospital, the family will still bring the body home to be mourned over, and there are usually a lot of people. I wonder what was going on in Rosie's mind as they gave her their condolences. She was probably inwardly congratulating herself for having accomplished her mission.

I left there, and as I was passing the mochele car, I saw people looking at me and still saying that I was a ghost, while others said that I was, in fact, alive. I ignored them and just kept on walking. For a little while, there were even children following behind me, but I ignored them also and kept walking. There was so much joy in my heart as I was walking. I didn't know where I was going, but I didn't stop walking. I walked until I ended up at the ocean; I just *had* to look at the water. As I stood there, my mind was so clear. After a while, a young man approached me and asked me to eat at the kiosk. I explained to him that I didn't have any money with me, and he replied that it was okay and that it would be free. I ate and then went back to look at the ocean until evening came. With night approaching, I wondered to myself where I would pass the time. I only had an empty suitcase with me that I had grabbed when I left Rosie's. I don't know why I grabbed it; I didn't even know where my clothes were. I had no idea where to go or how to get the money for a bus to get there. As I was standing there, a memory came to me about a hotel I had stayed at when I had first arrived in the area. It was about thirty miles from where I was though, but I was determined to get there.

I went to the bus stop and sat down. When the bus came, I pleaded with the driver to help me get to that hotel. I explained to him that I had no money to pay, but he told me to jump on anyway. When I arrived at the hotel, I went up to the receptionist and asked if he could help me because I had no place to stay and had no money. He offered to sneak me in when it was dark and said that he would give me a key to one of the rooms so that I could have a shower. I really smelled bad by the way! When I was in the room, it was only a few minutes later that this man came back and said that I could stay in the room and that someone had paid for it for me. Then he just left. I thought to myself that the man must think I was looking for someone to spend the night with and that he was so, so wrong! After I took my shower, I marched back to where that man was and told him in no uncertain terms was I looking for a man, and if that was what he was thinking, he was way outta line.

He denied that that was his intent and instead said that immediately after I had entered the room, a man had come in the hotel and paid for the room for a month! I asked him who this man was and where I could find him, but the receptionist said that he had never seen the man before and he didn't know where he was. I figured this was all a big joke and told him to stop messing around. He then produced the money the man had given him for the room. He told me that the mystery gentleman had said that he was paying for the room for me and had even described me to the receptionist. The receptionist said that he had assumed that the mystery man and I knew each other. After he said that, I remembered that God had told me that he would show me where to go and to not be fearful because he would be with me. So I knew then that this whole thing had been divinely arranged by God somehow. I left the front desk and went back to my room.

From that moment on, miracles started to happen in my life. God touched people's hearts, and they in turn blessed me. There was one thing in particular that happened to me that made me cry. There was this Rasta man by the side of the road who had a shop full of clothes that he was selling. One day I was walking by, and he called to me and asked me to have a look at the clothes he had. I said no and explained to him that I didn't want to look at anything because I didn't have any money. He said that he knew that I didn't have any money but that I was a good-looking girl and he wanted me to try his clothes on. I love to wear dresses and, well, I really had nothing better to do, so I went in and tried on the best dresses that he had, and oh, were they beautiful! After I was done, he packed up those dresses and told me that he wanted me to have them. He said that when I got some money, I could bring it to him. I refused his offer, but he was insistent. I asked him how did he know that I would even come back to pay him for the dresses, and he said that he trusted me and that he knew that I would pay for them when I could. He then insisted again that I should please take the dresses. I was so overwhelmed that I cried. I couldn't believe that he would do such a wonderful thing for me. I did come back and pay him for those dresses by the way. How?

Another wonderful thing happened to me. There was this guy who walked up to me and asked if he could speak with me. I said okay, and he said that he didn't know me, but he did know that I had been through a lot. He said that he wanted me to know that everything was going to be all right, and then he gave me $500! Yup, just like that! He then said, "See what you can do with it." I was speechless and told him so, and he said there was no need for me to say anything. I said thank you, and he left. After he left, I said to myself that that money was "funk" money and wondered how he could have that much foreign money. I wasn't as happy about what had happened because I didn't really believe that it was real money; for me, $500 was really a lot of money when changed into African currency. I took this money and travelled to the burette, and I must say that I was so frightened to enter there because I thought that I might somehow be arrested for having that "funk" money. When I got there, I just stood outside, thinking about whether or not I should go inside the building. I decided that it was worth a shot, that it might be real money, so I went in and spoke to a lady there and gave her the money. I just gave it to her to exchange, and when she was done, I walked as fast as I could out of there; I didn't even count it. After I had walked a distance, I was suddenly extremely happy, and I thought to myself that I hadn't really thanked that man enough for what he had done. I then went back to the man who had given me the dresses. I gave him the money I owed him and bought another dress while I was there. I also took some of that money and got myself a place.

A few months later, a guy called my name and approached me. I wondered who he was and how he knew me because I didn't really know anyone around there. He greeted me and told me that he was the man who had paid for my hotel room. He then asked me if I had liked it. I told him that the word *like* didn't describe how I felt about that room. I told him that I was surprised to find that he was a real person, for I thought that an angel had somehow procured the room for me. I asked him how he knew that I needed help. He said that he didn't really know, that it was just something that had been placed in his heart to do. He said that he had been seeing me around and wanted to let me know what he had done. I asked him why, if he had been seeing me around, had he now decided to tell me. He said that he had been busy, but that he also didn't want me to think that he wanted something from me in exchange. I appreciated that answer, and I told him how grateful I was for his help in my time of need. It was then, for the first time in my life, that I saw that kind people really existed. God uses good people to bless others, and it doesn't matter if they know him or not. If their heart is kind, he can use them. The devil also uses people with bad hearts to do his bidding.

It really is a significant thing when God will use people that you don't even know to help you. It is a great feeling to do for others that you don't know as well. I truly believe that God used these people to bless me, for without them, I really would have had nothing and no immediate means to help myself. I don't know why I was so shocked when these things happened to me; I mean, I had just seen inexplicable things while I was in heaven, but it was just so out of the ordinary for something like these things to happen to me on earth. I wonder sometimes which is greater, witnessing God's glory in heaven or being a witness to how he can use his power on earth?

Forgiving Rosie Was the Hardest Thing to Do

After having returned to my body and having some time to think, I really couldn't believe what Rosie had done to me. You would think after having seen hell's fire that I wouldn't even think of what Rosie had done, for it didn't compare to the suffering I had seen there, but I still thought about it. I couldn't stop thinking about how she had pretended to love me or how she had practiced witchcraft on me. The conversation we had when she said she was going to kill me and the way she looked and sounded when she was asking me why Jesus was not protecting me from her spun round and round in my head. It was beyond my comprehension, the hatred she had for me, and I wondered of the pain she must have been going through from having to be with me in order to receive the blessing she had been told she would get. Thinking of these things really made me hurt inside. The pain of thinking of what she did unknowingly planted roots inside of me. Every time I thought about her, the pain would grow and grow. It got to the point where I said that I would never become friends with a woman again because I felt that I couldn't trust another woman that way again. I started avoiding women. If I talked to a woman and she seemed to be getting to be so nice to me, I would cut her off and avoid her as much as possible. I guess you could say that I was shell-shocked at the thought that there could be a woman like Rosie in existence, but if there was one, there could be others, and I didn't want to take the chance.

I mean, really, who could conceive of a person pretending to like you, quitting their job to follow you to another country for their own devious ends? Who could believe that they could be so naive to not realize how this person really was on the inside or what they really thought of you? I would say that it was for about the first year that I would cry every time that I thought about her. The second year was when I was resentful of other women. I didn't really have any friends or have any trust in anybody, but more than that, I didn't trust myself. I blamed myself for not having listened to the people who had warned me about Rosie and the signs that God had shown me about her true character and the dreams I had about the snakes. You would think that two years would be enough, but the third year was the worst. The pains continued to grow bigger and bigger, and I started having heart problems because of it. Truly, I did pray and received healing.

One morning of the third year, I woke up, and the Lord told me to forgive her. I thought to myself that she should be asking me to forgive her for what she had done to me and that I shouldn't be going out of my way to forgive her, so I didn't forgive her at that time. I went on with my life, and things were going well. I prayed every day and was connected with God. You would think that because of that I would listen to God, but I refused to forgive her. I told God that it was unfair for him to ask me to forgive her and that instead, he should send her to my house and have her ask me for forgiveness. Well, my pains continued to grow. I even came across another former friend of mine who asked me to go to lunch with her, but I was scared that she might hurt me also, so I didn't go.

Well, time passed, and I went before the Lord, praying as I usually did, and after I had finished, the Lord spoke to me with a loud voice and told me to forgive Rosie and he promised to make my pain go away. I tell you that the voice I heard was crystal clear. This was only the second time I had heard him speak to me. Normally, he would speak to me through visions and dreams. I wonder if it is because I never believed in people who said they heard from God, because it could have just as easily been the devil talking to them. For me though, I knew that this was God speaking to me. Well, I tried to forgive her, but I couldn't. I went to God in prayer again and told him that I had tried to forgive Rosie but that I couldn't, and I asked him to help me, to open my heart and to place some forgiveness in there for Rosie because I didn't have it in me to do. A few days later, while in prayer, I felt a difference. I realized that I felt like forgiving Rosie. I started crying, and while I was, I could feel the pain leaving, as if a vacuum was sucking it out. What a difference that made. I had been so used to carrying that pain around, but being without it felt so good.

Unforgiveness is a killer of the human heart. My unforgiveness brought me pain both in my soul and in my physical heart as well. I was filled with thoughts of resentment and distrust of others. Not only that, but I felt justified in feeling that way. God does tell us to forgive others, not for them but for ourselves. Let's look at some verses on unforgiveness.

> I know you have heard that it was said, "Love your neighbor and hate your enemy." But I tell you: Love your enemy and pray for those who persecute you, that you may be sons of your Father in heaven.

He causes his sun to rise on the evil and the good, and sends rain on the righteous and the unrighteous. (Matt. 5:43-45)

Shouldn't you have had mercy on your fellow servant just as I had on you? In anger his master turned him over to the jailers to be tortured, until he should pay back all he owed. This is how my heavenly Father will treat each of you unless you forgive your brother from your heart. (Matt. 18:21-35)

Do not judge, and you will not be judged. Do not condemn, and you will not be condemned. Forgive, and you will be forgiven. (Luke 6:37)

Because judgment without mercy will be shown to anyone who has not been merciful. Mercy triumphs over judgment! (James 2:13)

God tells us in his Word to forgive others. How can we not do so after he has shown us forgiveness through the death of his son, Jesus Christ? When we refuse to forgive others, we open a door for Satan to use the very pain you received from being hurt by that person to destroy you. I opened the door with my constant thinking about what Rosie had done. Satan used the hurt from the incident to constantly torment me to the point that it was affecting my life and my relationship with God. Paul talks about this kind of thing happening in Corinthians.

The reason I wrote you was to see if you would stand the test and be obedient in everything. If you forgive anyone, I also forgive them. And what I have forgiven—if there was anything to forgive—I have forgiven in the sight of Christ for your sake, in order that Satan might not outwit us. For we are not unaware of his schemes. (2 Cor. 2:9-11)

Unforgiveness opens up a door for Satan to take those emotional feelings and use them against you. It becomes like a disease that worsens with complications as time goes by and it is left untreated. I have heard people say things like, "I will never forgive him/her for what they did. I will never love again. I will never trust again. I will never help anyone again. I will never open my heart to anyone again." When I hear people say those things, I really understand because I walked that road myself. But of those things said that we won't do, God want us to do those things. He doesn't want us to shut ourselves off from one another. You don't have to do it in your own strength; God is there for you to lean on. With his help, you can love again. You can trust again. You can be the person God created you to be, a whole and complete person without the stain of unforgiveness or revenge in your heart. Don't worry about what happens to that person that wronged you. God knows all about it, and he will judge them for their deeds.

I would like to also say that just because you have forgiven that person, it doesn't mean that you need to go back and hang around the person that wronged you. You are not obligated to go to them and rehash what happened or tell them that you forgave them or anything like that. Unless God tells you otherwise, forgive them and move on with your life. Pray for that person that they might come to know what they did wrong and for them to find God and ask for forgiveness for what they did. God will deal with them in his time and his way; you can't force it. There is no need for you to seek revenge on them, for their bad behavior is its own consequence, and God does not ignore our transgressions any more than he ignores the good things that we do.

The First People I Told about My Death Experience

Well, I guess the only question left to answer is, Who did I tell about the experience I had, and how did they react? I was so happy to share my death experience with my family, especially my mother, brother, and sister. After all, they were the main reason I decided to come back to earth. I remembered the experience when I was in heaven, and I was shown where my family was and how I was told that they didn't know about Jesus and that they could die without knowing. When I was in heaven, I couldn't imagine being there without them, so I was eager to tell them all that had happened and about Jesus Christ.

I waited until we were all gathered for lunch. I asked my mom to forgive me for not listening to her about Rosie, and then I told them how I had died and come back to life. I told them all about heaven and about hell. I told them about what the Lord had said about them accepting Jesus so that they would not end up in hell. The whole time I was speaking, they were quiet; even the children were quiet. I told my mom about the Protestant god and other gods that were attached to other religions. I even told them about how beautiful heaven was.

My brother was the first to stand up and leave. Then my mother and my sister left, followed by the children. They went outside and talked, and a few minutes later, my mother came inside and said that I was insane. She said that she thought that the witchcraft was still working on me. Funny that she would believe in that part and not the rest that happened afterward. She said that they would arrange for me to see someone before I became crazier. She said that she wouldn't tell anyone about anything I had just told them. She begged me not to tell anyone else and promised that she would make sure that my brother and sister wouldn't tell anyone either. I don't know why I was so disappointed, why I believed that they would have believed me right away. Still, I was sad in my heart and mind that my own family did not believe me.

Regardless, I didn't give up on them. I prayed and prayed to God that they would give their lives to Christ before it was too late. Years went by as I did this, and then I heard a rumor that a Nigerian man had died and came back to life while on a crusade with a German preacher named Reinhard Bonnke.

I can't explain how excited I was to hear about someone else who had come back to life, someone with a similar experience to mine. I went again to my mother, sister, and brother and told them that if they didn't believe me, they could see that such a miracle had happened to someone else, that it was on the news. We watched this man and heard his testimony on TV. This man had been dead for a few days, and he was now alive again. Well, that convinced my family finally, and they gave their lives to Christ. My mom apologized for not believing me. I told her that it really wasn't important. What was important was that God had answered my prayers and that they had accepted Jesus into their lives. They weren't the only ones, however. There were many people in Uganda who, after hearing this man's story, gave their lives to Jesus.

Want to hear something else? While we were talking, my mother told me that while she was pregnant with me, a woman had come up to her and laid hands on her stomach and said to her that the baby she was carrying would be a great woman of God and that she will serve him. I asked my mother why she had never told me that, and she said that she never believed anything those crazy born-again people said, so she had ignored her! Still, God brought me back to this earth because I have a purpose. Part of that purpose was writing this book, and it never would have happened this way if I hadn't gone through what I did. God is using the experience that I have gone though to minister to other people, to bring awareness and to intervene in the lives of his children and bring them closer to him, to make clear that there is no way but through Jesus Christ, for it says:

> "So how can we know the way?" Jesus answered, "I am the way and the truth and the life. No one comes to the Father except through me." (John 14:5-6)